An Encourager's Notebook

An Encourager's Notebook

Dennis G. Wood
compiled by Sandra M. Wood

WESTBOW
PRESS®
A DIVISION OF THOMAS NELSON
& ZONDERVAN

WestBow Press books may be ordered through booksellers or by contacting:

WestBow Press
A Division of Thomas Nelson & Zondervan
1663 Liberty Drive
Bloomington, IN 47403
www.westbowpress.com
1 (866) 928-1240

Because of the dynamic nature of the Internet, any web addresses or links contained in
this book may have changed since publication and may no longer be valid. The views
expressed in this work are solely those of the author and do not necessarily reflect the
views of the publisher, and the publisher hereby disclaims any responsibility for them.

Any people depicted in stock imagery provided by Thinkstock are models,
and such images are being used for illustrative purposes only.
Certain stock imagery © Thinkstock.

ISBN: 978-1-5127-4399-9 (sc)
ISBN: 978-1-5127-4401-9 (hc)
ISBN: 978-1-5127-4400-2 (e)

Library of Congress Control Number: 2016908873

Print information available on the last page.

WestBow Press rev. date: 06/21/2016

~ Introduction ~

> *We can rejoice, too, when we run into problems and trials, for we know that they help us develop endurance. And endurance develops strength of character, and character strengthens our confident hope of salvation. And this hope will not lead to disappointment. For we know how dearly God loves us, because He has given us the Holy Spirit to fill our hearts with His love.* (Romans 5:3-5, NLT)

We all struggle with life's many ups and downs, one trial followed by another. We ask ourselves the age-old questions: "Why? Why me? How much longer?" We crave an answer that would satisfy the deep aches in our minds, in our hearts, and in our spirits. Through our hurts and in all of these often-unanswered questions, we hope to make sense of life.

The world answers in so many different ways and with so many different voices. But the true answer can only be found in God. In these verses and as followers of Christ, we can begin to understand that the pattern of life which God has designed will help us to grow to be more Christ-like. In the midst of the trials of life, God miraculously uses those struggles to develop our endurance, to strengthen our character, and to give us hope. In this book, you will recognize the struggles of one man, Dennis Wood, and the journey of hope that grew in him - along with his zeal to share that message with everyone he met.

Throughout these challenges in life, we find a universal need for encouragement and some reassurance during our darkest times. The motivation to write a weekly devotional came from Dennis' awareness of that poignant truth as he daily engaged with people. He would see a hurt, a pain, a troubled soul; and God's prompting would lead him to give a "word of encouragement" in response to that need. Over the fifty years of Dennis' ministry as a pastor, he shared those encouraging words that would light up a face, providing much-needed guidance to those who were hurting and in need. It wasn't that Dennis believed he could convince a troubled soul of a quick fix or to ignore the pain, but he seemed to easily encourage another with the hope and promise Dennis himself found in his Savior and Lord.

So, as he retired from pastoring, he faced two struggles that nearly overwhelmed him. First, how could he continue to give words of encouragement to others when he no longer had a pulpit from which he could share weekly? The other was a far more serious concern: how could Dennis be an encourager in light of his own daily battle with stage-four, terminal liver cancer? How could the one who was called upon to be an encourager, find encouragement in his own hour of serious trouble?

After retirement, a friend challenged Dennis to write and share with others what was on his heart as well as the happenings in his ministry. The beginning of "The Encourager" sprang to life. Dennis' battle with cancer then found an even more critical purpose, and it was out of his own need that he could communicate and share his experiences.

The following chronological journal entries have been compiled from written devotions and personal messages that Dennis titled "The Encourager," and which he sent weekly to people worldwide via email and posted on an internet blog site. The entries will lead you on Dennis' journey with cancer and his precious walk with his Savior. You will recognize his struggles and his joys through the story, and he will draw you to Jesus - his true source of faith and hope. As you read along, perhaps you too may be encouraged.

It is my prayer that you would read the devotions with an open heart. As you read the Scripture passages, allow God to reveal Himself to you, and bring direction and comfort to your life. I consider it a privilege to share these messages, and the comments of our friends and family. Through this journey with Dennis, it is my hope (as it had always been his) to share Christ with you also. If you are on a "cancer journey" yourself or know someone who is, I pray Dennis' journey might bring some peace. I pray it will encourage many of you as Dennis lived victoriously through his own suffering.

~ Sandra M. Wood

Our Purpose: To Bring Glory to God

I have always been a planner. Maybe that is why I enjoy maps and calendars. God placed the planning gene in all of us when He created us in His image. God is a planner. The book of Ephesians reminds us of that character quality of God.

Ephesians 1:5 in the New Living Translation tells us that His unchanging plan has always been to adopt us into His own family by bringing us to Himself through Jesus Christ "and it gave Him great pleasure." WOW!!!

As a father and a grandfather, I know what great pleasure my family brings to me, but to imagine that the God of the universe and all creation receives pleasure through us, His family, is beyond comprehension. He chose us "in Christ" before the foundation of the world. It is in Christ that we are holy and blameless before Him.

God's plan is centered in Christ.
> *And this is the plan: At the right time He will bring everything together under the authority of Christ - everything in heaven and on earth.*
> (Ephesians 1:10, NLT)

As believers, we long for the day when everything is under the authority of Christ.

The ultimate purpose of God is that He will receive all the glory.
> *God's purpose was that we... who were the first to trust in Christ would bring praise and glory to God.* (Ephesians 1:12)

Whenever we place our faith and trust in Christ, God places His Holy Spirit within us as a guarantee that He will fulfill His promises to us. Ephesians 1:14 proclaims that this is just one more reason for us to praise our glorious God:
> *The Spirit is God's guarantee that He will give us the inheritance He promised and that He has purchased us to be His own people. He did this so we would praise and glorify Him.*

Although our plans and activities change day by day, we can rest assured that in Christ, we can fulfill our purpose as God's family by bringing glory to Him. As the song says, "To God be the glory, great things He has done."

~~

Our Plans, God's Plans

I AM ENCOURAGED!! Today is my 62nd birthday, and I am alive, well, and enjoying life. God has been good to spare my life in order that I may continue to serve Him and enjoy you.

The other day I went to the jar with the pens in it, selected a pen, and tried to write. The pen was out of ink. It took three or four pens before I found one that would write. I pitched many into the wastebasket and used the one that performed for the purpose it was intended. You also have a purpose. You were designed with the purpose of bringing glory to God:

> *God's purpose was that we… who were the first to trust in Christ would bring praise and glory to God.* (Ephesians 1:12, NLT)

The apostle Paul was very aware of our needs and continued with prayer for those who trust Christ. The prayer is quite simple:

1. Verse 17 - He prayed that we would have knowledge of God.
2. Verse 18 - He prayed for an understanding of our wonderful future.
3. Verse 18 - He prayed that we would know of our rich and glorious inheritance.
4. Verse 19 - He prayed that we would know the greatness of His power.

God has given us, those who trust in Christ, this same power and authority that He used when He raised Christ from the dead: resurrection power. As we celebrate Easter each year, remember it is more than just an event in history. It is the endowment of God's power on your life. No wonder the letter to the Philippians says, "That I may know Him and the power of His resurrection" (Philippians 3:10, NASB). God has given Jesus all power and authority over all rulers and authorities in this world and the world to come. God gave to Christ this authority for the benefit of His Body, the Church (Ephesians 1:22).

You and I have the authority of Christ as we are used of God for the purpose He created us: to bring glory to our Creator. Never sell short your importance as you fulfill your purpose. Bring glory to God today by allowing God to fill your life with His resurrected life. May you be richly blessed as you live the resurrected life and find purpose for your life today.

~~

Our Choices and God's Power in Us

> *Brothers, if you have any word of encouragement for the people, come and give it.* (Acts 13:15, NLT)

During the last few months the word "change" has filled the airwaves. It seems to be the buzzword for politicians. But I propose that for most people, change is difficult. Some people thrive on constant change - others reject the very thought of change. Now, I think most of us would like change if it benefited us. Like for instance, if the boss offered you a big raise, you would quickly accept that change.

The apostle Paul, in Ephesians 2:1-3, paints quite a grim picture of the sin and deep depravity of our lives. He concludes in verse 3, that because of the condition of the human heart, we were objects of God's wrath. I don't know about you, but having God angry at my sin is not a welcome thought.

But God brought about a change in the life of those who place their faith in Jesus Christ. We became objects of His grace and love, and were transformed from death to life. "He gave us life" (Ephesians 2:5).

He changed us into His masterpiece.
> *For we are God's masterpiece. He has created us anew in Christ Jesus, so we can do the good things He planned for us long ago.* (Ephesians 2:10)

Although we were without hope, lost and alienated from God, He brought us into His presence and into a loving relationship because of Christ.

You were changed. Belonging to Jesus has brought you privileges: changes in status and relationship. Instead of having peace with God by keeping laws and rules, you now have been received into God's presence and family through the blood of Christ and through the Holy Spirit.

You are no longer a stranger or alien; you are a citizen of the kingdom of God. You are a part of God's family. You are a holy temple, the very dwelling place of God. He has placed His Holy Spirit in you as a guarantee of the promises He has for you. I like that kind of change! How about you?!

Your purpose to glorify God is possible because of the change God has made in your life by faith in Jesus Christ. God is in the "Life-Changing Business." I pray God's blessing on you today and the new life He has given you.

~~

Growing in Christ

April 3, 2008

Our relationship with God in Christ is a growing relationship. The Bible admonishes us to "grow in the grace and knowledge of our Lord and Savior Jesus Christ" (2 Peter 3:18, NLT).

In order to help or be involved in growing spiritually, several things are needed. This list is certainly not conclusive, but I do pray it will be a motivation for you to grow:

1. Gain understanding of your position in Christ. The first two chapters of Ephesians are especially helpful for this understanding. You died with Christ on the cross, arose with Him in the resurrection, and stand in His grace.

2. Grow in your love for God's Word. The Bible is an amazing instruction book for life. Through its words we can gain knowledge, be reproved or corrected, and receive training for a life of righteousness. The end result is that we will be ready for the life that pleases God (2 Timothy 3:16-17).

3. Act on the spiritual disciplines. You are no doubt spending time in prayer, Bible study, worship, service, and ministry. You may even be fasting, spending time in solitude with God, and other areas of spiritual discipline. May I suggest you also practice the disciplines of humility and brokenness, submission and surrender? God's Holy Spirit must be in control of our lives for spiritual growth to occur. "Yielded-ness" to Him is a necessary spiritual discipline.

4. Allow God to conform you to the image of Christ (Romans 8:29). Paul says that God determined ahead of time that we should be conformed to the image of Christ. If being like Jesus is important to our spiritual growth, then only as we yield to Him can that happen. It is not "what would Jesus do" and then try to do it. We yield to Christ, and He works in and through us. Growth is not action as much as it is conformity brought about by surrender.

5. The last area of growth is our dependence on one another. We need to embrace the body of Christ. Each of us is a part of His body by new birth. Over thirty times in the New Testament, the Bible speaks of "one another." Whether it is love, serve, forgive, encourage, exhort, admonish, or submit to one another, it is obvious that we are not in this Christian life alone. We need one another. Growing in the grace and knowledge of our Lord Jesus Christ includes growing together. Embracing the fellow believers God places in our lives is a vital aspect of spiritual growth.

~~

Change!

April 10, 2008

Need a change in your life for the better? Have some habits, wrong behavior, "stinking thinking," bad decisions, or maybe downright sin in your life that needs a turn in God's direction? The apostle Paul gives us some insight into the "how-to of change."

Paul spends three chapters in Ephesians showing us that we are new people in Christ when we, by faith, receive Him as our Savior and Lord. Then he makes the application to daily life in the next three chapters. He assumes we are new. He also assumes we still struggle with our flesh. Thus he says in Ephesians 4:17, "With the Lord's authority I say this: Live no longer as the [ungodly] do, for they are hopelessly confused" (NLT). The walk of the believer is a "no longer" walk. But how do you change? Is it even possible?

I find defeated Christians who have given up on the power of the Holy Spirit to change their lives. I hope you haven't and that this may help you:

1. Believe you can.
    Since you have heard about Jesus and have learned the truth that comes from Him, throw off your old sinful nature and your former way of life, which is corrupted by lust and deception. Instead, let the Spirit renew your thoughts and attitudes.
    Put on your new nature, created to be like God - truly righteous and holy.
    (Ephesians 4:21-24)

You can change because you already are changed. Your thoughts and actions need to catch up with your identity. You are truly righteous and holy. Do you believe that or do you think of yourself as horrible, bad, and full of lies and deception? The first change must be in your thoughts. "Stinking thinking" produces stinking behavior, and negative attitudes result in negative actions.

2. Make right choices.
    So stop telling lies. Let us tell our neighbors the truth, for we are all parts of the same body. (Ephesians 4:25)

For the next eight verses, Paul reminds us that we need to make right choices. He makes it quite clear that those choices are made through the power of God's Holy Spirit - choosing truth over lies; taking control of our temper; working and giving instead of stealing; encouraging words as opposed to abusive language; being kind to one another instead of bitterness, rage, anger, and harsh words; forgiveness instead of grudges. You may think you cannot do this - and on your own you cannot.

3. Be dependent upon the Holy Spirit.
Ephesians 5:18 instructs us to let the Holy Spirit fill and control us. I like to think about the truth that we are totally dependent upon God's Spirit to think correctly and live godly lives. God did not create you to live without dependence upon Him for everything. If you want to change, He is the change agent. Lean on the Lord. You are involved, but the real power is from Him.

~~

God Uses People
April 17, 2008

The apostle Paul was stoned at Lystra and left for dead. He finally got up and went on. The story in Acts seems to fit the timetable of 2nd Corinthians, chapter 12. If this is so, it stands to reason that Paul did have an experience of death and then resuscitated. If so, he speaks of the unspeakable. He also says in order to keep him from bragging about that experience, God gave him a weakness.

The process by which God made him weak was described as "a thorn in my flesh, the messenger of Satan to buffet me" (2 Corinthians 12:17, KJV). The word "messenger" is angel or demon. "To buffet" means to be beat up, or pounded on. That is a great description of our weakness. It beats up on or pounds on us.

We experience attacks, and are vulnerable to attack and recurrences of weakness. The purpose of Paul's weakness was to keep him from being boastful or proud. Our pride is probably the greatest detriment to the work of God in all of us.
> *God gives grace to the humble.* (James 4:6 and 1 Peter 5:5, NLT)
> *Those who exalt themselves will be humbled.* (Luke 18:14)

Let me assure you that in spite of your weakness, God is in control. He is very aware of our weaknesses and has provided grace - His divine enablement - to see us through. Paul goes so far as to brag about his weakness. Not for the purpose of glorifying himself or his weakness, but to show the amazing power of God's grace. At some point all of us are broken, damaged, cracked, and imperfect. When Adam and Eve sinned in the Garden of Eden, the core of humanity was dismantled. Sin left its mark. Sin left humanity with shame, guilt, fear, blame, loneliness, anger, and powerlessness. These weaknesses caused us to become dependent upon God. We need to receive the thorn in our flesh as a gift from God. The thorn in the flesh has also been translated as the "gift of a handicap".

We are to serve and minister out of weakness. We are all struggling with our humanness. No wonder Paul wrote to the Philippians, "For I can do everything through Christ, who gives me strength" (Philippians 4:13). He realized it was Jesus and not himself that overcame his weaknesses to show forth the power and the glory of Christ.

Most people remind me of an eighteen-year-old behind the wheel of his car. "Nothing can ever happen to me. I am invincible." Get real. We are weak. We are, apart from God, a train wreck looking for a place to happen. I was told in seminary to not let my church folks know about my weaknesses. Let me tell you a secret: they already did. So does God, and only by His grace are we acceptable.

Did you ever take a look at the Bible crew that God used? Moses stuttered and disobeyed. David committed adultery, lied, and committed murder. John Mark deserted his mission. Timothy worried a lot. Hosea's wife was a prostitute. Amos was just a farmer. Jacob was a liar. Naomi was a widow. Paul was a persecutor. Jonah ran from God. Gideon and Thomas were doubters. Jeremiah stayed depressed and suicidal. Elijah was burned out and was depressed. Martha was a "worry-wart." Noah got drunk and committed incest. Solomon was rich and a sex addict. Abraham and Sarah were too old. Peter was afraid. Lazarus was dead. And a host of biblical characters struggled with a temper.

Yet God, in His grace, used them. The process by which God made you dependent upon Him is your own personal weakness.

The great lesson Paul learned through his weakness was that "when I am weak, then I am strong" (2 Corinthians 12:10). The reason he was strong in weakness was because he became so dependent upon God that the grace of God became his strength.

~~

Selfish Without Him

April 24, 2008

Have this attitude in yourselves which was also in Christ Jesus.
(Philippians 2:5, NASB)

Ever hear someone say, "Boy, they sure have an attitude!"? Normally that is not a compliment because it is insinuated that the person has a bad attitude. Actually, attitude can be very different from one person to another. The Scripture encourages us to have the attitude of Jesus.

Life is filled with relationships. From the relationship of parents and children, husbands and wives, friends, and many others, we exist in relationship with others. Words such as encouragement, love, fellowship, affection, and compassion are used in Philippians 2:1 to describe the essence of our relationship with Christ and people. The basis of a fruitful, fulfilling life is our attitude toward other people.

Jesus is our supreme example of how those relationships function in God's way. The key word is "unselfish." It is no wonder we have so many struggles. We are basically selfish to the core without Jesus. We are encouraged in Philippians 2:2-4 to be unselfish. The need is the expression of one mind, united in spirit, intent on one purpose. We are to have an attitude of humility, which is an unselfish mindset. That attitude thinks of others before thinking of yourself, and watches out for the interests of others before yourself.

Our example is Jesus who, though He was God, became a man - a servant; and gave Himself in death on the cross in order that we might truly live. Our attitude should be like Jesus'.

Why not try today to think of others before you think of yourself? Your attitude just might change your behavior and may have a major change, for the positive, in your relationships. TRY IT!!

~~

Your Primary Concern May 1, 2008

We so often refer to ourselves as "Christians," which means we are followers of Jesus Christ, yet fail to listen to or grasp His teachings. One of the most important passages in the Scripture is the Sermon on the Mount as presented in Matthew's gospel. Luke has a similar passage found in Luke 12:22-34.

> *Then, turning to his disciples, Jesus said, "That is why I tell you not to worry about everyday life - whether you have enough food to eat or enough clothes to wear. For life is more than food, and your body more than clothing."* (Luke 12:22-23, NLT)

How easy it is for us to become frustrated over "things." Jesus reminds His disciples that God takes care of birds and flowers, and you are far more important than they are. You cannot change a thing by worrying about it. In fact, the only thing you will accomplish is the negative impact on your emotions, your mind, and your body, as well as your spiritual wellbeing.

Worrying over the simple necessities of life is futile also because God knows your needs already.

> *Your heavenly Father knows your needs. He will always give you all you need from day to day...* (Luke 12:30-31, TLB)

By the way, God did not promise to give you all you "want." But here, God then adds the clincher. He says He will meet all of your needs, "... if you will make the kingdom of God your primary concern" (vs. 31).

What an encouraging thought that God is going to provide all our needs. "So don't be afraid, little flock. For it gives your Father great happiness to give you the Kingdom" (vs. 32). So don't worry. Make God happy.

~~

Can My Life Be Better?

May 8, 2008

> *And looking up to heaven with a deep sigh, He said to him, "Ephphatha!" that is, "Be opened!" (Mark 7:34, NASB)*

Jesus was compassionate and concerned for the wellbeing of the people He met. On this occasion, a deaf man was brought to Him. Jesus simply took a deep breath and spoke a word to heaven that meant "be opened." How often are your ears plugged to the spiritual things of God so that you cannot hear when God speaks to you? You may have tried many things to make life better and only failed, when the real need was to listen to God. Could you look to heaven on your own behalf and ask God to open your ears that you could hear and your eyes that you could see Him?

Paul prayed for the Ephesians:

> *I pray that the eyes of your heart may be enlightened, so that you will know what is the hope of His calling, what are the riches of the glory of His inheritance in the saints, and what is the surpassing greatness of His power toward us who believe.* (Ephesians 1:18-19)

Whether it is your spiritual eyes or ears that need to be opened, it would be God's desire that you pay attention to Him. The song says it well: "Open our eyes, Lord. We want to see Jesus." Let that be your prayer today.

~~

The Sizzle of Anger

May 15, 2008

I spoke with a man recently who had the misfortune of going through a nasty divorce. A lot of anger and resentment preceded the end of the relationship. I asked the man about his struggle. He simply said, "She got even. She took my bass boat and all my fishing tackle." Ouch! For a fisherman, that was a low blow.

We live in a "get even" world. Whether it is one country against another, a nasty divorce, a traffic altercation, a money deal gone badly, or numerous other events, the answer seems to be: "Vengeance is mine; I will get even."
God's Word encourages us against retaliation.

> *For God called you to do good, even if it means suffering, just as Christ suffered for you. He is your example, and you must follow in His steps. He never sinned, nor ever deceived anyone. He did not retaliate when He was insulted, nor threaten revenge when He suffered. He left His case in the hands of God, who always judges fairly.* (1 Peter 2:21-23, NLT)

Our Savior and Lord Jesus is our example. He was persecuted, insulted, and threatened; yet He left his case in God's hands. God will bring the justice.

Now let's personalize it. What happened to you today, or maybe years ago, that caused you to desire revenge by retaliating? Does that sizzle of anger still burn in your heart? Although you have been violated, hurt, or just threatened, remember that the real judge who will bring true justice is God. Don't get even by trying to be the prosecutor. "Justice is Mine," says the Lord.

You will be encouraged when you can "let it go" and let God handle your struggles. Jesus "left His case in the hands of God, who always judges fairly." Be encouraged: God always judges fairly for you, too.

~~

See the Hand of God May 22, 2008

Ever feel like second fiddle, or that you came up on the short end of the stick? These are terms that mean you feel cheated or that you are not given enough credit. I have often wondered what writers of the Bible feel like concerning their particular book of the Bible. Like for instance, if you were Nahum, how do you think you would feel if someone entered heaven and you (Nahum) met them and said, "How did you like my book?" and they shrugged their shoulders? The truth is, most of us would know nothing about the book and many would not even know it exists. Poor Nahum!

Such is the case of 1st and 2nd Corinthians. Although Paul wrote both letters, it appears to me that 2nd Corinthians is often overlooked because of its predecessor. 2nd Corinthians is a book of encouragement and deserves a close look. Paul begins his second letter with the announcement of the God of all comfort. What an encouragement! There is a God who cares enough about all of our needs that He comforts.

> God is our merciful Father and the source of all comfort. He comforts us in all our troubles... (2 Corinthians 1:3-4, NLT)

The Greek word used to describe God the Holy Spirit, used in John 14:26, is "parakletos" and is translated "comforter." God Himself is the comforter. He is always there to bring comfort in our times of trouble. There is an inner peace and joy that God sends our way to counterbalance the difficulties life sends us. Even when we are unaware of His presence, He is still there. We often say that "hindsight is twenty-twenty." That is certainly true as we look back and recognize the hand of the God of all comfort touching our fragile lives at those moments when trouble knocks at our door.

There is a reason for the comfort –

... so that we can comfort others. When they are troubled, we will be able to give them the same comfort God has given us. (2 Corinthians 1:4)

I have often said that God uses people. That means He will use you to be a comforter to the people He puts in your life. It is also true that God used people to bring you comfort. What a brilliant idea! God seems to have those quite often. Why not look for the opportunity today to comfort someone?

~~

You Can Experience God's Love and Peace May 29. 2008

Ever say, "I sure hope God will be with me!"? Maybe you have just needed God for some special event or occasion and wondered, "How can I make sure He is there?" We know He has promised to never leave us or forsake us, but the Scripture gives us a promise of His being with us in love and peace.

Dear brothers and sisters, I close my letter with these last words: Be joyful. Grow to maturity. Encourage each other. Live in harmony and peace. Then the God of love and peace will be with you. (2 Corinthians 11:13, NLT)

I have become so aware that practically every promise in scripture has a contingency clause. God promises He will, if you will. Here, the Bible admonishes us with four imperatives followed with a promise. The promise that the God of love and peace will be with you indicates the presence of God in a positive, encouraging, and uplifting way in your life.

What are those imperatives? First, He tells us to rejoice. Often in scripture we are told to rejoice, even if things are not going well. Second, He says to change our ways. There is obviously a link between our lack of sensing God's love and peace, and our unwillingness to change some things in our life. Third, He directs us to encourage others. Amazing how the love and peace of God comes as we focus on others rather than ourselves! Unselfish people experience God's love and peace. And fourth, He desires that we live in harmony and peace. When we are at peace with family, friends, and even our enemies, there is a love and peace that passes understanding.

Good counsel for the day: follow the four factors that produce the experience of God's love and peace.

~~

Who Cares?

June 5, 2008

Do you know you are very special? God loves you. You are made in His image. Christ died for your sins and rose again to give you His life.

Even with those truths in place, you may sometimes feel discouraged, defeated, and disappointed. It is then you need some encouragement - a jump-start to get you going again. God usually has a wonderful way of sending along someone to lift you up. God does use people, you know. That means He can use you to be an encourager.

> *Therefore encourage one another and build up one another, just as you also are doing. But we request of you, brethren, that you appreciate those who diligently labor among you... We urge you, brethren, admonish the unruly, encourage the fainthearted, help the weak, be patient with everyone.* (1 Thessalonians 5:11-12, 14; NASB)

Does someone minister to you? Do they care for your spiritual wellbeing? Show some appreciation. Maybe a note, an email, a phone call, a gift, or an uplifting word of gratitude would be appropriate. They need your encouragement.

Do you know someone who is out of step? Maybe they are headed into troubled waters or making some mistakes that could cause grief and difficulty. Warn them. Let them know you care and encourage them with a word of caution.

Do you know someone who has emotional struggles? Discouragement often leads to depression and distress. Come alongside and give them some aid. They need you today. There are those who cannot help themselves and you are in their life to help. Give yourself, and your time and energy to help them.

Lastly, be patient with everyone. You have needed, or will need, encouragement yourself sometime. You know that God will provide the encouragement to you at that time. Why not choose to be the one who gives the encouragement? It is, after all, more blessed to give than to receive. Take a look around. It won't be long before you find someone to lift up and build up through your encouragement.

~~

Under Pressure

June 13, 2008

> *And not only this, but we also exult in our tribulations, knowing that tribulation brings about perseverance;* (Romans 5:3, NASB)

> *We can rejoice, too, when we run into problems and trials, for we know that they help us develop endurance.* (Romans 5:3, NLT)

-OR-

Get all excited about difficulties you face in life, they will change you forever by giving you fortitude. (Romans 5:3, my paraphrase)

No matter how you interpret it, the Bible gives us a clue for getting through the difficulties of life. You undoubtedly have had those trials, tribulations, or difficulties. The Greek word "thlipsis" means pressure or stress. Surely you can relate to stress. God's solution is to rejoice, show and express joy. The only way you could possibly do that is the presence of the grace of God and His Holy Spirit. It is like reading the last chapter of the book and realizing that it all turns out good in the end. So it is with your life. There will be stress, but it has a purpose.

God wants us to be over-comers, victorious, and to bring glory to Him. The way that happens is that the stress and trials in life produce fortitude. William Barclay says that fortitude is more than endurance or patience. Fortitude, the translation of the Greek word "hupomone," means "the spirit which does not passively endure but which actively overcomes the trials and tribulations of life."

You may be experiencing tribulations, trials, or stress today. Let me remind you that God is in charge and He is providing you with fortitude for whatever may come your way.

~~

~ Note from Sandy ~

Dennis' cancer was first discovered in 2000 during an exploratory surgery. It was identified as a neuroendocrine tumor, which affects both the endocrine and nervous systems. These tumors can occur in different organs of the body but most commonly in the intestine, where they are often called carcinoid tumors. This type of cancer is often misdiagnosed because it is rare and the symptoms can present as another medical problem. The tumor was surgically removed and it did not reappear until 2006.

When his symptoms returned, another surgery was performed and by then, the cancer had metastasized to his liver and it was unusually fast growing. Chemotherapy could only slightly shrink the cancer, and radiation did nothing. Over the next nine years, Dennis had countless procedures to battle the tumors, and he learned everything he could about the neuroendocrine tumor. Because of his extensive research of the disease, doctors told him that he knew more about his own type of cancer than they did.

Dennis looked at the trial he faced as an opportunity to share with the medical profession the idiosyncrasies of this disease, but also as an opportunity to tell the doctors and nurses of the amazing God who was answering prayer and sustaining his life for a purpose.

~ Sandy

~~

God's Gracious Hand

June 20, 2008

I felt encouraged because the gracious hand of the Lord my God was on me. (Ezra 7:28, NLT)

Even the great men of God needed encouragement. As I read this verse, I was reminded how many times God has placed His hand on my life in order to encourage me. Ezra was encouraged by God's Word. Ezra 7:10 says, "Ezra had determined to study and obey the law of the Lord and to teach those decrees and regulations to the people..."

Ezra's encouragement came from God, but again, as usual, God used people. Ezra was greeted by the king, and he was given silver and gold in order to purchase animals to be used as an offering to God, plus he was given an exemption from paying taxes (now that would encourage anyone!). He was given the responsibility of ministry to the people of God. He was also honored by those in authority. What a great reason to be encouraged! Ezra merely counted his blessings and broke into praise.

Here is a great idea in order for you to receive encouragement today: why not count your many blessings? Praise God for His love, His Son, and His salvation. Praise Him for your family and friends, your job, your position in Christ. Praise God because no matter what is going on in your life, your family, your church, or your job - God is in control. The gracious hand of the Lord your God is on you!!

~~

Old Friends

June 26, 2008

I thank my God in all my remembrance of you, always offering prayer with joy in my every prayer for you all, (Philippians 1:3-4, NASB)

Ever have a good friend you had not seen in a while? Every time you think of them, you get a good feeling inside. You can remember those good times of fellowship, of sharing experiences, and of your talks about the Lord and His work. Maybe your memories are of a vacation together, or a dorm room, or a nice meal in your favorite restaurant. Those memories are pleasant and satisfying, but they can create an emptiness and a longing to see that person again.

God has allowed many people to cross your path and not by accident. God, in His infinite wisdom, knows that you need relationships and arranges those special people to impact your life. Over my years, God has certainly placed you and others in my life to make a difference. Thanks for crossing my path.

What action should you take about that special relationship? When you remember someone from the past, thank God for them and offer up a prayer. If you don't know what to pray for them, simply ask God to bless their life and protect them that day. Real purpose can be about an old friend who came to your mind today and you prayed for them. Who are you praying for today?

~~

Free! Free! Free! July 3, 2008

So now there is no condemnation for those who belong to Christ Jesus. And because you belong to Him, the power of the life-giving Spirit has freed you from the power of sin that leads to death. (Romans 8:1-2, NLT)

Happy Fourth of July! As we celebrate our freedoms as Americans, we also can celebrate our freedom in Jesus.

The book of Romans, chapter 8, encourages us with at least four kinds of freedom:
1. We are free from condemnation, guilt, and punishment. One commentator calls it freedom from "penal servitude" or in other words, continuing in servitude as if we had never been set free from sin's penalty. It means that as believers, we are no longer doing penance, or some action or punishment, in order to receive forgiveness and make up for our sins.
2. We are free to belong. One of our greatest needs is belonging, feeling a part of something or someone. We are connected to Jesus. We belong to Him.
3. We are free to live by the power of the Holy Spirit and not by the Law. Our ability to live freely and with power does not come from keeping rules but by the fruit of God's Spirit within us.
4. We are free from the power of sin that leads to death. "The wages of sin is death, but the free gift of God is eternal life in Christ Jesus our Lord"

(Romans 6:23, NASB). Sin was dealt a death-blow on the cross, and by God's grace, we have been forgiven and set free to live in victory.

Celebrate the freedom of the great country of America, but don't forget to celebrate your FREEDOM IN CHRIST!!

~~

Are You Facing Changes?
July 10, 2008

Throughout the Bible, God asked His people to make changes in their lives. Most of them found it difficult, as you probably do also. And yet, God's plans were always the best. Jacob found God calling him to Egypt. It was certainly not his first choice, but along with the call came the promise:

> He said, "I am God, the God of your father; do not be afraid to go down to Egypt, for I will make you a great nation there. I will go down with you to Egypt, and I will also surely bring you up again;" (Genesis 46:3-4, NASB)

God will never call us or ask us to make a change that He will not also provide for. Change is difficult because of the fear of the unknown, we are out of our comfort zone, it interrupts our routine, and it is sometimes painful. For a believer, change is embraced through the exercise of our faith. Take God at His word and follow, even if it requires major change.

Are you facing some changes? Maybe it is job related, maybe it is a relationship, or in a ministry that God is calling you to make a change. The answer to God's direction in your life is obedience. Remember, God is always with you. Make the change in confidence and faith, and praise God for the outcome.

~~

God Is Sovereign
July 17, 2008

> There is an appointed time and season for everything that happens to you, a time and purpose for everything under heaven.
> (Ecclesiastes 3:1, my paraphrase)

My grasp of the sovereignty of God increases each day of my life. I hope in your spiritual life that you are growing in your understanding that God is neither surprised nor panicked by your life's happenings. He does not wring his hands when gasoline costs four dollars a gallon, nor when you experience the struggles of suffering. There is a time for everything in life. The book of Ecclesiastes, written by a preacher, has the word "time" thirty-one times in the third chapter. He declares there is a time for everything and that everything has a purpose.

Let me encourage you to read that third chapter and contemplate your personal experience at this time. What is the time in life you are "in" right now? What is happening in your life, your family, your church, or your job that is appointed for your spiritual growth and wellbeing?

Remember today that God is in charge. He is the Sovereign Lord. Rejoice in His watch-care, protection, and provision for your every need.

~~

Enjoy Your Freedom   July 24, 2008

What happened on the cross and at the resurrection? Of course, Jesus died and rose from the dead, but what about you? When we place our faith in Christ's death and resurrection, we are changed. It is not a mind-game of convincing ourselves that we are different, nor an act of prayer, or of just believing something to be true. It is true. We are, as 2nd Corinthians 5:17 says, a "new creation" - old things are passed away and all things are new.

The word "reconciliation" means change. We have received the reconciliation.
> *We also exult in God through our Lord Jesus Christ, through whom we have now received the reconciliation.* (Romans 5:11, NASB)

You are a brand new person. You have gone from sinner to saint, lost to saved, old to new, and from death to life.

You are free! Free from the power and penalty of your sin. Free from the demands of the Law. Free to live in victory. You are free from the guilt and shame of the past. You are free from loneliness. You are free from inferiority and insecurity. You are free from performance. You are free from the fear of failure and lack of approval. YOU ARE IN CHRIST.

Galatians 5:1 says, "It was for freedom that Christ set us free." Rejoice in your freedom.

~~

Know HIM

More than that, I count all things to be loss in view of the surpassing value of knowing Christ Jesus my Lord, (Philippians 3:8, NASB)

Life without a personal relationship with Jesus Christ is a life without purpose or meaning. The Bible declares that in order for us to have that relationship, it is worth losing everything else. When values are measured, it is impossible to place a worth on our relationship with Christ. It is higher than the highest value known to mankind and to you.

Losing everything in order to know Jesus means that no possession, no person, no power, nor position brings as great a purpose to your life as knowing Jesus.

Seeking to know Christ becomes your ultimate purpose for living. Even near the end of his life, the apostle Paul was still saying, "that I may know Him and the power of His resurrection and the fellowship of His sufferings" (Philippians 3:10).

Purpose for you today is to know Jesus - nothing else is more important than that.

~~

Make Wise Choices

You may remember the story of the prodigal son (Luke 15:11-32), who took his inheritance early, left home, squandered it on all the wrong things, discovered himself in a pigpen eating slop, and decided to repent and go back home to his father. Of course, the story is of sin and its damage, and the way back to God through repentance and faith.

The other person in this story is the elder brother who was at home all the time and was terribly upset by the father's acceptance of the younger, rebellious son who had returned. There are three things that can destroy our lives even when we are in the presence of the Father, exemplified in the life of the elder brother: anger, a negative complaining attitude, and an inability to let go. You may struggle with these kinds of feelings.

First, let me suggest that you choose to forgive.
Be kind to one another, tender-hearted, forgiving each other, just as God in Christ also has forgiven you. (Ephesians 4:32, NASB)

Forgiveness is the choice to not take into consideration what has happened in the past or is existing in the present. The only reason to not forgive is vengeance, and that is God's job.

Secondly, a negative critical attitude never gave anyone a fulfilling life. We are admonished in Philippians 4:8, after a list of positive comments, to "dwell on these things." What we think about and toward people determines how we feel - not how they feel.

Lastly, let it go. The elder brother couldn't let go of the situation. He was angry and negative because he was unwilling to let the past go. You may be bound today in something from the past. Forgive, be positive, and let it go. It is not worth destroying your own life, no matter what happened in the past.

~~

Who Do You Look Like?   August 14, 2008

> *For I am confident of this very thing, that He who began a good work in you will perfect it until the day of Christ Jesus.* (Philippians 1:6, NASB)

PBPWMGINFWMY = Please be patient with me, God is not finished with me yet. You are still a work in progress. God is at work in your life to make you Christ-like. He will use people, experiences, things, struggles, and whatever is necessary to accomplish His purpose in you. God is in control of your maturity. The finished product will look and act like Jesus.

That means that whatever you face today, God will not panic or be surprised but will, ahead of time, know the purpose and accomplish it. You can also be confident that God's grace is sufficient to see you through whatever it may be. He loves you and cares for you. He will give you the strength needed to match the challenge. God never promised a life void of tribulation. In fact, He did promise that through many tribulations you will enter the kingdom of God (Acts 14:22). He also promised He will never leave you nor forsake you (Hebrews 13:5).

~~

God Is on Our Side   August 21, 2008

Ever feel insecure? Sure you have. All of us do. Certain situations in life lend themselves to our feelings of being unloved and uncared for. It is during those moments when we may feel insecure.

⋘ 19 ⋙

I am reminded of the words of the apostle Paul to the Roman church that gave them courage when insecurity knocked at their door. Maybe his words will help you:

If God is for us, who is against us? (Romans 8:31, NASB)

Who will bring a charge against God's elect? (Romans 8:33)

Who will separate us from the love of Christ? (Romans 8:35)

But in all these things we overwhelmingly conquer through Him who loved us. (Romans 8:37)

For I am convinced that neither death, nor life, nor angels, nor principalities, nor things present, nor things to come, nor powers, nor height, nor depth, nor any other created thing, will be able to separate us from the love of God, which is in Christ Jesus our Lord. (Romans 8:38-39)

Sounds like we are pretty secure if we are in Christ. God does love you, and He cares for you. No need to ever feel insecure. People will let you down, but God never will.

~~

Are You on the Bottom of the Sea?   August 28, 2008

How can you sleep at a time like this?... Get up and pray. (Jonah 1:6, NLT)

Ever feel like Jonah? The only way to describe your current situation is, "I am in a mess." Jonah found himself in the belly of a big fish. That was certainly a mess. He got there because he was running from God. My advice to Jonah and to you: stop running from God. You cannot get away.

The second thing Jonah had to do was to accept responsibility for the mess he was in at that moment. Not always, but often, the problem you are encountering is self-made and self-perpetuated. Accept responsibility and do something about it.

Third, look to God. He is the only way out. Jonah saw that living at the bottom of the sea in a fish's stomach was not the way to find abundant life. Maybe you need to come to the conclusion that you really need God. I believe God might even allow you to be "on the bottom of the sea" in order to wake you up to your need for God Himself.

Reach out to God right now. He is there waiting for you to come to Him.

~~

Express Your Freedom

It was for freedom that Christ set us free; …
For you were called to freedom, brethren; only do not turn your freedom into an
opportunity for the flesh, but through love serve one another.
(Galatians 5:1, 13; NASB)

Freedom is God's wonderful gift to us. The freedom to choose, the freedom to accept or reject, the freedom to live, and the freedom to restrict our personal freedoms are all gifts from God. As believers, we know that in Christ, we are free from the penalty and the demands of the Law. We are free to respond to God's love. This freedom is the calling of God upon our lives.

But the warning of scripture is to not turn that freedom (to do as we choose) into an opportunity for the flesh. We must not use our freedom for selfish reasons but use our freedom to serve one another.

The greatest expression of our freedom is to choose to love as God has loved us. Freedom to love or not to love is a gift from God, but to truly use our freedom as God would desire us to use it, is to choose to love one another. Selfish freedom is still called freedom, but instead of setting us truly free, it enslaves us. You were called to freedom. Use your freedom wisely.

~~

Pray for the Lost

Brethren, my heart's desire and my prayer to God for them is for their salvation. For I
testify about them that they have a zeal for God, but not in accordance with knowledge.
(Romans 10:1-2, NASB)

The Jewish people were the concern of the apostle Paul as he shared his great desire for their salvation. Paul recognized that the people who were his kinsmen in the flesh knew about God; and yet, their knowledge was not complete, for they had not accepted Jesus as the Messiah.

Every person who has not received Jesus needs to be the recipient of our burden. Pray that God will give you a heart's desire and a burden for people who do not know Christ as Lord and Savior. Although some people you know may have a belief in God, it takes an experience of faith in Jesus Christ to save them from their sin.

Pray for the people that you desire to come to know Christ. Speak their name to God. Your burden and prayer will not go unheeded. God cares for all people everywhere and is not willing that any should perish but for all to come to repentance and faith in Jesus.

~~

Is Your Wall Broken Down?   September 18, 2008

> They said to me, "The remnant there in the province who survived the captivity are in great distress and reproach, and the wall of Jerusalem is broken down and its gates are burned with fire." (Nehemiah 1:3, NASB)

The people of God had been taken into exile into Babylon, and the city of Jerusalem had been left behind and was now in shambles. Nehemiah had just received word back from his brother and some other men of the conditions in Jerusalem. There were only a few people left in the city and they were in poor condition, and the city wall was broken down. The destruction of the gates and wall of the city was so great that the city was unable to be protected.

Nehemiah's motivation, a great burden for the City of God, led him to inspect for himself the city of Jerusalem. When you are faced with little support, great distress, and broken down defenses, it is time to do what Nehemiah did and pray. Nehemiah realized this project was far more than he could handle. He needed the direct intervention of God.

Will you find purpose in your life today through the needs that face you, and then realize they are much bigger than you are and call out to God for His help?

~~

Master Controller   September 25, 2008

> For everything comes from Him and exists by His power and is intended for His glory. (Romans 11:36, NLT)

Do you need to be reminded, as I often do, that everything in life comes through the loving Father? No matter what happens, we need to remind ourselves that God is not surprised nor does He panic. Guess what? We don't need to panic or be surprised either.

Notice that the verse uses the word "everything." That means all things. Not only does everything come from Him, but everything that exists, exists by His power. He is in control of life, death, and everything in between. He knows what is happening to nations, people, and to you. He is aware of, and in control of, all things.

Your own comfort and peace are a result of God's control of all situations. Maybe most important of all is that God is going to receive glory from all things. Your life was intended for God's glory. To Him be the glory - great things He has done and is doing. Trust Him with your life's needs right now.

~~

Refreshment

October 2, 2008

> *And He said to them, "Come away by yourselves to a secluded place and rest a while." (For there were many people coming and going, and they did not even have time to eat.)* (Mark 6:31, NASB)

Are you tired? Even while doing the work of God, you will get tired. That kind of tiredness is physical, mental, emotional, and spiritual. Jesus recognized the need for the disciples to come away from the hustle and bustle of the city life and be alone. Interestingly enough, even Jesus needed to be refreshed.

We are certainly no stronger or better than Jesus. We need refreshing in body, soul, and spirit. We may be so involved with serving others, doing our job, or taking care of our home or family that we forget our own needs. The disciples were so busy that they did not even have time to eat. Take a break. Take some time today to refresh your life. Spend some time alone with God and let Him refresh you.

To renew your strength and find purpose in life, it may be necessary to withdraw, be alone for a while, and find some food for your body, your soul, and your spirit.

~~

Look Out for the Small Things

October 9, 2008

> *They returned to Joshua and said to him, "Do not let all the people go up; only about two or three thousand men need go up to Ai; do not make all the people toil up there, for they are few."* (Joshua 7:3, NASB)

Beware: it is sometimes the small, seemingly insignificant events, people, places, and experiences that will defeat you. After the great victory at the Battle of

Jericho, the children of Israel came up against a much smaller enemy - the City of Ai.

After spies checked out the city, they returned with a report of "easy victory." They noticed that Ai was a small city in size and in number, and after such an incredible victory at Jericho, it seemed relatively easy to capture.

They recommended that only two or three thousand soldiers go up to battle. Their reasoning was simply, "They are few." Few or small does not mean easy.

Some of our greatest spiritual battles are not the big things but the small and the few. As you face the spiritual battles in your life, never look at something as insignificant or easy. In the journey of life, the war is real and the enemy is ready to bring us down over the easy and the few.

The nation of Israel lost the battle to Ai for many reasons. One of the major reasons for failure was their assumption that just because the enemy was few in number that it was going to be a snap to defeat them. Your enemy may look small, but it is often the small things that defeat us. Be on the alert.

~~

How Much Love?   October 16, 2008

> *For I am convinced that neither death, nor life, nor angels, nor principalities, nor things present, nor things to come, nor powers, nor height, nor depth, nor any other created thing, will be able to separate us from the love of God, which is in Christ Jesus our Lord.* (Romans 8:38-39, NASB)

The little boy in Sunday School was asked how much God loved him. He stretched out his hands as if to measure the biggest fish he could imagine and said, "This much." I don't know how you measure God's love, but God's love is so great that it is hard for us to even imagine. The apostle Paul was so convinced that God's love is so amazing and powerful that he penned these great words which proclaim that nothing can separate us from His great love.

There is something wonderful to be said about love that nothing can destroy. Jesus' death and resurrection prove He is a God of love. He reached out to you, forgave your sin, and gave you freedom and a peace that passes understanding. Only love can achieve those ends.

God loves you because you are His creation, His child, and His inheritance. Through His Son, Jesus Christ, He expressed His love that can never be taken from you. Praise God right now that Jesus is your Savior and Lord.

~~

Attitude Check   October 30, 2008

> *Rejoice always; pray without ceasing; in everything give thanks; for this is God's will for you in Christ Jesus.* (1 Thessalonians 5:16-18, NASB)

Scores of books and articles have been written by authors concerning attitude. Charles Swindoll declared "attitude" as the most important criteria of a positive life. Norman Peale wrote the classic *The Power of Positive Thinking* to encourage everyone to express a positive attitude.

It was the apostle Paul, long ago, who admonished the Thessalonians toward an attitude of thanksgiving and rejoicing. He spoke to them of rejoicing always and of giving thanks for and in everything. Accomplishing this feat of constant gratitude and joy is truly an adventurous endeavor, and only to be fulfilled through prayer.

That is why, in the middle of the sentence, Paul said, "Pray without ceasing." Only through prayer can you truly express your heart of rejoicing and thanksgiving. God is concerned about everything in your life and knows that with prayer, you can have an attitude of gratitude.

~~

Preparations Can Hurt   November 13, 2008

> *All discipline for the moment seems not to be joyful, but sorrowful; yet to those who have been trained by it, afterwards it yields the peaceful fruit of righteousness.* (Hebrews 12:11, NASB)

Have you ever struggled to do just one more wind sprint, or one more pushup, or maybe one more mile, or maybe even one more Bible study or sermon, or one more worship service, or witness to one more person, and you thought to yourself, "Why am I doing this?"

Every athlete who has trained to compete in the game has known the struggle of getting in shape, working on the basics, and constant discipline. As we discipline ourselves in order to prepare for the game of life, we will discover the discomfort that it brings. The writer of the book of Hebrews called it not "joyful" but "sorrowful."

On the day of the race, we discover that, although the discipline was difficult at the time, it was worth it all. So it is in the Christian life. It may seem tough to be disciplined, but the results will bring meaningful purpose in your life.

~~

My Best Friend
November 20, 2008

> *And let us consider how to stimulate one another to love and good deeds, not forsaking our own assembling together, as is the habit of some, but encouraging one another; and all the more as you see the day drawing near.* (Hebrews 10:24-25, NASB)

Who do you hang out with? The answer might determine whether you are encouraged to love one another and serve one another. How can you be encouraged and stimulated to love others and do good deeds? The Scripture tells us that it is by "assembling together" with other believers.

The Church is the assembly of God's people. The word "church" means "the called-out assembly." That gathering in New Testament days was for the purpose of worship, but it also met for the purpose of helping one another. It is difficult for us to give or receive love, or express good deeds to someone we never see. God knew that for the Church to function as the Body of Christ, it was necessary for them to hang out together.

At the time of the writing of the book of Hebrews, several believers had decided it was not necessary to meet with other believers. The writer of the letter to the Hebrews reminded them of the need to not forsake assembling together. Even though there were those who saw no need, or chose not to meet with the assembly for one reason or another, the author of Hebrews said it was needed. Why? In order for you to be encouraged, and stimulated to love and serve one another, you need to see one another. Don't forget to meet together in order to worship and fellowship.

~~

Overflowing Thankfulness
November 27, 2008

> *Now He who supplies seed to the sower and bread for food will supply and multiply your seed for sowing and increase the harvest of your righteousness; you will be enriched in everything for all liberality, which through us is producing thanksgiving to God.*

For the ministry of this service is not only fully supplying the needs of the saints, but is also overflowing through many thanksgivings to God.
Thanks be to God for His indescribable gift! (2 Corinthians 9:10-12, 15; NASB)

Happy Thanksgiving!! You are probably celebrating today the wonderful "American Holiday of Feasting." As you eat your turkey and dressing and pumpkin pie, remember that God supplies all your needs. He does so for a reason. He gives to you in order that you may give to others. Not only can you meet the needs of people, but you can also bring an overflowing of thanksgiving to God.

You are bringing thanksgiving to God by the love and words of encouragement you share with Sandy and me. We are indeed thankful for the opportunities we have had to minister across the United States, and in Thailand and Canada. You made that possible. We are thankful to you and to God.

We are all most thankful for His indescribable gift that produces thanks from all His children. His greatest and indescribable gift was His Son, Jesus Christ.

~~

My Pile of Stones
December 4, 2008

"Let this be a sign among you, so that when your children ask later, saying, 'What do these stones mean to you?'..." (Joshua 4:6, NASB)

"What do these stones mean to you?" What a question! Have you contemplated the meaning of that phrase to Israel? They had just crossed the Jordan River on dry ground during the time of a flood. They watched as the waters of the river stood still and mounded up, and the two million or so Israelites crossed over on a dry riverbed. Then they erected a memorial to God and to the victory of the safe crossing by placing twelve stones in the middle of the river.

The question lingering over the pile of stones was, "What do these stones mean to you?" To Israel, it meant finality to forty years of wilderness wanderings. It meant freedom in the Promised Land. It meant God was faithful.

Do you have a pile of rocks somewhere? Not a literal pile but a place where you watched God at work and you took time to build a memorial? Why not find the middle of the river and build a memorial to God for yourself? It will be a ceaseless reminder that God was faithful to you in the past, and that He is there for you now and will be always.

~~

The "Why" Question
December 11, 2008

Difficult times have always been a cause for even God's people to question and yearn for answers. Several times in the book of Psalms, King David asks the inevitable question, "Why?" The author of Habakkuk writes a whole book in the Bible asking, "God, where are You?"

Israel had been captured by the Midianites and they were again asking God, "If the Lord is with us, why has all this happened to us? And where are all the miracles our ancestors told us about?" (Judges 6:13, NLT)

This may be the question in your mind today. The answer to all these questions is simply that God is in ultimate control. No matter what we face, God is always there. Romans 11:36 says it clearly, "For everything comes from Him and exists by His power and is intended for His glory. All glory to Him forever!"

Our comfort, hope, and encouragement are found not in material things, governments, economics, anyone or anything else. Our hope is in the Lord.

~~

From a Manger to a Kingdom
December 18, 2008

> *The angel said to her, "Do not be afraid, Mary; for you have found favor with God. And behold, you will conceive in your womb and bear a son, and you shall name Him Jesus. He will be great and will be called the Son of the Most High; and the Lord God will give Him the throne of His father David; and He will reign over the house of Jacob forever, and His kingdom will have no end." (Luke 1:30-33, NASB)*

Christmas is about Jesus. Jesus is the Son born to the virgin Mary. He was God in human flesh. The good news of His birth was announced to Mary in the midst of her fear, questioning, and elation. How can it be that a simple virgin should have the Child who would be the King of Israel and the King of the whole world?

Mary did not understand, but likely you don't either. The miracle of miracles became reality: the God of the universe and Creator of the world was to become a man and live on the earth. His kingdom would never come to the end, because

His kingdom would be found in the hearts of people who, by faith, trust Him as King of Kings and Lord of Lords.

No wonder Mary pondered these things in her heart. During this Christmas season, ponder in your heart that Jesus is able to establish His kingdom in you. Christmas, after all, is about Jesus.

~~

The Gift
December 25, 2008

> *He came to His own, and those who were His own did not receive Him. But as many as received Him, to them He gave the right to become children of God, even to those who believe in His name... And the Word became flesh, and dwelt among us, and we saw His glory, glory as of the only begotten from the Father, full of grace and truth.* (John 1:11-12, 14; NASB)

Merry Christmas! From the humble birth in a manger in the city of Bethlehem, Jesus came to bring salvation to the entire world. Leaving the glory of heaven and coming to earth, He provided for the nation of Israel a Savior, but they rejected Jesus. God had chosen Israel above all the nations to be a kingdom of priests in order that they might introduce Him to every nation and tribe. They failed to accept their mission. They rejected the Savior that was sent to save them.

But God, in His great love for all humanity, made it possible that through believing, everyone could become His child. If you receive Jesus by faith as your Lord and Savior, you can become a child of God. You simply have to believe. What a wonderful gift God has given to you through His Son! God asks you only to believe. Won't you receive Him now? What a great time, at this Christmas season, to become a believer in Jesus.

~~

Spiritual Privacy
January 8, 2009

> *"When you pray, you are not to be like the hypocrites; for they love to stand and pray in the synagogues and on the street corners so that they may be seen by men. Truly I say to you, they have their reward in full. But you, when you pray, go into your inner room, close your door and pray to your Father who is in secret, and your Father who sees what is done in secret will reward you."* (Matthew 6:5-6, NASB)

To whom do you pray? For what reason do you pray? What do you expect in return? Jesus knew His listeners well and approached their prayer life accordingly.

He warned them to be careful of their audience. Our prayers are to be directed to God and not to people. God desires for us to communicate with Him. If we pray in public in order that people might hear us and be impressed with our spirituality, then we have received all the answer we will get.

When we speak to God, we should go into a closet and shut the door. The God who is everywhere will meet with us and listen to us in private. Our communication and relationship with God, as well as the answers to prayer, are the true rewards.

God desires that you only pray to Him, and He promises to respond to your prayers. When you pray, talk to God in private and expect God to answer your prayers.

~~

Meditate on the Shepherd January 15, 2009

Ever say to God, "Where are You? Don't You care anymore?" Well, you are in good company. David the psalmist said the same thing in similar words:
> *Will the Lord reject forever? And will He never be favorable again?*
> *Has His lovingkindness ceased forever? Has His promise come to an end forever?*
> *Has God forgotten to be gracious, Or has He in anger withdrawn His compassion?*
> (Psalm 77:7-9, NASB)

It happened to David much like it does to us. It came in the night. The darkest times seem to be when all is quiet, you cannot sleep, and your mind is filled with disturbing thoughts. Then you wonder where God has gone. David finally realized that God had not changed. He realized that it was with his own emotions that he was struggling:
> *Then I said, "It is my grief, That the right hand of the Most High has changed."*
> (Psalm 77:10)

David then remembered how God had worked in his life in the past and said:
> *I shall remember the deeds of the Lord; Surely I will remember Your wonders of old.*
> *I will meditate on all Your work, And muse on Your deeds.*
> (Psalm 77:11-12)

Meditate on the ways God has blessed and cared for you over the years. Look back across the expanse of God's working in your life and rejoice. Take your eyes off of your own grief and meditate on God Himself. Remember, your God is a Great Shepherd. "You lead Your flock like a caring Shepherd" (Psalm 77:20, my paraphrase).

~~

The Perils of Distractions
January 29, 2009

> *But Martha was distracted with all her preparations; and she came up to Him and said, "Lord, do You not care that my sister has left me to do all the serving alone? Then tell her to help me." But the Lord answered and said to her, "Martha, Martha, you are worried and bothered about so many things; but only one thing is necessary, for Mary has chosen the good part, which shall not be taken away from her."*
> (Luke 10:40-42, NASB)

Distracted, worried, and bothered - sound like your life? Martha was serving Jesus, as you are, and was disturbed that her sister, Mary, was not as committed to serving Jesus as she was.

Martha decided to involve Jesus in a little reprimand for a lazy sister and found herself at the end of the correction. Jesus reminded her that she was so busy serving Him that she was missing the most important part.

Mary had discovered fellowship with Jesus at His feet. Jesus reminded Martha of the important part - sitting at His feet. She is described as "distracted, worried, and bothered" by serving to the point she had little fellowship with Jesus.

Could it be that, as a servant of Christ, your ministry has gotten in the way of love for, and time with, Jesus? Are you distracted, worried, and bothered by your ministry and serving God to the point that Jesus Himself is secondary? Jesus reminded Martha that there is only one thing that is important: you were created to fellowship with the Lord. Why not take an inventory of your life today and see if Jesus is first?

~~

A Reason Not to Complain
February 5, 2009

> *Do everything without complaining and arguing...* (Philippians 2:14, NLT)

"Easier said than done," you say? Sure it is. The natural tendency of life is to complain, gripe, bicker, grumble, and fight. To do even some things without complaining is quite difficult, but to do *all* things seems totally impossible. What is your excuse? How about, "You should live with my husband for a while," or maybe "be at my job," or "have to put up with my health," or "my neighbors," or maybe "my church." It is not easy to keep from complaining. Yet God reminds us often that we need not complain.

Complaining is really a lack of faith in a God who knows everything, including the knowledge of exactly where we are, what is happening to us, and what we need. Could it be that our choice is either to complain or to trust God? There is a reason not to complain:

> ... *So that you will prove yourselves to be blameless and innocent, children of God above reproach in the midst of a crooked and perverse generation, among whom you appear as lights in the world,* (Philippians 2:15, NASB)

Shine today as a light in a dark world as you trust God instead of complaining.

~~

Your Favorite Place
February 12, 2009

> *So when they got out upon the land, they saw a charcoal fire already laid and fish placed on it, and bread.* (John 21:9, NASB)

What kind of heat warms your home and cooks your food: gas, fuel oil, wood, coal, electricity, or a combination of more than one? Is your home equipped with a fireplace? Most often the fireplace is used for ambiance more than heat. The family gathers around the fireplace to enjoy the fire and one another. I am sure the disciples were hungry after a night of fishing, but the charcoal fire and the bread and fish were much more a place of gathering for closeness.

Six of Jesus' disciples met the resurrected Jesus around a fire. The warmth of the fire and food, as well as a place of fellowship with Jesus, drew them together. You probably have a favorite place where you meet with Jesus. It has a sense of warmth and closeness. It is a place of comfort and encouragement. When is the last time you sat around a fire with Jesus to eat from the Bread of Life? Why not today? Find someplace today where you can fellowship with Him.

~~

Go to the Bank!
February 19, 2009

> *For in hope we have been saved, but hope that is seen is not hope; for who hopes for what he already sees? But if we hope for what we do not see, with perseverance we wait eagerly for it.* (Romans 8:24-25, NASB)

Whether it is in the news or the weather, our "hope" is expressed in words of uncertainty. Maybe you hope the economy will again flourish, or you hope your cold will vanish with the next sneeze, or that someone will give you a new car. Hope is such an illusive word except when it comes to God's promises. We used to say, "You can go to the bank with that." That is probably not a good analogy to use right now. We probably should be saying, "My hope is built on nothing less than Jesus' blood and righteousness."

Our hope today is based on Him who died for us and arose from the dead to give us His life. Sure, we can't see it yet because it is assured to us through faith. After all, it was "by grace you have been saved through faith" (Ephesians 2:8). Trust in the only One who really gives you hope. His name is Jesus.

~~

My Desires or God's Desires March 12, 2009

*Trust in the Lord and do good; Dwell in the land and cultivate faithfulness.
Delight yourself in the Lord; And He will give you the desires of your heart.
Commit your way to the Lord, Trust also in Him, and He will do it.*
(Psalm 37:3-5, NASB)

Ever have something of a passion in your life, something that you just wanted so much you could hardly stand to wait? The verse "Delight yourself in the Lord; and He will give you the desires of your heart" is often used out of context to prove that by delighting in God, we can have whatever we want.

However, the idea of getting "whatever you desire" is couched between two very important verses. First, we need to trust God and do good. Second, we need to commit our way to the Lord. "Delight yourself in the Lord" means He is first - His will and His way.

When you delight in Him, trust Him, and commit your way to Him, then the desires that are placed in your heart are His desires. The question is not "How can I get what I want?" but rather, "How can I make sure that what I desire is what God desires?" Quite a difference.

~~

No More Than I Can Handle March 19, 2009

No temptation has overtaken you but such as is common to man; and God is faithful, who will not allow you to be tempted beyond what you are able, but with the temptation will provide the way of escape also, so that you may be able to endure it. (1 Corinthians 10:13, NASB)

You have, no doubt, heard that God will not put more on you than you can handle. This verse is the text used to support that statement. The word "temptation" can mean a test, trial, or adversity. You have experienced those trials in your life. The promise of the Scripture is that what we experience is normal.

It also promises that God is faithful to not allow us to have more than what we are able to handle. The way of escape is merely the process by which God gives us the strength to endure what is coming our way. It may not be that the trial is less, but the grace is more. After all, did not God promise in 2nd Corinthians 12:9 that "My grace is sufficient"?

~~

A Tough Question March 26, 2009

Then Peter said to Him, "Behold, we have left everything and followed You; what then will there be for us?" (Matthew 19:27, NASB)

Peter is so much like you and me. He wanted an answer to a tough question. He asked Jesus the question you probably also ponder: "What am I going to get out of this?" Sounds pretty selfish on the surface, but don't you ever want to know answers like that?

For a Christian who is following Christ with their whole being and has given up family, possessions, jobs, money, and recognition to follow Jesus, that question is a legitimate one. Peter truly wanted to know what would happen to those who had left everything to follow Jesus. Peter had given up everything. "What am I getting out of this?" is a normal question.

Jesus' answer to Peter was that he would rule with Him in His kingdom and have eternal life. In other words, Jesus was promising the disciples eternal life in exchange for their total surrender to Him in this life.

To give your life to God and to allow Him to direct you day by day is a guarantee that your next life will be in heaven. It is not wrong to ask what you will receive from following Christ. The answer is very simple: you will have eternal life.

~~

Shortsighted?   April 2, 2009

> *But Joseph said to them, "Do not be afraid, for am I in God's place? And as for you, you meant evil against me, but God meant it for good in order to bring about this present result, to preserve many people alive. So therefore, do not be afraid; I will provide for you and your little ones." So he comforted them and spoke kindly to them.*
> (Genesis 50:19-21, NASB)

God is the Great Comforter and Encourager. Often His words to us will encourage us to not be afraid. You may be facing situations and circumstances that seem fearful. God, through His servant Joseph, reminds us that although it appears that evil is against us, God is for us. The evil brought against us by the enemy is going to be used for good by God Himself.

Joseph had been sold into slavery, spent time in jail as a result of a false accusation, and was raised to the office of the prime minister of Egypt - all in order to provide food for the entire world in the midst of a great famine. When his brothers sold him into slavery, it was evil; but God turned the tables and brought good from it.

Our perspective is very shortsighted. God looks at the realms of history and sees it all working together for good to those who love God and are called according to His purpose. We are not to be afraid. Be comforted. We are in the hands of the Sovereign Lord, the God of the universe.

~~

Abundant Givers   April 16, 2009

> *A poor widow came and put in two small copper coins, which amount to a cent. Calling His disciples to Him, He said to them, "Truly I say to you, this poor widow put in more than all the contributors to the treasury; for they all put in out of their surplus, but she, out of her poverty, put in all she owned, all she had to live on."*
> (Mark 12:42-44, NASB)

> *Then He said to them, "Beware, and be on your guard against every form of greed; for not even when one has an abundance does his life consist of his possessions."*
> (Luke 12:15)

Giving is such a Godly quality. Jesus used the opportunity of a poor widow, giving all she had into the temple treasury, to teach a valuable lesson. Giving from our abundance in an abundant way is not wrong. But this widow gave from her poverty, all that she had. Jesus quickly pointed out the abundant givers and stated that the widow gave more than all the rest, because she gave her all.

Whether it is our money, our time, or our abilities, God desires us to give our all. He warns us to guard against greed. Life does not consist of possessions.

Although Jesus' teachings are two thousand years old, it is amazing how relevant they are to our current world. Ask yourself, "Am I greedy?" Ask yourself, "Am I giving my all?" Let me encourage you to be an unselfish giver and run from greed.

~~

Speed Bumps

April 23, 2009

... Being greatly disturbed because they were teaching the people and proclaiming in Jesus the resurrection from the dead. And they laid hands on them and put them in jail until the next day, for it was already evening. (Acts 4:2-3, NASB)

Do you have speed bumps in your neighborhood? The purpose of those bumps is to slow down traffic. You don't want to fly over them at a high speed. Do you have potholes in your street? They will slow you down, too. Peter had preached the great sermon at Pentecost with three thousand people coming to faith in Christ. He had just healed a lame man in the temple and had preached another powerful sermon. And then the bump came.

The religious leaders of the day were really bothered that Peter was teaching people about Jesus and the resurrection. So into jail he went. Probably not what Peter wanted or expected.

What kind of bump or pothole have you just hit? The victory came to Peter. He was released and was once again in ministry mode. Praise the Lord for short-lived potholes and speed bumps that grow your faith even greater.

~~

Think Like God Thinks

April 30, 2009

But turning around and seeing His disciples, He rebuked Peter and said, "Get behind Me, Satan; for you are not setting your mind on God's interests, but man's." (Mark 8:33, NASB)

Ever feel singled out for the attack? I am sure that is how Peter felt when Jesus rebuked him in front of all the other disciples. Rebuke from anyone is difficult to take, but a direct rebuke from the Lord Jesus must have been especially hard. Peter had just made the great confession of his faith in Jesus as the Christ, the Son of the Living God. Then Peter took Jesus aside and reprimanded Him because Jesus told the disciples He was going to suffer and die. Peter probably deserved rebuking.

On top of being rebuked, Jesus called him "Satan." Not exactly a compliment. Peter's problem was much like ours. There are times we probably are not thinking like God thinks. Jesus said Peter was thinking like a mere human. His thoughts were self-centered and self-serving. Jesus would remind us to have the mind of Christ - a mind focused toward God, and His ways and interests.

Real purpose and a meaningful life will never be a reality with a mind set on our own selfishness.

~~

What Are You Asking God for Today?   May 6, 2009

> But Peter said, "I do not possess silver and gold, but what I do have I give to you: In the name of Jesus Christ the Nazarene - walk!" (Acts 3:6, NASB)

What are you asking God for right now? Is it the right thing to ask? As Peter and John approached the temple, they encountered a crippled man who could not walk. Upon inquiry of their assistance in the form of money, Peter replied that he had none to give. For a beggar who made his living from the coins dropped in the tin cup he carried, Peter was not much help.

Sometimes what we think we really need is NOT what we really need, and even what we ask God for is not what He really wants to give us. Peter did not respond with cash but with something far better. He declared that, in the name of Jesus Christ the Nazarene, the man was to get up and walk. He not only got up and walked, but with profound praise to God, he went leaping into the temple.

Maybe you should re-evaluate your current requests to God. Are you asking for the wrong thing? Maybe, like the lame man, you are not receiving God's very best. Why not let God declare what you need, and receive His best for you?

~~

~ Personal Message from Dennis ~ September 30, 2009

Dear Family, Friends, Co-Laborers, and Prayer Warriors,
As you can see, I am finally getting strong enough to write The Encourager this week. The previous one was in May. Little did I know then what the next 4½ months would bring. If you have been keeping up with the blog site, then you know maybe more than I do. For many days and weeks during that period of time, I remember little.

It was through your prayers that I am better today. I was surrounded by the best family and group of friends that anyone could ever ask for. Sandy's personal care for me has been an especially wonderful blessing.

I am still in need of prayer. I am weak, on four infusions a day of very high-powered antibiotics, seeing several doctors, and anticipating more procedures soon in October.

God has been so good to allow me to live. Twice in the hospital, I quit breathing and had to have breathing tubes. One was a result of a brain bleed with a grand mal seizure, and the other septic shock. Prayers from you and many others, along with some quick actions by some wonderful nurses, provided me another chance at life.

As time goes on, I hope to tell you some of the things God has taught me - from what it feels like when God seems very distant, to having a ministry in the hospital that I never dreamed God would accomplish. I love all of you, and thank God for you and your prayers. PLEASE DON'T STOP PRAYING!!! I still have a long way to go.

~ Dennis

The Greatest Encourager

> *"Now My soul has become troubled; and what shall I say, 'Father, save Me from this hour'? But for this purpose I came to this hour. Father, glorify Your name." Then a voice came out of heaven: "I have both glorified it, and will glorify it again."*
> (John 12:27-28, NASB)

Does the one who encourages others ever become discouraged? Have you found that the circumstances of life bring you to a point of wanting to give up, or as Jesus said, "For this purpose I came to this hour"? Jesus was the greatest encourager who ever lived, and yet, as He approached the upcoming suffering of the cross, He was troubled. Some translations say He was depressed, others even despondent. He was an encourager who became discouraged.

He was even to the point of not knowing what to pray: "What shall I say?" Have you ever been speechless before God? It seems that Jesus did find the right words: "Father, glorify Thy name." That is our purpose for living: to glorify God. The Father responded that He has glorified His name before and He would do it again. He did it in the most splendid of ways as He gave His Son to die on a cross to give eternal life to all who would believe.

You may be troubled, depressed, or despondent. Just remember that the greatest Encourager of all time also experienced your feelings.

~~

A Mighty Work Through You October 9, 2009

Now to Him who is able to do far more abundantly beyond all that we ask or think, according to the power that works within us, (Ephesians 3:20, NASB)

Did you ever consider what God is doing in you? His Holy Spirit lives in every believer and that means you. As a result, you have His power in you. His power is not only in you but is at work in you. You may say, "At work for what reason?"

The answer is that He will accomplish far more abundantly beyond anything we could ask or think. Consider the possibilities. The Scripture says that He is able to do more than that which we could ask or think. What a tremendous thought! He is at work in and through your life to bring about the amazing miracles that only God can do, but He will be working through you.

God uses people to accomplish His works and you are no exception. He wants to do mighty works. He is using your thoughts and your requests to fulfill His mighty deeds. To God be the glory.

~~

Discouragement October 15, 2009

Now it was in the heart of my father David to build a house for the name of the Lord, the God of Israel. But the Lord said to my father David, "Because it was in your heart to build a house for My name, you did well that it was in your heart. Nevertheless you shall not build the house, but your son who will be born to you, he will build the house for My name." Now the Lord has fulfilled His word which He spoke; (1 Kings 8:17-20, NASB)

Have you ever been disappointed? Sure you have. Discouragement is often a result of having a dream, desire, hope, or expectation and then seeing it come to an end. You find yourself disappointed. David desired to build a temple for God and told the prophet Nathan about it. Nathan then had a vision in which God revealed to him that David would not build a temple. God gave credit to David's desire but then gave the assignment of the construction of the temple to his son, Solomon.

Disappointment on your part might also mean that God has a new direction for the fulfillment of His perfect will. You may have not gotten the raise, didn't make the volleyball team, or a host of other dashed dreams. Remember that God still is in charge.

The greater joy for David was to realize that his son would fulfill his dream of building a house for the Lord. God is in charge not only of your dreams, desires, and aspirations but also of His intended outcome. His Word will be fulfilled in you.

~~

Repent Today

October 22, 2009

> *He prayed to the Lord and said, "Please Lord, was not this what I said while I was still in my own country? Therefore in order to forestall this I fled to Tarshish, for I knew that You are a gracious and compassionate God, slow to anger and abundant in lovingkindness, and One who relents concerning calamity." (Jonah 4:2, NASB)*

Anne Graham Lotz, Billy Graham's daughter, recently said that her passion was to daily know God more and more. How well do you know the nature of God?

Jonah was called of God to preach to the wicked city of Nineveh. The message was simply to repent or perish. Jonah preached it to them and they did repent. It was not Jonah's desire for them to do so, but it was the will of God.

God forgave them and saved them from destruction. Jonah was furious, and yet, he knew what God would do because he knew the nature of God. God is gracious and compassionate, slow to anger, and abundant in lovingkindness. Do you understand the nature of God as Jonah did?

Maybe you need to meet the God of love. Or maybe someone you know needs to meet Him. God is a forgiving God, just waiting for people to repent in order to express that forgiveness. Won't you repent of your sin today and place your faith in Christ?

~~

Monuments of Success

November 5, 2009

Samuel rose early in the morning to meet Saul; and it was told Samuel, saying, "Saul came to Carmel, and behold, he set up a monument for himself, then turned and proceeded on down to Gilgal." (1 Samuel 15:12, NASB)

Ever accomplish something and feel like you need some credit? Sort of human. But what if we don't get the recognition we think we deserve? We might resort to Saul's approach. Saul had just returned from his attack on the Amalekites. God's instruction to Saul was to destroy them completely, even their livestock. As Saul returned, he was so proud of his accomplishment that he stopped at Carmel to erect a monument to his own success. Think maybe pride was a motivation?

The real problem was that he had not obeyed God. He had captured Agag, king of the Amalekites, and brought back spoils of livestock, which was in direct disobedience to God.

Do you ever desire to erect monuments to your success but fail to take into consideration God's commands and His plans? We fail when we only partially obey. Partial obedience is really nothing more than disobedience.

True purpose in life can never be discovered if you insist on tooting your own horn and not following the Word of God.

~~

More Than Lip Service

November 11, 2009

Trust in the Lord with all your heart;
do not depend on your own understanding.
Seek His will in all you do,
and He will show you which path to take. (Proverbs 3:5-6, NLT)

Have you ever had a hard time trusting God? Someone said, "I have never lost my faith in God, but sometimes I have a hard time trusting Him." Semantics maybe, but you probably can relate. Trusting God "with all your heart" means more than lip service. It is being totally yielded to God's wisdom and guidance to the point we quit trying to figure it out or fix it.

Whatever "it" might be for you, the only true way to be directed is God's voice. If we will listen, then everything we do, everywhere we go, and whatever we face, we can rest assured that God is there to keep us on track.

Listen to Him. Follow Him. Quit trying to do it yourself, or even figure it out. Just trust God.

~~

Don't Worry, Be Thankful
November 26, 2009

> *Be anxious for nothing, but in everything by prayer and supplication with thanksgiving let your requests be made known to God. And the peace of God, which surpasses all comprehension, will guard your hearts and your minds in Christ Jesus.*
> (Philippians 4:6-7, NASB)

Do you have anything to worry about? "Don't worry, be happy." It may be a phrase you've heard a lot, but it does have a biblical basis. The apostle Paul, author of Philippians, tells us to not worry about anything. The alternative to being anxious is prayer and supplication. We worship and approach God, and then ask for what we need.

The prerequisite is that the request should not go without "thanksgiving" to God. You, no doubt, have many needs. From the financial needs to physical needs, emotional and relational needs, family needs, and deep personal needs - we can always ask God to meet those needs. But during this Thanksgiving season, don't forget to also be thankful.

You can thank God for many things, and can show your love and appreciation to Him. The end result is that you will find a peace with God that surpasses all comprehension. Your heart and your mind will be guarded by Christ Himself.

~~

Go in Faith
December 3, 2009

> *Then Gideon said to him [the angel of the Lord], "O my lord, if the Lord is with us, why then has all this happened to us? And where are all His miracles which our fathers told us about, saying, 'Did not the Lord bring us up from Egypt?' But now the Lord has abandoned us and given us into the hand of Midian." And the Lord looked at him and said, "Go in this your strength and deliver Israel from the hand of Midian. Have I not sent you?"* (Judges 6:13-14, NASB)

Are you not glad that even great men of faith like Gideon struggled with that which appeared to them as the absence of God in the struggles of this life? Why would we be encouraged by that? Because we ourselves wonder from time to time, "Where is God?"

When Gideon looked around at the situation of Israel, he could not understand why the God who delivered Israel from slavery at the hands of the Egyptians could not help them now to rescue them from the enemy, the Midianites. God's answer was Gideon himself. "Gideon, I will use you. Go in this your strength and I will deliver you."

You may be the answer to your prayer. God is a God of deliverance. Go in faith. Gideon is listed in the New Testament in Hebrews 11:32 as a man of faith. Your greatest miracle may be in the future. It is helpful for you to look back to see how God has worked in your life in the past, but maybe it is more important to look forward in faith to what God has ahead for you.

~~

Do You Need a Savior?   December 10, 2009

As He approached Jerusalem and saw the city, He wept over it…
(Luke 19:41, NIV)

Of all the characteristics of Jesus, compassion may stand near the top of the list. He expressed His compassion for the Holy City with tears. He had already shed tears at the tomb of His friend, Lazarus. His love for the inhabitants of Jerusalem was expressed in tears as He saw their need of a Savior.

Earlier, Jesus spoke to the city:
O Jerusalem, Jerusalem, the city that kills the prophets and stones those sent to her! How often I wanted to gather your children together, just as a hen gathers her brood under her wings, and you would not have it! (Luke 13:34, NASB)

He knew the destruction of the city was imminent. Do you see someone whose life is headed for destruction? Maybe you yourself are in need of a Savior. Let me assure you that Jesus loves you. His compassion toward you took Him to the cross to die for your sins and give you life. Would you trust Him today?

~~

What Do You Wish For?

December 17, 2009

> *And God is able to make all grace abound to you, that always having all sufficiency in everything, you may have an abundance for every good deed;*
> (2 Corinthians 9:8, NASB)

At this Christmas season, do you find yourself wishing you could give more gifts to your family and friends? If you had a bundle of money and untold resources, would that abundance make it easier? Let me assure you that nothing is more abounding than the grace of God.

God is able to make all grace abound to us. The result of God's grace, as always, is sufficiency. Not necessarily a bankroll or our own toy store or car dealership - but God's sufficient grace. The grace of God is adequate to meet the intentions of God for us in everything. The objective of God's grace is our ability to accomplish the good deeds, or works, that God wants us to accomplish.

Could it be that your idea of "adequate and sufficient" is not necessarily God's idea? Could you possibly have, right now, all you need to provide for every good deed? God does not expect more from you than His grace provides for you. And, by the way, that is sufficient.

God bless you as you meet the needs of others through God's grace.

~~

Putting Christ First

December 24, 2009

In Matthew 3:2 and 4:17, John the Baptist and Jesus are both attributed as having said: "Repent, for the kingdom of heaven is at hand" (NASB).

Christmas is about the establishment of the Kingdom of Heaven. It is about the Savior, who was God in human flesh, coming to earth to save us from our sins and establish His kingdom in our lives. Every kingdom needs a king, and Jesus is that King. Thus Matthew said:

> *But seek first His kingdom and His righteousness, and all these things will be added to you. So do not worry about tomorrow; for tomorrow will care for itself. Each day has enough trouble of its own.* (Matthew 6:33-34)

To seek His kingdom first, we must be allowing the reign of Christ in our lives and acknowledging His rule in our hearts. Before all else in our lives, He must be first. Anytime that order is changed or transposed, then we are not allowing His kingdom to be first. Our strength to not worry about tomorrow comes from the knowledge that Christ is in charge of our present and future - we are seeking His kingdom first.

Trouble in this life is inevitable, and each day has enough of its own. Commit to Christ the King this Christmas and find the meaning of His kingdom's rule over your life.

~~

Be Grateful   December 31, 2009

> *I will not die, but live, And tell of the works of the Lord.*
> (Psalm 118:17, NASB)

David the psalmist penned the words of Psalm 118 with words of encouragement. He was filled with the wonder of the Great God that he served. The words were of gratitude for the mighty works of God in his life. He celebrated the mercy and grace of God. He rejoiced in the victories over his enemies at the hand of God. He praised God for answers to prayer.

David recognized that it was God who preserved his life even when death was ringing at the door. He found himself trusting in God who was on his side. He praised God for the hope of continued comfort and victory. He concluded with the decision that God would have him to speak of the wonderful works of God. He would be given life with a purpose.

Your life is no different. God has blessed you in so many ways. He has given you life in order that you might fulfill the purpose of telling what God has done and is doing in your life. Be grateful and praise God for His mighty works. God is good.

~~

~ Note from Sandy ~

2009 marked the most difficult year in Dennis' fifteen-year cancer struggle - he endured seventy-six days in the hospital that year. He had multiple surgeries, scans, and procedures. He had a seizure, went into septic shock, fought off various infections with multiple doses of antibiotics, and he survived three near-death experiences. One day, the infectious disease specialist told Dennis he had only a short time to live and suggested that Dennis needed to prepare for the end of his life.

I remember that day as Dennis looked the doctor in the eye and said, "I am not giving up!" The doctor said, "If you aren't, then I won't either." The doctor ordered another six weeks of daily antibiotic injections.

During his hospitalization, Dennis read Psalm 118:17 (see previous devotion). Excitedly, he shared with me his realization that he was not going to die – not just yet; God was answering his prayers and the prayers of many. Dennis had a job to do. His mission was clear, and like King David, Dennis knew that he was to tell everyone of all the things that God had done in his life. He knew God had spared his life in 2009 (and would sustain it for almost six more years) for a reason.

Dennis' response through all of this was gratitude. He approached this mission with a greater urgency. He told everyone what God had done for him in 2009. He spent many days at his favorite coffee shop sharing with people what God was doing in his life. Many wanted to know about his cancer and because of Dennis' testimony, many more dug deeper to ask about his faith and hope in God.

~ Sandy

~~

Can't Keep Quiet

January 7, 2010

> *But Peter and John answered and said to them, "Whether it is right in the sight of God to give heed to you rather than to God, you be the judge; for we cannot stop speaking what we have seen and heard." (Acts 4:19-20, NASB)*

Peter never seemed to struggle for words. Often he stuck his foot in his mouth. But on this occasion, he was speaking from the heart about a heart conviction. Do you have heart convictions - things you believe so strongly that nothing can change your mind, your response, or your words?

Peter and John had just experienced the healing of a lame man at the gate of the temple. They were reprimanded and told to never speak in the name of Jesus again. Peter's boldness in face of the religious leaders of the day was simply, "I cannot keep from speaking what I have seen and heard."

Could your own boldness use an energizing of the work of God? It appears that when God is at work in our lives and we see Him accomplishing His will, it becomes easier for us to say something.

Have you ever said, "I just don't know what to say"? Maybe the issue is that you haven't seen God's hand in your life for a while. Why not look around and see what God is doing, and what He would like to do if you would just trust Him? Peter and John saw God at work in healing the lame man and refused to keep their mouths shut.

~~

I Stand Amazed!   January 14, 2010

> *And when he realized this, he went to the house of Mary, the mother of John who was also called Mark, where many were gathered together and were praying. When he knocked at the door of the gate, a servant-girl named Rhoda came to answer. When she recognized Peter's voice, because of her joy she did not open the gate, but ran in and announced that Peter was standing in front of the gate. They said to her, "You are out of your mind!" But she kept insisting that it was so. They kept saying, "It is his angel." But Peter continued knocking; and when they had opened the door, they saw him and were amazed.* (Acts 12:12-16, NASB)

Ever have an answer to prayer and then discover you were totally amazed that it was answered? Strange how we say we have faith and then when the answer to our prayer comes, we are amazed at the outcome.

The early Church was in the same situation. They prayed for the release of Peter from jail; and yet, when he appeared at the home where they were meeting, they determined it must be his angel. On the surface that seems like a major lack of faith.

Amazement to answered prayer is more than likely our response, also. Maybe because of lack of faith, we are amazed. More than likely, it is the realization that we are in the presence of a God who answers prayer. Amazement is our only true response. Stand amazed at His answer to prayer and in His presence.

~~

Harmony and Peace   January 21, 2010

> *In this way aim for harmony in the church, and try to build each other up.* (Romans 14:19, TLB)

Here in the book of Romans, Paul stated that differences of opinion existed in the Roman church concerning food that had been offered to idols and then eaten. He reminded the Roman church that not everyone's opinions are the same. He concluded that harmony, peace, and the building up of one another is more important than personal opinions or preferences. Sometimes it is necessary to yield our personal preferences for the sake of others.

No one was any more adamant about freedom in Christ than was the apostle Paul. He often spoke of the freedom to live life without the restraints of the Law. The basis of his belief was that, through God's grace, we have been set free through the blood of Christ. Yet our freedom should never cause a brother or sister to stumble in their faith. Don't allow your freedoms to harm another believer. Aim high! Work at harmony, peace, and the building up of one another.

~~

Life Through the Cross
January 29, 2010

> *For the word of the cross is foolishness to those who are perishing, but to us who are being saved it is the power of God.* (1 Corinthians 1:18, NASB)

The cross is definitely a defining line. The work of Christ on the cross was the complete redemption of mankind. If you are a believer in Jesus and His death, burial, and resurrection, then you will understand what the verse means when it says, "But to us who are being saved it is the power of God." It would seem foolishness to a person who rejects the cross as the way of salvation. The dividing line is faith in the person of Jesus and His death on the cross.

Maybe you have felt a need to find meaning in life beyond anything you could imagine. It requires death. It means death to yourself and acceptance of life in Christ. What a great trade! It is easy to understand why it would seem foolish to those who have rejected Jesus. But if you have trusted Him, then you know the power of God over sin, self, and the world. Praise God for the opportunity to live through the cross.

~~

Rules or People?
February 11, 2010

> *Then Jesus went over to their synagogue, where He noticed a man with a deformed hand. The Pharisees asked Jesus, "Does the law permit a person to work by healing on the Sabbath?" (They were hoping He would say yes, so they could bring charges against Him.) And He answered, "If you had a sheep that fell into a well on the Sabbath, wouldn't you work to pull it out? Of course you would. And how much more valuable is a person than a sheep! Yes, the law permits a person to do good on the Sabbath." Then He said to the man, "Hold out your hand." So the man held out his hand, and it was restored, just like the other one! Then the Pharisees called a meeting to plot how to kill Jesus.* (Matthew 12:9-14, NLT)

Jesus' enemies came from the religious crowd. They constantly sought for a way to condemn Jesus for breaking the Law of Moses. Working on the Sabbath was strictly forbidden by the Law. The opportunity for pushing the envelope came when Jesus saw a man with a deformed hand. Jesus asked the Pharisees if a sheep fell into a well on the Sabbath, would they have to work to pull it out, and would they pull it out? Of course, the answer was "yes." Then Jesus showed the value of a man over not only a sheep but over the Law. He turned to the man and healed him. The Pharisees were so upset that they called a meeting to determine the best way to kill Jesus.

Does your understanding of the Law of Moses place it above people needs? It is easy to put rules above people needs. Jesus reminded the Pharisees, at another time, that "the Sabbath was made for man, not man for the Sabbath." Be careful how you judge one another.

~~

New Hope

February 18, 2010

"For this reason I say to you, her sins, which are many, have been forgiven, for she loved much; but he who is forgiven little, loves little." Then He said to her, "Your sins have been forgiven." (Luke 7:47-48, NASB)

Religious movements or political ventures are generally started by an individual with followers willing to believe in what the leader says or does. Throughout history, the leaders have proven to either lead people astray or establish something positive for the good of mankind.

Jesus invaded first century Palestine with a new message and new hope. As His followers, we need to take a good look at His words and actions. As the founder of not only our faith but of a new approach to life, He challenges His followers with His lifestyle and His words.

Jesus found Himself in the home of Simon, the religious one. At that time, a prostitute settled at the feet of Jesus and began to wash His feet with her tears - tears of remorse, repentance, and faith. Jesus, knowing of her sin and her repentant heart, announced her forgiveness. The reason was because of her faith and her great love for Jesus. At the same time, He condemned Simon for his lack of love, repentance, remorse, and faith.

When you realize what a sinner you are and how much you need forgiveness, you will look for the Savior to change your life through His forgiveness and His love. Your faith will save you.

~~

Tired of Waiting

March 15, 2010

For this reason also, since the day we heard of it, we have not ceased to pray for you and to ask that you may be filled with the knowledge of His will in all spiritual wisdom and understanding, so that you will walk in a manner worthy of the Lord, to please Him in all respects, bearing fruit in every good work and increasing in the knowledge of God; strengthened with all power, according to His glorious might, for the attaining of all steadfastness and patience; (Colossians 1:9-11, NASB)

The pastor, the mother of preschoolers, the contractor, the school principal, the doctor, and the farmer all prayed the same prayer: "Lord, give me patience, but please hurry up about it." Ever need patience? Ever wish God would give you more patience but you were a little tired of waiting?

The apostle Paul wrote to the Colossian church to assure them he was praying for them, and desired that they know God's will and walk in such a way that their lives would please God. In order for that to be accomplished, they needed God's power to receive the patience. Patience is a fruit of the Spirit, not a contrived mental state or emotion derived from our determination. Pray for the Holy Spirit to be your power and to fill your life with God's patience. You might need it even today.

~~

Give What You Have

March 25, 2010

One of His disciples, Andrew, Simon Peter's brother, said to Him, "There is a lad here who has five barley loaves and two fish, but what are these for so many people?" (John 6:8-9, NASB)

Has God ever used you to serve others? The young lad left home with a lunch of five barley loaves and two fish. It was not a large amount of food but likely just enough to satisfy his own hunger. Jesus had asked the disciples to feed the thousands of people who had come to hear Him teach the words of life. As the multitude became hungry, Jesus knew He needed to feed them. The disciples were overwhelmed with the task of meeting people needs beyond their means. They checked around and found a young lad with five loaves and two fish. Their response was simply, "What are these for so many people?" Jesus knew He could use this young lad and his lunch to meet a great need. Do you know God can use your life to bless many?

God has chosen to use you in His mighty plan. A young lad with a small amount of food fed 5,000 with food left over. He merely gave what he had into the hands of Jesus.

Will you give what you have into His hands, and allow Him to use your life to meet needs and glorify God? You may not see that you have much to give, but remember the disciple's evaluation of the lad's lunch was, "What are these for so many people?" In God's hands, you can be used of God also.

~~

Faith Struggles

> *Thomas answered and said to Him, "My Lord and my God!" Jesus said to him, "Because you have seen Me, have you believed? Blessed are they who did not see, and yet believed."* (John 20:28-29, NASB)

Doubting Thomas, as he was known, may remind you of yourself. Doubting our own faith in Christ and His resurrection is not abnormal. There may be times when we feel like the man who said to Jesus, "I do believe; help my unbelief."

Thomas remarked that unless he had proof, he could not believe. When the hands and the side of Jesus were shown to Thomas, he cried out, "My Lord and my God!" You have not seen Jesus as Thomas did, yet you believe. Jesus declares you blessed because you believe without the proof of an actual body. Faith is based on the unseen.

The Scripture says, "We walk by faith, not by sight" (2 Corinthians 5:7). That is what makes it faith. We do not know what tomorrow will bring because it is unseen. As Thomas struggled with faith because he had not seen Jesus as the other disciples had seen Him a week earlier, you too may be struggling with your faith. Remember that if you see it and have absolute proof, it requires no faith; and "without faith it is impossible to please [God]" (Hebrews 11:6).

As we celebrate this Resurrection Sunday, express your faith in Jesus. Although you have not seen Him or touched His hands or His side, through faith say with Thomas, "My Lord and my God!"

~~

Something Missing

April 15, 2010

But when Simon Peter saw that, he fell down at Jesus' feet, saying, "Go away from me Lord, for I am a sinful man!" (Luke 5:8, NASB)

Is there a missing element in your life that keeps God from using you more in the work of His kingdom? Could that missing character trait be humility and brokenness? Peter and the other disciples were fishing and had caught nothing. They were on the shore preparing their nets for the next fishing expedition when Jesus showed up on the scene. His words to them were, "Put out into the deep water and let down your nets for a catch" (Luke 5:4). Peter was quick to point out to Jesus that they had already fished all night and caught nothing, but he was willing to follow the wishes of Jesus. When they drew up their nets, the catch was so great that the nets began to break. They called the other disciples to bring another boat, and the load of fish caused both boats to begin to sink. Now that is a fishing trip anyone would want to be on!

The response of Peter gives us insight into the future of his involvement in Jesus' mission. Peter was humbled and broken as he recognized his own inadequacies and sin. His words and actions show this as he fell to his face before Jesus and acknowledged his sin.

We will never be used of God for His glory as long as we see ourselves as anything other than a person needful of God's grace. We may put too much emphasis on our own abilities and talents, and not enough on God's amazing power and our need of Him.

Humility and brokenness will lead you to surrender to God and trust Him. Like Peter, you will fall at His feet in humility, brokenness, and amazement.

~~

~ A Personal Note ~

My wife, Tommie, and I have known Dennis and Sandy for almost forty years. So, naturally we were burdened for our dear friend when he told us the news regarding his health. I remember the phone call when Dennis informed us that he would be starting chemotherapy treatments. His voice was very emotional and tearful, however, I never heard or saw high emotion after that point in time.

During that call, Dennis asked us to join him and Sandy camping as he began those treatments. The chemo made him so sick that he could expend energy only to sit (and if you knew Dennis, you understand this to be abnormal).

Despite the pain and sickness, I marveled that he never complained. Dennis' mind was set *"on things above"* with a strong intent to endure for Sandy's sake and for his grandchildren, the boys who called him "Tapaw."

Over the years of his fight with cancer, Tommie and I would often meet Dennis and Sandy at a campground or a state park. He seemed to find a special peace away from the city, and some of his best *Encourager* messages came during those times of respite. Many phone calls during those years of struggle were positive and full of discussion about faith in the face of difficulty. Dennis always focused on two things: his family, and sharing his faith with whoever would listen. I named him the "Preaching Machine" before cancer was even on the horizon, and he lived up to that name right to the end. He lived to preach the Word *"in season and out of season"* and he told anyone who would listen that "Jesus is Lord."

Dennis' long battle with cancer demonstrated to us the truth of living out Romans 12:12, *"Be joyful in hope, patient in affliction, faithful in prayer"* (NIV). Dennis lived this verse every day while fighting the cancer — even during his worst times. The message Dennis exemplified: "Make each day count to God's glory; spend time with your family; use the spiritual gifts God has entrusted to you; and never, never give up!"

~ Don

~~

Are You a Quitter?   April 22, 2010

> *Do not be deceived, God is not mocked; for whatever a man sows, this he will also reap. For the one who sows to his own flesh will from the flesh reap corruption, but the one who sows to the Spirit will from the Spirit reap eternal life. Let us not lose heart in doing good, for in due time we will reap if we do not grow weary.*
> (Galatians 6:7-9, NASB)

"I QUIT!" Ever feel like screaming those two words at the top of your lungs because you were ready to throw in the towel? Are you ready to stop struggling over your personal demon? You have tried and tried, and it seems like you cannot overcome the struggle. It could be your marriage - the dream you had of marriage bliss never materialized and now you want to walk away. Maybe you are ready to quit as a parent - you have tried everything and your child or teenager still is causing you grief.

For some of you, it is the ministry. Ministry was supposed to be the greatest and most wonderful, rewarding experience in life, but nobody told you that the people to whom you were to minister could and would be cruel. They failed to tell you how ruthless, mean, unforgiving, and unimpressed they would be with your love and care for them. It may seem to you the only answer is to quit.

You may be struggling with a health issue that seems to never go away, and quitting means you would close your eyes and hope to be with Jesus in the next few minutes because you have lost your desire and fight to live. You may find yourself in a boring, unfulfilling job that seems to be going nowhere - you are looking for any way out; but with the economy in shambles, you can't quit even though every thought is about walking away to any other job.

You are no different than most folks. Everyone has the desire to quit once in a while. You may have lost your passion, your drive, your happiness, and your love for God and people. How about remembering a few things? We do not reap the rewards of life immediately. We will reap, but in due time. Instant gratification is not God's way. Our heart's desire to bring about a better world will bring a reward if we don't quit.

The words of John the Baptist might do you good: "He must increase, but I must decrease" (John 3:30). Our reason for being on this earth is to glorify God, not to bring recognition to ourselves. A heart and life submitted to God will bring glory to Him. Who is at the center of your life, your family, your job, or your ministry? If it is God, then you won't quit. Live your life with God at the center of everything. Quitting is not an option.

~~

True Freedom
April 29, 2010

> *So Jesus was saying to those Jews who had believed Him, "If you continue in My word, then you are truly disciples of Mine; and you will know the truth, and the truth will make you free."* (John 8:31-32, NASB)

Jesus knew the desire in everyone's heart was to be free. To the Jews of His day, their freedom meant they would no longer be under the rule of Rome. Jesus announced to the Jews who had believed in Him that they could have true freedom. They were the Jews who had found the truth that Jesus was their true Messiah.

The freedom was of the spirit and soul. It was a release from the control of sin and self and Satan. His admonishment was, "If you abide in My word, you are truly My disciples" (John 8:31, ESV). Those who followed Christ lived by, believed in, and practiced His teachings. Real disciples, real followers, learners of Christ, were people of the Word. Freedom was based on truth. Without truth there is no true freedom. The Word was, and still is, truth.

Do you want to be a disciple of Jesus? Do you desire truth and freedom? It has been said that the most important discipline of the Christian life is to hear, read, study, memorize, and meditate on the Word of God - the Bible. Take the challenge of Jesus today and abide in His Word. It will set you free through the discovery of truth.

~~

Prayer Time

May 13, 2010

> *But Jesus Himself would often slip away to the wilderness and pray.*
> (Luke 5:16, NASB)

Jesus communicated with the Father in prayer. He was known for His praying, and the strength and power He received from prayer. It was the only subject that His disciples specifically asked that He teach them:

> *It happened that while Jesus was praying in a certain place, after He had finished, one of His disciples said to Him, "Lord, teach us to pray just as John also taught his disciples." (Luke 11:1)*

No doubt you have been in a prayer meeting when several believers joined together to ask God to meet a specific need or to just praise Him. Never underestimate the power of corporate prayer. But it appears from scripture, that the major dynamic of Jesus' prayer life was slipping away to pray alone:

> *It was at this time that He went off to the mountain to pray, and He spent the whole night in prayer to God. (Luke 6:12)*

His prayer time was alone, in a secluded place, at a specific time, for a specific reason. When was the last time you went to a place to pray, by yourself, for a specific reason? Alone times with the Father are a vital part of our spiritual life and growth. It is also the secret to answered prayer.

Why not take time this week to remove yourself from the hustle of life; the struggles of work, school, family, or ministry; and be refreshed in a time of prayer? Remember: find the time to be alone, in a secluded place, and with a specific reason. God will meet you there.

~~

What Plans?

> *"For thus says the Lord, '...For I know the plans that I have for you,' declares the Lord, 'plans for welfare and not for calamity to give you a future and a hope. Then you will call upon Me and come and pray to Me, and I will listen to you. You will seek Me and find Me when you search for Me with all your heart. I will be found by you,' declares the Lord, 'and I will restore your fortunes...' "*
> (Jeremiah 29:10-14, NASB)

The nation of Israel had been taken into exile as captives of the Babylonians. It appeared from every perspective that all hope was lost of ever going back home to Israel. They needed the prophet of God, Jeremiah, to remind them that God was in charge of their present and their future. God had plans.

Notice how many times Jeremiah used the pronoun "you." God has plans for *you*. God has a future and a hope for *you*. If *you* call on Him and come to Him and pray to Him, He will listen to *you*. If *you* seek Him with all your heart, *you* will find Him. He will restore *you*.

What a great God we serve and love. He is for YOU. He cares about YOU. No matter what your circumstances or situation, He promises His plans for your future and gives YOU hope. Never give up or give in. Trust in the Lord with all your heart and He will direct your steps to fulfill His plans for YOU.

Never forget that God loves you and knows what is best for your life. You may not understand why things are happening to you until you step into eternity. But rest assured - God does have plans for you and He does cause all things to work together for good.

~~

Hurtful Words

> *So also you, since you are zealous of spiritual gifts, seek to abound for the edification of the church. What is the outcome then, brethren? When you assemble, each one has a psalm, has a teaching, has a revelation, has a tongue, has an interpretation. Let all things be done for edification.* (1 Corinthians 14:12, 26; NASB)

> *Let no unwholesome word proceed from your mouth, but only such a word as is good for edification according to the need of the moment, so that it will give grace to those who hear.* (Ephesians 4:29)

Ever been hurt by a word from a friend, teacher, parent, relative, coach, or another important person in your life? It has been said that for every negative word spoken, it takes seventeen positive ones to undo the damage. Maybe you have been the recipient of such discouragement or maybe you were the one who let those hurtful words flow from your lips. The Bible is very clear that words we utter should be to edify. The word means to "build up."

In the use of spiritual gifts within the church setting, it is possible to either destroy or to edify one another. Paul encourages uplifting one another with the use of spiritual gifts. All things are to be done for edification. Words should be good for building up one another for the need of the moment. The result is that words which edify give grace to those who hear.

Why not be committed to building up other believers and say words that edify, and use your spiritual gifts to build up one another?

~~

Do You Care?   June 3, 2010

But I hope in the Lord Jesus to send Timothy to you shortly, so that I also may be encouraged when I learn of your condition. For I have no one else of kindred spirit who will genuinely be concerned for your welfare. (Philippians 2:19-20, NASB)

If someone was separated from you by time and space, and you desired to know how they were doing, what would you do? Paul was apart from the Philippians yet loved and cared for them very much. He was in prison so he could not visit them. He had a solution: send someone who cared as much as he did.

That person with kindred spirit was Timothy. Timothy was a strong believer in Jesus Christ, and had learned his spiritual walk from Paul. Paul was like a spiritual father to Timothy. He cared for the people, loved them deeply; and when Paul wanted someone to minister to their needs, Timothy was the man. He was a pastor at heart - a shepherd who cared for the sheep.

How great it would be to send someone in your place to check on those you love. Paul's commentary on Timothy was that no one genuinely cared for the Philippians like Paul except Timothy. Are you Paul or Timothy? Do you care for a flock of people? Maybe it is your family, your church, your small group, or your work mates. It is an encouragement to know that someone is being loved and cared for, whether you are Paul or Timothy.

~~

Hope Lives

June 10, 2010

> *This I recall to my mind, Therefore I have hope. The Lord's lovingkindnesses indeed never cease, For His compassions never fail. They are new every morning; Great is Your faithfulness. "The Lord is my portion," says my soul, "Therefore I have hope in Him." The Lord is good to those who wait for Him, To the person who seeks Him.*
> (Lamentations 3:21-25, NASB)

What is the source of your hope? Jeremiah, who is credited with writing the book of Lamentations, says his hope is in the Lord. Whenever he recalls with his mind where his hope originates, he is assured it is from the Lord.

The reason the Lord gives us hope is because His lovingkindness never ceases. He is full of compassion that never fails. Every day, the faithfulness of God brings hope. Deep in Jeremiah's soul he says, "I have hope."

What are you seeking to give you hope today? Is it in the job you have, or the money in the bank, or your health, or your knowledge, or status? The only hope that will truly last is based on the lovingkindness, faithfulness, and compassion of the Lord. Trust Him, not what He can do for you, or even has done for you in the past. True hope is in the Lord Himself.

Make today a special day by trusting only in the Lord and His character.

~~

Been Blessed?

June 17, 2010

> *God be gracious to us and bless us,*
> *And cause His face to shine upon us - Selah.*
> *That Your way may be known on the earth, Your salvation among all nations.*
> *Let the peoples praise You, O God; Let all the peoples praise You.*
> *Let the nations be glad and sing for joy;*
> *For You will judge the peoples with uprightness*
> *And guide the nations on the earth. Selah.*
> *Let the peoples praise You, O God; Let all the peoples praise You.*
> *The earth has yielded its produce; God, our God, blesses us.*
> *God blesses us, That all the ends of the earth may fear Him.*
> (Psalm 67:1-7, NASB)

Has God blessed you, your family, your church, or your job lately? Did you ask Him to bless you? Would you feel right about asking for a special blessing from

God? According to the psalmist King David we should ask God for a blessing, but for a reason.

David asked for God to be gracious to Israel, to bless them, and to cause His face to shine on them. The reason was so that the ways of God would be known to the whole earth, and then salvation would spread to the ends of the earth.

The blessings of God also brought praise to God's name. We were created to praise God, and His blessings encourage us to praise Him. No doubt the main reason God would bless us is so that others would know Him. "That all the ends of the earth would fear [respect, honor, and know] Him" (vs. 7).

Why not ask God for a blessing today, not in order to brag about your worthiness to receive a blessing, but in order to brag on God and tell people about Him? Ask and you will receive.

~~

From Crying to Smiling   June 24, 2010

Now it came about, as she continued praying before the Lord, that Eli was watching her mouth. As for Hannah, she was speaking in her heart, only her lips were moving, but her voice was not heard. So Eli thought she was drunk. Then Eli said to her, "How long will you make yourself drunk? Put away your wine from you." But Hannah replied, "No, my lord, I am a woman oppressed in spirit; I have drunk neither wine nor strong drink, but I have poured out my soul before the Lord. Do not consider your maidservant as a worthless woman, for I have spoken until now out of my great concern and provocation." Then Eli answered and said, "Go in peace; and may the God of Israel grant your petition that you have asked of Him." She said, "Let your maidservant find favor in your sight." So the woman went her way and ate, and her face was no longer sad. (1 Samuel 1:12-18, NASB)

Do you have a need so great that even your face shows the sadness you feel? Hannah wanted a child and was unable to have one. She cried unto the Lord to send her a son. Eli the priest saw her and thought she was drunk. She explained her need and Eli told her that because of God's graciousness, she would receive her son. Her face was no longer sad.

God desires to meet your need today. Cry unto Him and expect an answer to your request. He is full of grace and love for you, and His grace is sufficient to meet your deepest desire. Thank God and smile.

~~

The Simple Message

July 8, 2010

After the usual readings from the books of Moses and the prophets, those in charge of the service sent them this message: "Brothers, if you have any word of encouragement for the people, come and give it." (Acts 13:15, NLT)

"When they had done all that the prophecies said about Him, they took Him down from the cross and placed Him in a tomb. But God raised Him from the dead! And over a period of many days He appeared to those who had gone with Him from Galilee to Jerusalem. They are now His witnesses to the people of Israel. And now we are here to bring you this Good News." (Acts 13:29-32)

"Brothers, listen! We are here to proclaim that through this man Jesus there is forgiveness for your sins. Everyone who believes in Him is declared right with God - something the law of Moses could never do." (Acts 13:38-39)

Paul and Barnabas found themselves in the temple with an invitation to teach the Hebrew Bible to all present. The men in charge of the temple called it "a word of encouragement." Paul, of course, had the greatest word of encouragement possible. The simple message was that Jesus had been crucified on a cross, three days later arose from the dead, never to die again, and appeared to countless witnesses; and that this same Jesus, because of His death and resurrection, could forgive all their sins and free them from guilt and make them right with God. They called this the "Good News" which it truly was and still is.

The Jewish people had been given the Law, which gave them knowledge of sin but no way to remove or forgive it. The coming of Christ, the Messiah, assured all of us a way to a true relationship with God. The death of Jesus on the cross was a substitute for us, who truly deserve to die for our sin. The resurrection brought justification for our sin.

Paul and Barnabas saw that their mission was to declare this Good News. Encouragement, hope, eternal life, forgiveness, freedom from guilt, and a right relationship with God were all theirs through Jesus.

Have you found the "good news" or have you only heard the condemnation of the Law and not the freedom of the cross and resurrection? Jesus came to give you life and life abundantly. Trust Him today.

~~

The Secret
July 15, 2010

Not that I was ever in need, for I have learned how to be content with whatever I have. I know how to live on almost nothing or with everything. I have learned the secret of living in every situation, whether it is with a full stomach or empty, with plenty or little. For I can do everything through Christ, who gives me strength.
(Philippians 4:11-13, NLT)

Much has been written about the secrets to this and that - maybe the secret to happiness, success, a great marriage, the right job, gaining wealth, and on and on. The apostle Paul gives a secret to living in every situation. Can you imagine life that is never changing, always the same? Of course that is not the case. You may find yourself in one situation one day and it could be totally changed the next. The Bible's answer to the secret of living in every situation is: CONTENTMENT.

Obviously, it is difficult to be content. The reason is the lack of strength to overcome viewing life by the situation of the moment. To view life as only the struggle of the moment will bring discouragement and hopelessness.

Paul explained his life as one in which he had experienced living on almost nothing or having everything. The secret he learned was that Christ provided the strength in order for him to face anything. The power of Christ led him to contentment because he realized and accepted that Christ was in charge of his life.

Do you need to find that secret? Do you need to find strength for your situation in the strength that only Christ can provide? Trust Him today because you can truly do all things through the One who gives you His strength. To Him be the glory.

~~

An Encouraging Heart
July 22, 2010

Is there any encouragement from belonging to Christ? Any comfort from His love? Any fellowship together in the Spirit? Are your hearts tender and compassionate? Then make me truly happy by agreeing wholeheartedly with each other, loving one another, and working together with one mind and purpose. (Philippians 2:1-2, NLT)

Is your heart tender and compassionate? What a probing question. What is inside of you? The encouragement you are to others is determined by what is in your own heart. Is it a heart of an encourager? Is it a heart of love? Is your heart at one mind and purpose with another? Then you can be an encourager.

The theologian William Barclay once wrote, "One of the highest of human duties is the duty of encouragement... It is easy to laugh at men's ideals; it is easy to pour cold water on their enthusiasm; it is easy to discourage others. The world is full of discouragers. We have a Christian duty to encourage one another. Many a time a word of praise or thanks or appreciation or cheer has kept a man on his feet. Blessed is the man who speaks such a word."

Is your heart a heart of encouragement? Be aware that every day God will send someone into your life who needs to be uplifted. He will send them your way in order that you can "be there" for them. Look for them. They may be as near as your spouse or child. It may be a discouraged student or a co-worker. It may be in a hospital room, or a nursing home. You are God's emissary of the moment. Be available with a heart ready to encourage.

~~

Deep Roots

July 29, 2010

"Blessed is the man who trusts in the Lord and whose trust is the Lord.
For he will be like a tree planted by the water, that extends its roots by a stream and will not fear when the heat comes; but its leaves will be green,
and it will not be anxious in a year of drought nor cease to yield fruit."
(Jeremiah 17:7-8, NASB)

Do you wish God would bless you? God wants to bless us. He desires to fill our lives with blessings. But the question is: "What does God want of us?" The answer is simply that He wants us to trust Him. That would mean we are no longer in control of our lives - God is. It means that in all things, and every situation and circumstance, our trust is not in anything that we can do, anyone we know, or any influence we can exert. Our trust is in the Lord.

Jeremiah explains that the person who trusts in the Lord is like a tree with a deep root system - it is planted by the water with an endless supply of moisture. The roots extend into the stream and when heat comes, it never lacks the strength to survive. The result is a tree whose leaves are ever green and which does not fear drought nor cease to produce fruit.

So it is with your life. When you trust in the Lord, your roots are grounded in Him. You have no reason to be afraid or lose sight of your purpose for life. Your life will produce the fruit of God's Holy Spirit: love, joy, peace, patience, kindness, goodness, faithfulness, gentleness and self-control. Trust, depend on, lean on, rely upon, yield to, and be supported by the Lord; and you will be blessed.

~~

Are You Part of the Flock?

August 5, 2010

So when they had finished breakfast, Jesus said to Simon Peter, "Simon, son of John, do you love Me more than these?" He said to Him, "Yes, Lord; You know that I love You." He said to him, "Tend My lambs."
He said to him again a second time, "Simon, son of John, do you love Me?" He said to Him, "Yes, Lord; You know that I love You." He said to him, "Shepherd My sheep."
He said to him the third time, "Simon, son of John, do you love Me?" Peter was grieved because He said to him the third time, "Do you love Me?" And he said to Him, "Lord, You know all things; You know that I love You." Jesus said to him, "Tend My sheep." (John 21:15-17, NASB)

The Bible uses many metaphors to describe the Church. It is compared to a bride, a field, a flock, a building, a people for God's possession, sheep, an assembly. Jesus Himself said, "I will build my church; and the gates of hell shall not prevail against it" (Matthew 16:18, KJV).

Jesus confronted the apostle Peter with the imperative of caring for the flock. Jesus saw the Church as sheep needing leadership - a leader that would tend, care for, and shepherd the flock of sheep He called His Church. It should show us the importance of the Church in our lives to realize that Jesus left disciples to care for His Church.

Today, He still has those whose calling is to shepherd the sheep. We all need the fellowship, the teaching, the worship, the ministry of the Church, but especially the care we receive from the Church. Are you a part of the flock? Join with a local church in your area this Sunday and experience, along with the other sheep, what it means to be a part of Jesus' flock.

~~

What a Warranty!

August 12, 2010

It is God who enables us, along with you, to stand firm for Christ. He has commissioned us, and He has identified us as His own by placing the Holy Spirit in our hearts as the first installment that guarantees everything He has promised us.
(2 Corinthians 1:21-22, NLT)

Ever buy something with a warranty? It means that if anything goes wrong with the product, you can return it. Of course, the warranty is usually short-lived. It has certain requirements that must be upheld in order to remain in effect. After a few months or years, it is no longer good. Often, the store wants you to buy an extended warranty that goes for another length of time.

Aren't you glad God doesn't have the same approach to your walk with Him? Instead of us being the ones who meet the requirements, it is God who gives us the ability to stand firm for Christ. He is the One who delivers the product - eternal life - and then guarantees it for all eternity.

It is God who commissions us and identifies us as belonging to Him. He even goes so far as to place His Holy Spirit within us as the symbol of His ownership of our lives and a guarantee that we will never lose what He has given us. And the Scripture says that the Holy Spirit is the first installment of everything He will give us throughout eternity. What incredible assurance, hope, and encouragement that we have because of the indwelling Holy Spirit.

God lives in you and makes you confident that "He who has begun a good work in you will complete it" (Philippians 1:6, NKJV). What a terrific guarantee! God paid for your eternal life in Christ with Jesus' death and resurrection, and then gave you His Spirit as a guarantee. You serve an amazing God. Praise Him today and thank Him for His Holy Spirit.

~~

Removing the Veil   August 19, 2010

Since this new way gives us such confidence, we can be very bold. We are not like Moses, who put a veil over his face so the people of Israel would not see the glory, even though it was destined to fade away. But the people's minds were hardened, and to this day whenever the old covenant is being read, the same veil covers their minds so they cannot understand the truth. And this veil can be removed only by believing in Christ. Yes, even today when they read Moses' writings, their hearts are covered with that veil, and they do not understand. But whenever someone turns to the Lord, the veil is taken away. For the Lord is the Spirit, and wherever the Spirit of the Lord is, there is freedom. So all of us who have had that veil removed can see and reflect the glory of the Lord. And the Lord - who is the Spirit - makes us more and more like Him as we are changed into His glorious image. (2 Corinthians 3:12-18, NLT)

The New Covenant (the covenant of grace) extending through Jesus' death and resurrection - the privilege of being right with God by grace through faith - is the basis of our confidence before God. Unlike the Old Covenant, written on tablets of stone and given to Moses as the Law, the New Covenant was written on the human heart. Whenever we attempt to live by laws, rules, and regulations, and believe that the achievement of that attempt gives us a real relationship with God, we are fooling ourselves and a veil of non-truth is over our eyes.

Moses came from Mt. Sinai with the Ten Commandments, and because of being in the presence of God and receiving the Law, his face shone with the glory of God. Yet the glory faded. Moses wore a veil over his face so Israel could not see glory fading away. The New Covenant in the blood of Christ does not fade.

The glory of God is reflected in the life of everyone who comes to believe in Christ. The veil is removed and God's glory is reflected as the Spirit of God, the Holy Spirit, lives in us.

What an incredible thought: God is in you and is working in your life to make you like Jesus, for His glory. No wonder Romans 11:36 says: "For everything comes from Him and exists by His power and is intended for His glory. All glory to Him forever! Amen."

~~

The Precious Treasure August 26, 2010

> *Therefore, since God in His mercy has given us this new way, we never give up.*
> *We now have this light shining in our hearts, but we ourselves are like fragile clay jars containing this great treasure. This makes it clear that our great power is from God, not from ourselves.*
> *We know that God, who raised the Lord Jesus, will also raise us with Jesus and present us to Himself together with you. All of this is for your benefit. And as God's grace reaches more and more people, there will be great thanksgiving, and God will receive more and more glory. That is why we never give up. Though our bodies are dying, our spirits are being renewed every day.* (2 Corinthians 4:1, 7, 14-16; NLT)

The ministry of the New Covenant is a ministry of reflecting the light of the glory of God into a world of people who need hope, encouragement, and life. God receives glory as His light is reflected by those who believe in Jesus. Because this ministry is of God and for His glory, we never give up in proclaiming the Good News of salvation by grace through faith.

The struggle we have is that the Gospel, the wonderful treasure, is contained and proclaimed from a perishable house - the human body. All of us live in bodies that will eventually die and are in that process now. The precious treasure of the

Gospel is proclaimed from the frailty of the human life and body in order that it becomes obvious to all that it is God at work, and not us.

The hope of the believer in Christ is that as God raised Jesus from the dead after His death on the cross, we too will be raised to life through Christ. Our hope is of eternal dimensions. Through the light of God we reflect in our lives, the more people will come to know Jesus as their own Savior. God's grace will bring more and more people to Christ and in turn, God will receive more and more glory.

That truly is why, no matter the circumstances you are experiencing, God is at work in your life for His glory. That is why we do not give up. Our bodies may be dying, but our Spirits are being renewed day by day. To God be the glory.

~~

Any Room Left?   September 9, 2010

> But when Peter saw this, he replied to the people, "Men of Israel, why are you amazed at this, or why do you gaze at us, as if by our own power or piety we had made him walk?" (Acts 3:12, NASB)

Where does the credit go when something great happens in your life? We easily like to think we achieved a great accomplishment or that somehow we can take credit and brag about it. Peter was eager to not allow the healing of the lame man to be credited to himself but to the Great Physician. Often, people will try to shower you with credit when only God is the One who deserves the glory. Peter quickly reminded everyone that it was not by his power, nor was it because he was pious enough, but only by the power of God alone that a lame man was healed. Our purpose is always to glorify God and give Him credit for all good that comes our way.

There is a story of a young martial arts student who was having tea with his master. He said, "I have learned all you have to teach me about defending myself. I want to learn one more thing now. Please teach me about the ways of God."

The master took the tea kettle and started pouring the student's cup full of tea. Soon the cup was full and began to spill over onto the saucer. The master continued to pour the tea until it spilled over the saucer and then onto the floor.

The student finally said, "Stop, stop, the tea is spilling over. The cup can't take any more." The master then looked at the student and said, "You are so full of yourself that there is not room in your life for God. It is not possible for you to learn the ways of God until you learn to empty yourself."

And He was saying to them all, "If anyone wishes to come after Me, he must deny himself, and take up his cross daily and follow Me." (Luke 9:23)

~~

True Purpose   September 16, 2010

> *After these things the word of the Lord came to Abram in a vision, saying,*
> > *"Do not fear, Abram, I am a shield to you;*
> > *Your reward shall be very great."*
> *And He took him outside and said, "Now look toward the heavens, and count the stars, if you are able to count them." And He said to him, "So shall your descendants be." Then he believed in the Lord; and He reckoned it to him as righteousness.*
> (Genesis 15:1, 5-6; NASB)

Faith is our response to the revealed Word of God. When Abram was told he was to be the father of a great nation, his response was to believe God. How often do we not respond in faith? We try to "flesh it out" or do it our way.

Romans 14:23 says that "whatever is not from faith is sin." We try by all our power and abilities and means to make something happen. God does not receive the glory nor is He pleased with that which is not done in faith. We also try to enlist other people to help us "flesh it out." Nothing in our flesh, or in anyone else's flesh, pleases God. Why not allow God to work through His Spirit to accomplish the miraculous and to bring glory to Himself?

"Faith" is believing that God is able - and He only needs our cooperation to accomplish what He wants to be done. Then, and only then, can it be said, "To God be the glory; great things He has done."

What is God saying to you today? Is He asking you to trust, to have faith in Him to accomplish what He wants done in your life? Why not say "yes" to God and allow Him to have His will in your life? You may be facing trials and struggles; and God is asking you to just believe He is able and willing to come to your side, and lend you the grace and love to see you through your need. True purpose in life is to bring glory to God.

~~

Light Reflectors

September 23, 2010

So all of us who have had that veil removed can see and reflect the glory of the Lord. And the Lord - who is the Spirit - makes us more and more like Him as we are changed into His glorious image. (2 Corinthians 3:18, NLT)

Therefore, since God in His mercy has given us this new way, we never give up. For God, who said, "Let there be light in the darkness," has made this light shine in our hearts so we could know the glory of God that is seen in the face of Jesus Christ. We now have this light shining in our hearts, but we ourselves are like fragile clay jars containing this great treasure. This makes it clear that our great power is from God, not from ourselves. (2 Corinthians 4:1, 6-7)

The Bible gives us great insight into life. It says that our lives in Christ are like mirrors that reflect the glory of God. Our ultimate purpose in life is to glorify God. We are not here for our comfort or happiness but for Him and for His glory. As believers in Christ, the Holy Spirit lives in us to reflect the image of God. The more mature we become, the more we become like Jesus, and the more we bring glory to Him. Our ministry is to be reflectors of His glory so that God is known, praised, and worshipped.

The light we reflect is the image of Jesus. His love, mercy, compassion, grace, and truth are reflected to everyone as the image of God. The interesting thing is that God does that through imperfect, weak, and dying bodies. That, in turn, gives more glory to God because His power is expressed, and not ours. Our weak bodies are the vessel by which God shows Himself. To Him be the glory.

Why not let your light shine? You may think you are weak or undeserving. Well, guess what - God can still use you. It is because of your weak earthly vessel, which we call the human body, that you cannot take the credit for who you are or what you do. God receives all the glory. Let Jesus shine through you today.

~~

Shine Your Light

September 30, 2010

Then Jesus again spoke to them, saying, "I am the Light of the world; he who follows Me will not walk in the darkness, but will have the Light of life." (John 8:12, NASB)

In Him was life, and the life was the Light of men. The Light shines in the darkness, and the darkness did not comprehend it. (John 1:4-5)

"You are the light of the world. A city set on a hill cannot be hidden; nor does anyone light a lamp and put it under a basket, but on the lampstand, and it gives light to all who are in the house. Let your light shine before men in such a way that they may see your good works, and glorify your Father who is in heaven." (Matthew 5:14-16)

Spelunkers travel through caves. They understand the meaning of "pitch black." The minute the lights go out, it is impossible to see your hand in front of your face. Turning on a flashlight or a carbide light illuminates the cave. Darkness is dispelled and light permeates the interior of the cave. Why? Because light overcomes the darkness.

We are the light of the world because the life and light of Jesus are in us. His Holy Spirit reflects the image of Christ. Our light shines in a dark world (a world without the light of God) and brings glory to God. The basis of the New Covenant that God established through the life and death of Christ, His precious blood, and His resurrection is the life of Christ in the heart of every believer.

... giving thanks to the Father, who has qualified us to share in the inheritance of the saints in Light. For He rescued us from the domain of darkness, and transferred us to the kingdom of His beloved Son, in whom we have redemption, the forgiveness of sins. (Colossians 1:12-14)

We have been transferred from the kingdom of darkness into the kingdom of God through the blood of Christ by His granting us the forgiveness of sins and deliverance from darkness into His marvelous light. And it was all for the glory of God.

Celebrate your freedom from darkness into light. Rejoice in the forgiveness of your sins. Praise God that you are a part of His kingdom.

~~

DEEP Faith October 7, 2010

Then He told them many things in parables, saying: "A farmer went out to sow his seed... Some fell on rocky places, where it did not have much soil. It sprang up quickly, because the soil was shallow. But when the sun came up, the plants were scorched, and they withered because they had no root...
The seed falling on rocky ground refers to someone who hears the word and at once receives it with joy. But since they have no root, they last only a short time. When trouble or persecution comes because of the word, they quickly fall away."
(Matthew 13:3, 5-6, 20-21; NIV)

What is the depth of your walk with Christ? In Jesus' own words, He admonishes those who are shallow in their faith. Actually, He gives an emphatic warning that those who have a superficial faith will find their faith withering away when trouble or persecution comes. Some translations use the word "tribulation" to describe the cause of falling away.

Notice that this person is an "immediately" person. They respond to the Word with enthusiasm, quickly, and with joy. They like what they hear. The problem is that they have no root within themselves. The effect of the Word only lasts a short time. Then, as quickly as the Word was received, it also abruptly leaves with no lasting evidence.

Trials, tribulations, persecution, and adversity are all causes for the recipients of the Word to fall away. It is like a river that is a mile wide but only six inches deep. The river is easily disturbed by drought, floods, and algae - much like the way in which someone who receives the Word into a life that is shallow is easily disturbed.

What kind of recipient are you? Do you have roots that run deep into Christ? Do you flounder when things get tough? Anchor your life into the depths of Jesus and find strength to weather the worst of storms. God bless you in your spiritual growth into a deep relationship with Jesus.

~~

Only by Faith

October 14, 2010

> *What then shall we say that Abraham, our forefather according to the flesh, has found? For if Abraham was justified by works, he has something to boast about, but not before God. For what does the Scripture say? "Abraham believed God, and it was credited to him as righteousness." Now to the one who works, his wage is not credited as a favor, but as what is due. But to the one who does not work, but believes in Him who justifies the ungodly, his faith is credited as righteousness,* (Romans 4:1-5, NASB)

How important to you is your faith? What are you trusting in to give you a right relationship with God? You may believe that how you live, things you do or don't do, or your own performance would cause God to accept or reject you. Let me encourage you: you are right with God by faith, and faith alone.

Our father, Abraham, received a relationship with God because he believed in God and God's promises. Abraham was justified, or made righteous, by his faith and his faith alone. If he could have done works or deeds which would have given him a right relationship with God, then he could have bragged or boasted of himself and not given glory to God.

Abraham believed God and it was credited to him as righteousness in Genesis 15:6. Our relationship with God is not based on keeping laws or rules, or on our deeds and works, or our performance. It is based on our faith in God Himself, Jesus Christ. We all have sinned and fall short of the glory and holiness of God. The only way for that sin to be forgiven, and for a relationship with God to be established, is faith in God the Son, Jesus. He died for us on a cross and arose from the dead to give us life. But life, forgiveness, and right-standing with God are received only by faith.

Your faith determines not only your right relationship with God, but also, your faith keeps you daily assured of your relationship with God. Trusting God brings hope and encouragement.

Trust God with your life today. He loves you and cares for you. He desires to save you from your sin and guide your life.

~~

Taking Advice October 21, 2010

Finally, Paul called the crew together and said, "Men, you should have listened to me in the first place and not left Crete. You would have avoided all this damage and loss. But take courage! None of you will lose your lives, even though the ship will go down. For last night an angel of the God to whom I belong and whom I serve stood beside me, and he said, 'Don't be afraid, Paul, for you will surely stand trial before Caesar! What's more, God in His goodness has granted safety to everyone sailing with you.' So take courage! For I believe God. It will be just as He said. But we will be shipwrecked on an island." (Acts 27:21-26, NLT)

The apostle Paul was on his way to Rome to stand trial before Caesar as a common criminal. The ship he was on had not only a crew but other prisoners as well. Paul had warned the crew of impending disaster if they did not follow his instructions. They refused and found themselves in major difficulties. As things grew worse, Paul gathered the crew together and reprimanded them for not paying attention and following his advice. The problems and difficulties they faced could have been avoided, if only they had listened and heeded his warnings.

Do you ever find yourself in trouble for not taking the advice of those who are wise and knowledgeable? Paul did give them encouragement and hope in spite of their failure to follow his counsel. "Take courage" because none would lose their lives even though the ship would sink.

Sometimes our ship sinks because of our poor decisions, yet life is not over. There is still hope. God had spoken to Paul and assured him that he would arrive in Rome and stand before Caesar. God's purpose would be fulfilled. He also assured him that everyone on board would be safe as well. This was because of no reason other than the goodness and grace of God.

Even though we often fail in our obedience to God and fail to follow His directives, He still promises that His goodness will see us through. So Paul concluded with, "Take courage!" How could they take courage in light of the future prophesy of Paul concerning the ship's destiny? They could be courageous because Paul believed God.

Your faith will see you through even though the ship will sink, because God said it would. You may be on a sinking ship, but God is still in charge. Take courage and believe God. He will see you through to His intended purpose.

~~

Who's in Charge?

October 28, 2010

> Then the Lord answered Job out of the whirlwind and said,
> "Who is this that darkens counsel
> By words without knowledge?
> Now gird up your loins like a man,
> And I will ask you, and you instruct Me!
> Where were you when I laid the foundation of the earth?
> Tell Me, if you have understanding," (Job 38:1-4, NASB)
> "Have you ever...?" (Job 38:12)
> "Where is the way...?" (Job 38:19)
> "Can you send forth lightning...?" (Job 38:35)
> "Is it at your command that the eagle mounts up...?" (Job 39:27)
> Then the Lord said to Job,
> "Will the faultfinder contend with the Almighty?..."
> Then Job answered the Lord and said,
> "Behold, I am insignificant; what can I reply to You?
> I lay my hand on my mouth." (Job 40:1-4)

Job and his friends had questioned God and His intentions. After thirty-seven chapters, God finally spoke and gave wise counsel. The declaration of God and the conclusion of Job is that the Creator makes the decisions, determines outcomes, and directs the action.

Job's friends tried to blame Job for his problems. His wife asked him to curse God and die. Finally, God spoke and said that, as His creation, you cannot challenge His decisions. He is in charge. HE IS GOD!! You're not!!

Job's understanding of himself was that, in the scheme of things, he was insignificant. It does not mean he was of no worth but simply that in comparison to God, he was insignificant. Whenever we recognize the almighty nature of God and His sovereignty, we will see and exclaim along with the psalmist, "What is man that You are mindful of him, the son of man that You care for him?" (Psalm 8:4, ESV)

God has a purpose for your life, and He will fulfill it.

> Then Job answered the Lord and said, "I know that You can do all things, And that no purpose of Yours can be thwarted." (Job 42:1-2, NASB)

Rest assured that God knows all that is happening to you, through you, for you, and in you. He has a purpose that will bring glory to His wonderful name. Praise Him today for His watch-care and providence in your life.

> And looking at them Jesus said to them, "With people this is impossible, but with God all things are possible." (Matthew 19:26)

Take time right now to thank God that He is in charge.

~~

Got Trouble?

November 3, 2010

> We now have this light shining in our hearts, but we ourselves are like fragile clay jars containing this great treasure. This makes it clear that our great power is from God, not from ourselves.
> That is why we never give up... For our present troubles are small and won't last very long. Yet they produce for us a glory that vastly outweighs them and will last forever! So we don't look at the troubles we can see now; rather, we fix our gaze on things that cannot be seen. For the things we see now will soon be gone, but the things we cannot see will last forever. (2 Corinthians 4:7, 16-18; NASB)

The vacation was going well until it became evident that it was going to take a long time to reach Disneyland. That's when the complaining started. "How much further?" "Are we there yet?" Mom and Dad are thinking, "WILL IT EVER BE OVER?"

Does that sound much like life as well? What time did you wake up last night with the "stinking thinking" and the thoughts that could be labeled as "catastrophizing?" Was it at 2 AM, or 3 AM? How long was it before you were able to return to sleep? Maybe your thoughts were based on the assumption that all bad things will continue in eternity. How easy it is to forget that God is in charge of life and that He will see us through.

Whatever troubles we are experiencing are quite small compared to the eternal reward of heaven. They are producing immeasurable great glory that will last forever. The psalmist understood the feeling of endless trouble, yet wrote that "joy comes in the morning." No wonder, when we wake up in the middle of the night rehearsing the tragedy of living, that we long for the sun to arise so the night thoughts will go away.

What is the solution? Don't look at the troubles, but rather, look forward to what we have not yet seen. The troubles will soon be over, but the joys to come will last forever.

Praise the Lord for hope and encouragement. May God bless you today.

~~

Only Jesus

November 10, 2010

> *... Although I myself might have confidence even in the flesh. If anyone else has a mind to put confidence in the flesh, I far more...* (Philippians 3:4, NASB)

> *But whatever things were gain to me, those things I have counted as loss for the sake of Christ.* (Philippians 3:7)

> *Indeed, we had the sentence of death within ourselves so that we would not trust in ourselves, but in God who raises the dead;* (2 Corinthians 1:9)

The Bible reminds us that there is security in no one else, or no place else, other than in God. The apostle Paul's security, value, worth, trust, and confidence were not in his credentials. Because of his religious background, his heritage, his family, his wealth, and his social standing, he could have easily bragged about his standing with God and his fellow man. Yet his true trust was in the person of Jesus Christ.

Jesus was the One who had died for him, called him, and given him eternal life. Paul realized that anything and everything else in life would never give him that kind of security and hope. It was Jesus, and Jesus alone, that was worth counting all things as loss. It was Jesus that brought him to the realization that he could not trust in himself.

It was the God who raises the dead and gives eternal life that gave Paul worth. He did not need to brag about his personal accomplishments or his heritage, because it was Jesus and Jesus alone that gave him hope of resurrection and eternal life. For that reason, he counted everything loss.

Paul gave up his credentials and standing in the world in order to follow Jesus. He found in Christ, someone who could not only forgive his sins but could give to him life in its fullness. He counted victory in loss.

Could you find purpose for your life by ceasing to trust and have confidence in anything other than Jesus?

~~

One of Ten

November 25, 2010

As He entered a village, ten leprous men who stood at a distance met Him; and they raised their voices, saying, "Jesus, Master, have mercy on us!" When He saw them, He said to them, "Go and show yourselves to the priests." And as they were going, they were cleansed. Now one of them, when he saw that he had been healed, turned back, glorifying God with a loud voice, and he fell on his face at His feet, giving thanks to Him. And he was a Samaritan. Then Jesus answered and said, "Were there not ten cleansed? But the nine - where are they? Was no one found who returned to give glory to God, except this foreigner?" And He said to him, "Stand up and go; your faith has made you well." (Luke 17:12-19, NASB)

Are you thankful? Do you take the time to thank someone for their kindness to you? Jesus entered a village and met ten lepers who were begging for Him to heal their leprosy. Their plea was for Jesus to show them mercy. They had a dreaded terminal illness with physical and social implications. They were separated from family and friends, made to walk the streets declaring themselves to be "unclean," and were total outcasts from society. No wonder they begged for healing.

Jesus gave them their desire and healed them all. As they were going to the priest, one of them noticed he was healed and returned glorifying God. He fell on his face thanking Jesus for the miracle of life. How sad that only one out of ten returned with a thankful heart.

As we celebrate Thanksgiving Day, ask yourself if you would have been that one. Or would you have gone on your way and not returned to fall before Jesus, thanking Him for a new beginning in life? You can thank God right now for giving you life, and life more abundant. Thanksgiving Day, as you celebrate the multitude of blessings God has given to you, BE the one who returns to God, and show your gratitude. Happy Thanksgiving Day to you.

~~

In Every Nation
December 2, 2010

Then Peter replied, "I see very clearly that God shows no favoritism. In every nation He accepts those who fear Him and do what is right. This is the message of Good News for the people of Israel - that there is peace with God through Jesus Christ, who is Lord of all. You know what happened throughout Judea, beginning in Galilee, after John began preaching his message of baptism. And you know that God anointed Jesus of Nazareth with the Holy Spirit and with power. Then Jesus went around doing good and healing all who were oppressed by the devil, for God was with Him.

And we apostles are witnesses of all He did throughout Judea and in Jerusalem. They put Him to death by hanging Him on a cross, but God raised Him to life on the third day. Then God allowed Him to appear, not to the general public, but to us whom God had chosen in advance to be His witnesses. We were those who ate and drank with Him after He rose from the dead. And He ordered us to preach everywhere and to testify that Jesus is the One appointed by God to be the judge of all - the living and the dead. He is the One all the prophets testified about, saying that everyone who believes in Him will have their sins forgiven through His name." (Acts 10:34-43, NLT)

Christmas is right around the corner. What does Christmas mean? The biblical story of Peter visiting the home of Cornelius gives us a picture of the Gospel. Christmas means God sent Jesus for everyone of every nation. He does not show partiality. It is Good News because Jesus' coming to earth brought peace with God - because He is Lord of all. Jesus went about doing good by healing the sick and those oppressed by the devil. He died on a cross but arose from the dead three days later. He appeared to a select group that He charged with the responsibility of telling everyone about Himself. They were to tell that Jesus was the Appointed One of God to judge the living and the dead.

He was also the One of whom the prophets foretold. He was more than just a prophet Himself. He was Emmanuel - God with us. The message of Christmas is summarized in the statement: "Everyone who believes in Him will have their sins forgiven through His name." Have you put your trust and faith in the One who was God in human flesh, who came to die for the sins of all who believe in Him? Why not now?

~~

Fear or Faith?

December 9, 2010

> *And there arose a fierce gale of wind, and the waves were breaking over the boat so much that the boat was already filling up. Jesus Himself was in the stern, asleep on the cushion; and they woke Him and said to Him, "Teacher, do You not care that we are perishing?" And He got up and rebuked the wind and said to the sea, "Hush, be still." And the wind died down and it became perfectly calm. And He said to them, "Why are you afraid? Do you still have no faith?" They became very much afraid and said to one another, "Who then is this, that even the wind and the sea obey Him?"*
> (Mark 4:37-41, NASB)

Jesus had just finished teaching the people and casting out demons. As He often would, He led His disciples to a retreat away from the crowds. This was one of those times. They climbed into a fishing boat and headed out across the Sea of Galilee. Jesus was tired and found a place to recline and take a much-needed nap. While He was sleeping, a storm arose that threatened the fishing boat and the disciples. The winds were so fierce and the waves were so high that the little boat was in danger of sinking. The disciples were very afraid. They awoke Him in desperation and asked a most interesting question, "Don't You care that we are perishing?"

They had just watched Jesus teaching, healing, and casting out demons from the crowds that gathered. They knew Him to be more than an ordinary man, yet questioned His care of them. If we were asked if Jesus cares for people, what would we say? Of course, we would encourage them to trust that God not only cares but is prepared to come to their aid. But how many times do we face issues in our lives when we, like the disciples, ask God, "Don't You care about me?" Deep down inside we know He does, but it is easy to question Him when things are difficult.

You may be facing something today that is overwhelming - a storm in your life. Do you wonder where God is? Is fear your number one emotion? The disciples woke Jesus from sleep and, with fear and not faith, they asked for Him to do something. He spoke the word and the storm ceased. He then asked them the key question. It is a question He may be asking you right now: "Why are you so afraid? How is it that you have no faith?"

After the quieting of the storm, the disciples had a new fear. It was the awe and reverence and amazement of being in the presence of God. That kind of fear is needed. It acknowledges that you are in the presence of, and cared for by, a God who loves you. Let Him quiet your storm. Why not place your faith in Him right now?

~~

Who Is Jesus?

December 16, 2010

And the Word became flesh, and dwelt among us, and we saw His glory, glory as of the only begotten from the Father, full of grace and truth. (John 1:14, NASB)

What is Christmas all about? Why do so many millions of people celebrate the birth of Jesus? Is it because He was a great prophet? Is it because He lived a good life and went about doing good things for people? Is it because He was able to heal people of disease and cast out demons from them? Is it because it is fun to give and receive gifts, decorate trees, put up lights on your house, or have office parties and family gatherings?

Surely some people celebrate for just those reasons, but the real reason is because of who Jesus is. The Greek word "logos," translated "word" in chapter 1 of the book of John, is a way of declaring that Jesus was and is God Himself. "The Word became flesh" means that God became a man in Jesus. The Son of God has always been. Jesus even declared in John 8:58, "Truly, truly, I say to you, before Abraham was born, I am." He is declaring here His eternal nature as God. He came to earth to reveal God and to die for the sins of humanity.

"... He who has seen Me has seen the Father; how can you say, 'Show us the Father'? Do you not believe that I am in the Father, and the Father is in Me? The words that I say to you I do not speak on My own initiative, but the Father abiding in Me does His works. Believe Me that I am in the Father and the Father is in Me; otherwise believe because of the works themselves." (John 14:9-11)

Can you celebrate Christmas for the right reason? Would you place your faith in Jesus as God, who came in the flesh in order that you might have eternal life? WHAT A GREAT CELEBRATION OF CHRISTMAS THAT WOULD BE!!

~~

The Christ Child

December 23, 2010

This is how Jesus the Messiah was born. His mother, Mary, was engaged to be married to Joseph. But before the marriage took place, while she was still a virgin, she became pregnant through the power of the Holy Spirit. Joseph, her fiancé, was a good man and did not want to disgrace her publicly, so he decided to break the engagement quietly. As he considered this, an angel of the Lord appeared to him in a dream. "Joseph, son of David," the angel said, "do not be afraid to take Mary as your wife. For the Child within her was conceived by the Holy Spirit. And she will have a son, and you are to name Him Jesus, for He will save His people from their sins." All of this occurred to fulfill the Lord's message through His prophet: "Look! The virgin will conceive a

Child! She will give birth to a son, and they will call Him Immanuel, which means 'God is with us.' " (Matthew 1:18-23, NASB)

The birth of Jesus is the story of a man and woman, a miracle, hope, and God. Joseph was engaged to Mary, and in a dream it was revealed to him that she was already pregnant by God, the Holy Spirit. Instead of shaming her, he was going to break the engagement; but an angel of the Lord appeared to him - a mystery and miracle - and told him to marry her because the Child in her was conceived of God.

The Child would be named Jesus and would save His people from their sins. His birth was a fulfillment of the prophesy declaring that a virgin would conceive a Child who would be different from all others. This Child was God in human flesh. This Jesus would be called Immanuel, meaning "God with us." Truly the miracle of Christmas is that the Sovereign Lord, the God Almighty, would become one of us in order to save us from our sins and give us eternal life.

Not only was Joseph allowed to be the earthly father of Jesus, he was privileged to see the miracle of Immanuel, God with us, and the hope of eternal life through faith in Jesus Christ. Have you discovered that Hope?

~~

Just Do It! December 30, 2010

And on the third day there was a wedding in Cana of Galilee, and the mother of Jesus was there; and both Jesus and His disciples were invited to the wedding. When the wine ran out, the mother of Jesus said to Him, "They have no wine." And Jesus said to her, "Woman, what does that have to do with us? My hour has not yet come." His mother said to the servants, "Whatever He says to you, do it." (John 2:1-5, NASB)

Ever make a New Year's resolution? Sure you have. How long did you keep it? Usually a few days is a long time to keep a resolution. Almost seems like a waste of time to determine the future by making a promise you are more than likely not going to remember a few weeks down the road.

If there ever existed a resolve worth following to completion, it would be the one Mary suggested to the servants at the wedding feast at Cana of Galilee. The words from Mary were in the context of a wedding with a major problem: they had run out of wine. Mary went to Jesus with the bad news, "They have no wine." Jesus responded with what may appear as words of disrespect but were not. They were expression from the Savior that the time for Him to begin His ministry had not yet arrived. She ignored His words and simply told the servants, "Whatever He says to do, do it."

What a tremendous New Year's resolution! Could you consider your resolution to do whatever God wants you to do? He calls us to a life of submission and surrender. That call means He is Lord of our life. As Lord, He is in charge. What a great opportunity to find purpose and fulfillment, simply by doing what our Lord says.

The servants followed Jesus' instructions and filled the water pots with water. As they drew out the water, it was no longer water but the finest wine possible. The "best" came as a result of doing what He said. This New Year, entrust your life to the Life Giver, Jesus, and DO WHAT HE SAYS. There is no greater New Year's resolution you could make. May this New Year be filled with His blessings to you.

~~

Inside Out
January 6, 2011

And I will ask the Father, and He will give you another Advocate, who will never leave you. He is the Holy Spirit, who leads into all truth. The world cannot receive Him, because it isn't looking for Him and doesn't recognize Him. But you know Him, because He lives with you now and later will be in you. (John 14:16-17, NLT)

"He who believes in Me, as the Scripture said, 'From his innermost being will flow rivers of living water.' " But this He spoke of the Spirit, whom those who believed in Him were to receive; for the Spirit was not yet given, because Jesus was not yet glorified. (John 7:38-39, NASB)

Living life from the inside out is the goal of God for you. Jesus was nearing the end of His life on earth. Meeting with His closest disciples, He brought the plan for their future. Although He Himself would die and return to the glory of heaven, He was not leaving the disciples alone. His plan was to send the Holy Spirit (the Counselor, Advocate, Helper) to live not only WITH them but IN them.

The faith they had in Jesus was the guarantee that the Holy Spirit would indwell them. On the day of Pentecost, the Holy Spirit came to indwell the believers for the first time. He would, from that point forward, indwell every believer.

Just think of it: the living God lives IN YOU. He provides you with power, comfort, peace, love, joy, and the list goes on. You don't have to go beyond yourself to find God. He dwells in you. Thus your life is not lived by things outside but through the God who lives within - life from the inside out.

The indwelling Holy Spirit, Jesus said, would be like a spring or river of living water springing forth from your life. This great Advocate, Counselor, Helper, and Comforter is within you. Allow His life to flow from you today.

~~

Conforming to His Image   January 13, 2011

> *But we should always give thanks to God for you, brethren beloved by the Lord, because God has chosen you from the beginning for salvation through sanctification by the Spirit and faith in the truth. It was for this He called you through our gospel, that you may gain the glory of our Lord Jesus Christ.*
> (2 Thessalonians 2:13-14, NASB)

The ministry of the Holy Spirit in our lives is to sanctify us, or make us holy. Our spiritual life is dependent upon the Holy Spirit. We cannot make ourselves holy. We cannot grow ourselves spiritually. We can, through our openness to the Holy Spirit's molding and making us like Jesus, give Him a door for His work, for our spiritual growth.

We can place ourselves under the control of God's Spirit, and He will grow us in Christ-likeness. The Holy Spirit lives in us. The Bible tells us that the purpose of God is to conform us into the image of Jesus. In your life right now, He is at work to make you like Jesus.

The fruit of the Spirit is love, joy, peace, patience, kindness, gentleness, faithfulness, and self-control. These are characteristics of Jesus. He is developing these qualities in your life as the Holy Spirit sanctifies you - makes you holy.

In what areas of your life is God working to conform you to His image? How is He accomplishing that transition and change in you? Are you like a piece of clay allowing the potter to mold you into the image of Christ, or are you like a piece of iron - hard and unyielding?

God wants to use your life for His glory. He accomplishes that result by conforming you to the image of Christ. Whether it is in your relationship with God or with others, your lifestyle, or your attitudes and actions; God is completing what He began in you. He is making you like Jesus, sanctifying you, and making you holy in order that your life would glorify God. Today, allow God to mold you like soft clay into His likeness.

~~

Under the Circumstances

> *Now I want you to know, brethren, that my circumstances have turned out for the greater progress of the gospel,* (Philippians 1:12, NASB)

Ever find yourself in a mess? Most of us have. We might say we are "under" the circumstances. Although some would question you as to why you were under the circumstances, it still is an accurate description of how we often find ourselves.

How we view those circumstances will have a profound effect on our lives. Paul, the apostle, was serving a jail sentence. As a result, he found that he had a greater opportunity than ever to share the Gospel of Jesus Christ. He saw his circumstances as the hand of God on his life, and the result was progress for the kingdom of God.

What is happening today that causes you to question the goodness of God and His provisions for you? Are there trials that seem to be overwhelming? Will you see those trials as an opportunity for the Gospel?

Although Paul struggled through the trials of imprisonment, he saw a much larger picture. He knew that God was at work in and through his trial, to bring more people to Christ. He wrote to the Corinthian church:

> *For all things are for your sakes, so that the grace which is spreading to more and more people may cause the giving of thanks to abound to the glory of God.*
> (2 Corinthians 4:15)

God receives glory as we encounter our trials and circumstances through which the Gospel is spread to more and more people. Real purpose may be the very circumstance that you find yourself in or "under" at this very moment.

~~

Worship and Will

> *Therefore I urge you, brethren, by the mercies of God, to present your bodies a living and holy sacrifice, acceptable to God, which is your spiritual service of worship. And do not be conformed to this world, but be transformed by the renewing of your mind,*

so that you may prove what the will of God is, that which is good and acceptable and perfect. (Romans 12:1-2, NASB)

What is your heart's desire as a follower or Jesus Christ? The Bible tells of two very important aspects of our walk in Him. One of those is worship, and the other is doing the will of God.

In the book of Romans, the apostle Paul encourages our spiritual service of worship through the surrender of our bodies to God. Paul begs the believers in Rome to be totally yielded to God by presenting their bodies as a living sacrifice. The usual condition of a sacrifice is dead, but in this case, Paul urges a living sacrifice.

Though the body is alive, it is not to be alive to sin. The sacrifice is made by God's mercy, and results in holiness. This living and holy sacrifice, God accepts. As we yield ourselves to God in surrender and submission, the body that contains our flesh and the sin that indwells us, is under the control of the Spirit of God. The least we can logically do is submit to God. God accepts this sacrifice as worship. In fact, the beginning of worship is the bowing down of your life before a holy and righteous God who has given you the grace and the mercy to be a living sacrifice. Our God is an awesome God. He seeks and urges us to be surrendered to Him. Our purpose for life is discovered in that act of surrender.

The second aspect of our walk with God is to do His will. The good, acceptable, and perfect will of God is discovered as we are transformed by the renewing of our minds by God's Holy Spirit. The admonishment of the Bible is to refrain from conformity to the world and its systems. The will of God is accomplished as we are not conformed but are transformed.

Today, why not discover the wonderful experience of worship and the knowledge of His good, acceptable, and perfect will?

~~

God Wants to Use You   February 3, 2011

And He called the twelve together, and gave them power and authority over all the demons and to heal diseases. And He sent them out to proclaim the kingdom of God and to perform healing. (Luke 9:1-2, NASB)

Now after this the Lord appointed seventy others, and sent them in pairs ahead of Him to every city and place where He Himself was going to come. And He was saying to them, "The harvest is plentiful, but the laborers are few; therefore beseech the Lord of the harvest to send out laborers into His harvest." (Luke 10:1-2)

The song says, "People Need the Lord." It is so true that people need the Lord, but equally true is that the Lord needs people. God, in His infinite wisdom, determined that He would use people to accomplish His purposes. When Jesus chose His disciples to go into all the world to proclaim the kingdom of God, He had in mind that He would use people. He first sent the twelve, then the seventy. As He sent the seventy, He not only sent instructions to precede Him to every city into which He was going but to also pray for more laborers. Why would He ask for more laborers?

His reason was that He uses people to spread the Gospel of the Kingdom. He chose you. He saved you by His grace, called you into service for the King, and sent you to be His servant to those in need of the hope of eternal life.

William Carey, the father of modern missions, was confronted with the words, "When God pleases to save the heathen, He will do it without your aid and mine." His response came later as he said, "Expect great things from God; attempt great things for God." His conviction that God uses people to proclaim the Gospel was so strong that it became the motivation for establishing the Baptist Mission Society in 1792.

God wants to use your life to share the Good News. He has chosen to use people like you to be the laborers in the mission field of the world. He desires that every person hear the message of salvation by grace through faith in Jesus Christ.

Allow God to use you today. He still uses people just like you to accomplish His purposes.

~~

Beware of the Destroyers

February 10, 2011

And the disciples came to the other side of the sea, but they had forgotten to bring any bread. And Jesus said to them, "Watch out and beware of the leaven of the Pharisees and Sadducees." They began to discuss among themselves, saying, "He said that because we did not bring any bread." But Jesus, aware of this, said, "You men of little faith, why do you discuss among yourselves that you have no bread? Do you not yet understand or remember the five loaves of the five thousand, and how many baskets full you picked up? Or the seven loaves of the four thousand, and how many large baskets full you picked up? How is it that you do not understand that I did not speak to you concerning bread? But beware of the leaven of the Pharisees and Sadducees." Then they understood that He did not say to beware of the leaven of bread, but of the teaching of the Pharisees and Sadducees. (Matthew 16:5-12, NASB)

Ever notice how there is often a lesson within a lesson? Jesus and His disciples had traveled to the other side of the Sea of Galilee. As they approached the other side, the disciples realized they had forgotten to bring anything to eat. The first words from Jesus' mouth were about leaven. Leaven causes bread to rise. The disciples' immediate thoughts went to the times in the past when they had forgotten to bring bread. Feeling a bit guilty, they began to discuss their forgetfulness.

Enter the first lesson… "Where is your faith? Do you not remember?" How easy it is to forget the provisions of God. Two different times, Jesus had fed the disciples as well as four thousand people one time and five thousand another. Could they never get the lesson straight? God will provide.

Enter the second lesson… Jesus was speaking of the leaven of the Sadducees and Pharisees - the legalism and hypocrisy that invaded the life of freedom that Jesus brought to His followers. Beware! There will always be those who would destroy the freedom you have in Christ, with rules and laws that promise what they cannot produce. Jesus always was concerned that what He came to give, "life and life more abundantly," would be snatched from His followers by a substitute religion based on performance and not grace.

Never forget the lessons of Jesus. First, He can meet your needs; and second, He came to give life through grace, not life through rules.

~~

Pride, Humility, and Worth   February 17, 2011

Humble yourselves in the presence of the Lord, and He will exalt you.
(James 4:10, NASB)

Therefore humble yourselves under the mighty hand of God, that He may exalt you at the proper time. (1 Peter 5:6)

The world we live in has lost sight of the great truths of the Bible. Insights into the Word of God reveal the forgotten truths that seem to be absent in this twenty-first century world. Concepts such as "we gain strength through weakness," "grace through helplessness," "mercy from need," "hope through suffering," "holiness from brokenness," "life from death," "power from the Holy Spirit," and "exaltation through humility" have been replaced with self-centered theology.

Both James and Peter, early disciples in the Jerusalem church, gave a proper presentation of the truth that our humility in the hands of God produces an exalted life. Instead of exalting ourselves, God encourages us to humble ourselves. It is not thinking of ourselves in negative condescending terms but to realize that we are who we are by God's grace.

> ... *clothe yourselves with humility toward one another, for God is opposed to the proud, but gives grace to the humble.* (1 Peter 5:5b)

The opposite of humility is pride. Pride is our exalted estimation of our value and worth apart from God. Pride is believing that we don't need God or others to achieve our worth because we are sufficient within ourselves. God desires for us to humble ourselves under His mighty hand, humble ourselves toward God and others, and recognize that God is opposed to self-worth apart from Him. We may try to impress, but if we look at ourselves as worthy apart from God, then God will oppose us.

It is as you humble yourself before God and recognize that He alone can give you your worth, that you will be exalted. A proud and boastful heart will only lead to humiliation, not exaltation. Give to God the glory and the credit for who you are, what you are, and what you have accomplished. God will then exalt you. Jesus, our example, humbled Himself by going to the cross to die, but at His name every knee will bow and every tongue confess that He is Lord. Humble yourself today and give glory to God. He will exalt you when His time is right.

~~

From Tragic to Triumphant   February 24, 2011

> *Pilate said to them, "Then what shall I do with Jesus who is called Christ?" They all said, "Crucify Him!"* (Matthew 27:22, NASB)

> *And Jesus cried out again with a loud voice, and yielded up His spirit.* (Matthew 27:50)

Death seems so tragic and senseless. We struggle to find meaning in the death of a baby or teenager. When someone is killed in an accident, we question the reason why anyone would have to die in such a meaningless way. Yet there was one death that, on the surface, looks tragic and senseless and meaningless but, when observed through the eyes of God, makes all the fog roll away.

Jesus' death was not an ordinary one. He died for a reason. He died to be a substitute and a sacrifice for us. He died with the sin of the whole world on Himself. He took our place in order that we might have eternal life. He also died to forgive us of our sin. We sin against a Holy God and need forgiveness. Jesus' blood, that He shed on the cross, washes away our sin. He also died to give us direct access to God.

His death was unique in that He did not remain dead. Three days after His death and burial, He arose from the dead. His resurrection not only proves He is God but also provides each of us with life - His life. Religion offers rules and laws that give a false hope of eternal life. Jesus' death and resurrection provides a relationship with God that gives true hope. That hope is not only for life in eternity but life right now. Jesus declared that He came to give us life, and life more abundantly.

By faith and trust in God's way of salvation through Christ, we can experience the life He has for us. God is only a prayer away for each one of us. Ask God to forgive you and come into your life. Place your faith in Jesus' death and resurrection, and you can be saved. Jesus made the way possible. He died that you might have hope - not only in this life but for eternity in a place called heaven.

Have you come to faith in Jesus? Do you know Him? Have you heard that He loves you? Trust Him for life today.

~~

Hypocrites in Action March 3, 2011

> *And He was teaching in one of the synagogues on the Sabbath. And there was a woman who for eighteen years had had a sickness caused by a spirit; and she was bent double, and could not straighten up at all. When Jesus saw her, He called her over and said to her, "Woman, you are freed from your sickness." And He laid His hands on her; and immediately she was made erect again and began glorifying God. But the synagogue official, indignant because Jesus had healed on the Sabbath, began saying to the crowd in response, "There are six days in which work should be done; so come during them and get healed, and not on the Sabbath day." But the Lord answered him and said, "You hypocrites, does not each of you on the Sabbath untie his ox or his donkey from the stall and lead him away to water him? And this woman, a daughter of Abraham as she is, whom Satan has bound for eighteen long years, should she not have been released from this bond on the Sabbath day?" As He said this, all His opponents were being humiliated; and the entire crowd was rejoicing over all the glorious things being done by Him. (Luke 13:10-17, NASB)*

Jesus had an incredible ability to aggravate religious people. His method: do something against their rules. In this case, as in many others, He healed someone on the Sabbath. The Sabbath was the day of rest and not a day for work. The religious Pharisees' interpretation of the law of the Sabbath did not allow for healing anyone. Jesus did it anyway. He freed the woman of an infirmity in which her back was bent double. Her response was praise to God. The religious crowd was indignant.

Jesus immediately labeled them hypocrites - play actors. They lived from the written script of their interpretation of the Law, which meant no healing on the Sabbath. Jesus reprimanded them and expressed the value of this crippled woman over their interpretation of the Sabbath. The crowd turned on the Pharisees, and the Bible says they were humiliated.

People are pretty important to God. In spite of the religious rules of some people in which they question your worth, He still loves you and wants the best for you. Rejoice over the glorious things He has done.

~~

On Guard

March 10, 2011

> For God has not given us a spirit of fear and timidity, but of power, love, and self-discipline. So never be ashamed to tell others about our Lord. And don't be ashamed of me, either, even though I'm in prison for Him. With the strength God gives you, be ready to suffer with me for the sake of the Good News. For God saved us and called us to live a holy life. He did this, not because we deserved it, but because that was His plan from before the beginning of time - to show us His grace through Christ Jesus. And now He has made all of this plain to us by the appearing of Christ Jesus, our Savior. He broke the power of death and illuminated the way to life and immortality through the Good News. And God chose me to be a preacher, an apostle, and a teacher of this Good News. That is why I am suffering here in prison. But I am not ashamed of it, for I know the One in whom I trust, and I am sure that He is able to guard what I have entrusted to Him until the day of His return. Hold on to the pattern of wholesome teaching you learned from me - a pattern shaped by the faith and love that you have in Christ Jesus. Through the power of the Holy Spirit who lives within us, carefully guard the precious truth that has been entrusted to you. (2 Timothy 1:7-14, NLT)

"Standing Alone" is more than just words or a slogan - it is where many of us find ourselves. We may be the only Christian in our family, neighborhood, or work. That could mean that in order for us to walk with God, it takes real courage and strength. The Bible gives to us some wonderful words of encouragement. We need not be ashamed of the Gospel, who we are, or in Whom we believe. We also have been given, from God's Holy Spirit who lives within us, a Spirit of power, love, and self-discipline. For that reason, we need never be ashamed of speaking of Jesus. The apostle Paul found himself in jail as a result of the testimony of his hope in Christ but also found the strength God gives to endure the suffering.

He realized his reason for being in jail was his faith. We may not face jail but instead ridicule, rejection, lack of respect, and persecution.

The word of encouragement from the Bible is simply to guard the truth of what God has given to you. He has given you salvation and guards your eternal life. You entrusted your eternity to Him, and He will protect and guard you until the end. Guard this truth of what was given to you.

~~

Climbing Into the Chariot   March 17, 2011

> Then the Spirit said to Philip, "Go up and join this chariot." Philip ran up and heard him reading Isaiah the prophet, and said, "Do you understand what you are reading?" And he said, "Well, how could I, unless someone guides me?" And he invited Philip to come up and sit with him. Now the passage of Scripture which he was reading was this:
> "He was led as a sheep to slaughter;
> And as a lamb before its shearer is silent,
> So He does not open His mouth.
> In humiliation His judgment was taken away;
> Who will relate His generation?
> For His life is removed from the earth."
> The eunuch answered Philip and said, "Please tell me, of whom does the prophet say this? Of himself or of someone else?" Then Philip opened his mouth, and beginning from this Scripture he preached Jesus to him. (Acts 8:29-35, NASB)

Can you imagine taking a walk and suddenly God's Holy Spirit speaks to you and requests that you sit in a chariot of a total stranger? That is exactly what happened to Philip. He was a leader in the early Church and ready for God to use his words as an encouragement to a court official from Ethiopia. He heard the man reading from the book of Isaiah - a passage about the suffering servant. The suffering was compared to a lamb taken to slaughter.

Philip asked if he understood what he was reading. He said he did not, and at that moment Philip opened his mouth with the greatest message ever. The message was of the God-Man, Jesus. The Bible says Philip spoke unto him about Jesus.

What great things we learn from the Bible. We learn that God is looking for people who have something to share. If you have met Jesus as your own Savior, you know Him and can tell others of Him. We learn there are people searching for the way, the truth, and life. The Bible records the words of Jesus, "I am the way, the truth, and the life" (John 14:6).

We learn that Jesus was a suffering servant. He came to die for the sins of the entire world. God so loved the world that He gave Jesus as a sacrifice and substitute for our sin. He is our Savior.

We also learn that much like the Ethiopian, people are desirous to know Jesus and become His followers. Often they are waiting for you or someone like Philip to tell them. If you do not know Jesus, I pray that today you will believe in Him and find true salvation. God loves you and wants you to know Him through His Son, Jesus Christ.

~~

Need Rest?
March 24, 2011

> *Then Jesus said, "Come to me, all of you who are weary and carry heavy burdens, and I will give you rest. Take My yoke upon you. Let Me teach you, because I am humble and gentle at heart, and you will find rest for your souls. For My yoke is easy to bear, and the burden I give you is light."* (Matthew 11:28-30, NLT)

It is difficult to conceive that someone knows everything, but God does. Thankfully, God knows and understands. Our weariness and burdens will likely not be the same that someone else carries, but they are real and overload us - body, soul, and spirit. Thank God that He is aware of our needs and has done something about it. He overcomes our struggles with His rest. It is not a nap, or a good night's sleep, or even a long vacation. His rest provides a supernatural strength we cannot muster or create. He is our rest.

A yoke is a wooden crossbeam placed on the shoulders of two animals that allows them to pull a load together. It was used as a symbol of the teachings of the rabbis. Jesus used the word to describe His relationship with us. We are never alone. As we are under the yoke of God, we are being led and taught by Him. We are to take the yoke of God and place it on ourselves to learn of, and from, Him.

Jesus, as our rabbi, is humble and gentle. Jesus drew a comparison between the wonderful yoke of a Christian believer, and the discouraging yoke of heaviness and slavery placed on the people by the rabbis of the day. Jesus' gentle and humble heart results in a yoke that is easy and a burden that is light.

You can make a great trade today. Why not trade your heavy burdens, your weariness in life, for the yoke of Jesus? He is ready to give you REST FOR YOUR SOUL. What a wonderful trade!

~~

Moving On

> *On the contrary, I am going away so that the world may know that I love the Father. Just as the Father commanded Me, so I do. "Get up; let's leave this place."*
> (John 14:31, HCSB)

Where do we go from here? Ever been unsure of the next step? The disciples had just spent some lengthy time listening to Jesus give them His last minute instructions as He prepared them for His death. He comforted them with the hope of eternal life. "Do not let your heart be troubled; believe in God, believe also in Me" (John 14:1, NASB). He told them, "I am the way, and the truth, and the life" (John 14:6). He gave hope that they would not be left alone but that He would send another Comforter, the Holy Spirit, to be with them. He also promised a peace that passes understanding which would come within them through the presence of God's Spirit.

After finishing His discourse, Jesus announced in John 14:31, "Arise, let us be going from here" or "Get up; let's leave this place." His mission at that time and place had been accomplished. He was now preparing for His arrest and ultimately His crucifixion.

Are there times in our lives that we need to move on? Sure there are. Often, our mission has been accomplished but we continue to drag on. In chapter 15, Jesus continued teaching but with a new purpose. His betrayer was awaiting the opportunity to turn Him over to the Roman soldiers and He would be led to His death. Jesus' response, instead of running away, was: "Arise, let us go from here." He had a new mission, a new purpose, a new direction; and wasted no time in moving on.

After praying with His disciples and by Himself, the reason for Jesus "moving on from here" became apparent. Judas had led the Roman cohort to Jesus. With weapons drawn, they entered the Garden of Gethsemane and dragged Jesus away. His reason for moving on was accomplished. It was not the time for more teaching or instructions - it was time for action.

Have you considered that today may be a day for action? Today may be your time to move on. That which is ahead is God's direction for you, and He is waiting for your obedience. In Jesus' own words in John 14:31, "But so that the world may know that I love the Father, I do exactly as the Father commanded Me. So let's move on" (my paraphrase). Is God asking you to move on today? Why not listen, and follow His instructions?

~~

Praise! Praise! Praise!

April 7, 2011

> *And in that day you will say,*
> *"Give thanks to the Lord, call on His name.*
> *Make known His deeds among the peoples;*
> *Make them remember that His name is exalted."*
> *Praise the Lord in song, for He has done excellent things;*
> *Let this be known throughout the earth.* (Isaiah 12:4-5, NASB)

"What a day this has been!" Normally, if those were the words from your mouth, it would indicate that you have had a "not so good" day. Maybe things didn't go as you had hoped and planned, maybe you received some news that broke your heart, or maybe the knowledge of the unknown came to reality and it was not good. Whatever caused you to lament concerning the not-so-desirous experiences of the day, it has a counterpart.

The prophet Isaiah found the counterpart: "In that day you will say..." These were the words of an encouraged man of God who recognized the goodness of God and all His blessings. He burst into praise as he said, "Give thanks to the Lord, call on His name." He continued his praise as he said, "Make known His deeds among the peoples." He knew that God is good, holy, gracious, compassionate, and full of love.

How did he know that? He had watched and contemplated the deeds of God. He knew the God who had provided for His people, protected them, guided them, and given them salvation. Isaiah could only burst into song and express his gratitude for the excellent things that God had done. Not only did he remember them, but he shouted from the housetops so all the world would know that God is good, excellent, and worthy of praise.

What a difference it makes when we dwell on the goodness of God and all that He has done for us to show His love, rather than live in the state of a negative, critical attitude focused on something or someone other than the God who has blessed us so much. Try a refocus today. Praise God for all the good things God is, and tell others of the excellent things God has accomplished in your life.

~~

Where's Your Joy?

April 14, 2011

> *Then he said to them, "Go, eat of the fat, drink of the sweet, and send portions to him who has nothing prepared; for this day is holy to our Lord. Do not be grieved, for the joy of the Lord is your strength."* (Nehemiah 8:10, NASB)

Are you celebrating today? The nation of Israel had just rediscovered the Law of Moses and the people were grieving over their sin. In the midst of their failure, God spoke through Nehemiah and encouraged the people to celebrate.

The reason for their celebration was the strength they received from the joy of the Lord. God declared the day a Holy Day. The day that God declared "holy" gave occasion to have a part. Joy can turn mourning and weeping into strength. Joy is such an integral part of the nature of God. He is a God who not only brings rejoicing to His people, but He Himself is a God of rejoicing.

The book of Galatians lists the fruit of the Spirit and includes in that list "joy." Joy is a result of God's presence in our lives.

> *But the fruit of the Spirit is love, joy, peace, patience, kindness, goodness, faithfulness, gentleness, self-control; against such things there is no law.* (Galatians 5:22-23)

No matter what is happening in our lives, God can bring us His joy. Through joy we will discover and experience His strength. Trials and tribulations will come to us from time to time; but our complete reliance upon the Lord, and the joy that only He can bring, will give us hope, strength, and encouragement.

God has your best interest at heart. He cares for you and loves you. His desire is to bring joy to your heart. Why not ask Him right now to give you His joy? Joy is not the absence of problems but comes from the knowledge that His strength will see you through any and all circumstances. No wonder Nehemiah could say that the "joy of the Lord" was his strength.

~~

The Finisher

April 21, 2011

> *Therefore when Jesus had received the sour wine, He said, "It is finished!" And He bowed His head and gave up His spirit.* (John 19:30, NASB)

How are you at finishing what you start? Some people finish all projects early, and some never finish anything. As Jesus was hanging from the cross, He uttered the words, "It is finished." The meaning is far deeper than just the fact that He died at that moment. He had finished the work God gave Him. He came to earth to be the Savior of the world. As He died on the cross, the work of salvation was finished. God always finishes what He starts. "I know that You can do all things, and that no purpose of Yours can be thwarted" (Job 42:2).

When God's amazing grace invaded your life and you were born again, God's Spirit began a good work in you:
>For I am confident of this very thing, that He who began a good work in you will perfect it until the day of Christ Jesus. (Philippians 1:6)

Remember that what God starts, He always finishes. When we come to faith in Christ, God begins that good work. His purpose, that cannot be thwarted, will be completed in each life as He makes us like Jesus. What a comfort and hope to know that everything which comes our way - pleasant or unpleasant, expected or unexpected, easy or difficult - is used of God to bring us to completion.

It is God who is the Finisher. Like the finish carpenter who comes into a new home to bring the finishing touches to the woodwork, cabinets, and such; God is the Finisher. But He is more than that - He is also the One who starts the good work in us:
>Looking unto Jesus the author and finisher of our faith; who for the joy that was set before Him endured the cross, despising the shame, and is set down at the right hand of the throne of God. (Hebrews 12:2, KJV)

God started you towards your intended conclusion - and what God starts, He finishes. You will be like Christ.

~~

Believe It or Not!   April 28, 2011

>"Therefore let it be known to you, brethren, that through Him forgiveness of sins is proclaimed to you, and through Him everyone who believes is freed from all things, from which you could not be freed through the Law of Moses. Therefore take heed, so that the thing spoken of in the Prophets may not come upon you:
>>'Behold, you scoffers, and marvel, and perish;
>>For I am accomplishing a work in your days,
>>A work which you will never believe, though someone should describe it to you.'" (Acts 13:38-41, NASB)

Can you believe it? Believe it or not. The book of Acts records words of encouragement: God is a forgiving God. Through Jesus Christ's death and resurrection, He provided a sacrifice and a substitute for us and our sins. Through His death, He provided not only forgiveness but freedom.

The writer called it freedom "from all things" which could not be accomplished through the Law of Moses. Freedom from guilt, freedom from condemnation, freedom from fear, freedom from failure, and freedom from punishment were all accomplished through Christ.

Yet the skeptics are prevalent among us - those who would scoff at the freedom found in Christ and the forgiveness He provides to all who believe. Instead, we can marvel at God's work in us, who without Him are perishing.

God is at work. Observe His will and His work through you, and the circumstances of your life that, even if someone described it to you, would be hard to believe or understand. Rest assured that God is accomplishing His work in you.

You might think that nothing positive is happening in your life. Maybe it is because you don't see the big picture of the hands of a mighty, sovereign God who is at work in you and your life - but He is. Praise Him today for His work in you; and even if you don't see it, CAN YOU BELIEVE IT?!

~~

Love and Be Loved

To you who are loved, be loving in return, for the power to be loving is from God; and everyone who is loving is born of God and knows God. If you are not loving, you do not know God, for God is loving. (1 John 4:7-8, my paraphrase)

But now faith, hope, love, abide these three; but the greatest of these is love.
(1 Corinthians 13:13, NASB)

The greatest virtue in the world is love because it is the expression of God - because He is Love. The Bible presents the three great virtues of faith, hope, and love; and declares love to be the greatest. Jesus taught us the way to love. He simply said, "A new commandment I give to you, that you love one another, even as I have loved you, that you also love one another" (John 13:34).

The qualification of our love for another is this: as Jesus loved you. Jesus goes so far as to say that the way people will know if we are truly a disciple of Jesus, is if we love others: "By this all men will know that you are My disciples, if you have love for one another" (John 13:35).

Two additional scriptures give us more insight into what love means:
Therefore, accept one another, just as Christ also accepted us to the glory of God.
(Romans 15:7)

...forgiving each other, just as God in Christ also has forgiven you.
(Ephesians 4:32b)

The Bible teaches clearly that to be loving, is to be accepting and forgiving. Jesus did both for you. He accepted you and received you as His child. He also forgave you of your sin and gave you a new life. Praise the name of Jesus for His love, and in return be a loving person by accepting and forgiving others.

~~

Coincidence? May 12, 2011

The child grew, and she brought him to Pharaoh's daughter and he became her son. And she named him Moses, and said, "Because I drew him out of the water."
(Exodus 2:10, NASB)

Of all the great men who have walked on this earth, Moses was obviously one of them. He is recognized as the leader of Israel who delivered them from Egyptian slavery, the one who received the Ten Commandments, and the one who is an obvious type of Christ. But how did he come to this place in history? He was born to an Israelite woman named Jochebed and adopted into the house of the Pharaoh by Bithia, the Pharaoh's daughter. It was from that position that God used his life to free Israel from slavery.

"Just a set of coincidences," you might say. He just happened to be in a wicker basket placed in the Nile where Pharaoh's daughter found him. He just happened to be nursed by his birth mother, Jochebed, who was paid for nursing her own child. He just happened to be raised in the home of Pharaoh where he received the finest of everything in order to prepare him for the task ahead.

Could it be that God was actually in charge of it all? He is, after all, God. He is sovereign. He knows ahead of time what is to happen. He has foreknowledge. He is also a God of providence. He provides ahead of time for our needs. Because He is sovereign, a God of foreknowledge, and a God of providence, He is never surprised nor does He panic. He has your life in His hands. You may not see it but rest assured: He sees and knows. He provides far in advance of your need.

The nation of Israel was in Egypt four hundred years before God delivered them from slavery. God prepared ahead of time (providence) for them to eventually return to their homeland through the selection of Moses as their leader four hundred years in advance.

God is at work in your life today in order to provide for you, not only now but for your future. He is a sovereign God, a God of foreknowledge, and a God of providence. You may not know what the future holds, but rest assured you can know Who holds the future.

~~

What Directions?

May 19, 2011

> *Now this He said, signifying by what kind of death he would glorify God. And when He had spoken this, He said to him, "Follow Me!" Peter, turning around, saw the disciple whom Jesus loved following them; the one who also had leaned back on His bosom at the supper and said, "Lord, who is the one who betrays You?" So Peter seeing him said to Jesus, "Lord, and what about this man?" Jesus said to him, "If I want him to remain until I come, what is that to you? You follow Me!"*
> (John 21:19-22, NASB)

When all else fails, read the directions. Great advice but maybe it should be, "When all else fails, FOLLOW the directions." How often have you received instructions only to ignore them? Most everyone has, at some time, read the instructions only to proceed to "do it your way."

Whether it was a school assignment or putting together the Christmas gift that simply said, "Some Assembly Required," you did it your way and ended up with a mess. Usually that "Some Assembly Required" meant a degree in engineering was required, but you still ignored the instructions and jumped full speed ahead into the project without heeding any guidance.

The apostle Peter had been following Jesus three years by this time. He had witnessed miracles, heard Jesus teach, and he had himself denied three times that he knew Jesus. After a miraculous fishing trip, Jesus spoke to Peter about his future. He told Peter to follow Him, and Peter responded by asking about John, "What about him?" The instructions to Peter were clear, "Follow Me." Peter appeared determined to take attention off of the instructions he had received and make sure John followed his instructions. Jesus merely responded that what He requested of John was between Him and John, and not Peter's business.

Peter's instruction was clear and simple: follow Jesus. You may ignore your instructions, do it your way, try to get someone else to follow your directions, or do as you are instructed. The choice is yours. Today is decision day.

~~

Fear Factor!

May 26, 2011

For God has not given us a spirit of fear and timidity, but of power, love, and self-discipline. (2 Timothy 1:7, NLT)

Ever feel afraid? Not the kind brought about by snakes, spiders, and high places but the fear of failure, the unknown, or rejection. Fear can be debilitating; can cripple your ability to think, make decisions, or relate to other people; and can cause major worry and even health issues.

The Bible has a lot to say about fear, but the words to the young pastor Timothy from his mentor, the apostle Paul, may say it best: fear and timidity do not come from God. They are from the enemy whose desire it is to steal, kill, and destroy. Our spiritual, emotional, and physical health is greatly influenced by fear. But truth can nullify fear.

You will know the truth and the truth will set you free. (John 8:32)

The truth is that not only does God NOT give us fear and timidity; He gives us something to replace it. God is the author of power, love, and self-discipline. Some translations say "sound mind" instead of self-discipline.

What do you believe? Do you look at a situation or circumstance, and shudder with fear and back away in timidity; or do you accept God's truth that you have power, love, and a sound mind? The Bible says, "Perfect love casts out fear" (1 John 4:18, NASB). We have power over fear because God gives it to us. We have love instead of fear because God gives it to us. We have a sound mind instead of fear because God gives it to us.

How would you like to make a trade? Trade your fear and timidity for what God can give you. Trust His word; not how you feel about your life, situation, or circumstance. God is far greater than any fear we will ever encounter.

Never forget that it is God's desire to change the way we think. He wants us to know and experience truth. Trust Him today, instead of the fear that the enemy throws into your mind. The battle is in your mind - it is truth versus the lies of the enemy. God loves you and wants you to move from fear to faith.

~~

Coping With Life

June 2, 2011

A song for pilgrims ascending to Jerusalem. A psalm of David.
Lord, my heart is not proud; my eyes are not haughty.

I don't concern myself with matters too great
or too awesome for me to grasp.
Instead, I have calmed and quieted myself,
like a weaned child who no longer cries for its mother's milk.
Yes, like a weaned child is my soul within me.
O Israel, put your hope in the Lord – now and always.
(Psalm 131:1-3, NASB)

If you were asked the question, "How are you?" would your answer include the words, "I am tired"? Most people are overcommitted, overworked, and expecting too much of themselves and others. Are you one of those? David the psalmist discovered himself to be the overachiever who was proud and haughty, concerned with matters above and beyond his strength.

David found that he could no longer keep up the pace, and finally found in God a place of quiet and peace. The need of his soul was recovered deep in the presence of a God who deeply cared for his wellbeing. He discovered that his tireless efforts generated by his prideful, haughty spirit only led to emotional and physical exhaustion.

The answer was to make some choices. He simply decided to not involve himself in matters too difficult. He also made a conscious effort to be still and quiet his soul. He pictured his life as a small child resting against its mother for comfort and peace. David saw himself as that child resting in the arms of God.

He could only do that because he knew the God of comfort and peace - a God in whom he could take refuge. What, today, is overwhelming to you? What are you attempting to do or be, in order to prove your value or worth? Do you remember that your true value and worth only come from God? Is your pride in your accomplishments destroying your life? How are you coping with the issues you are facing? Could it be that you need to back off from the devastating issues that are destroying you, and take a place of stillness and quiet in the arms of the Lord?

God loves you and accepts you as you are. He desires to hold you in His presence and bring a calm to your soul. Allow Him right now to be your Comfort, Consoler, and Encourager.

~~

Serve Along the Way June 9, 2011

Then the mother of the sons of Zebedee came to Jesus with her sons, bowing down and making a request of Him. And He said to her, "What do you wish?" She said to Him, "Command that in Your kingdom these two sons of mine may sit one on Your right and one on Your left." But Jesus answered, "You do not know what you are asking. Are you able to drink the cup that I am about to drink?" They said to Him, "We are able."

Jesus called them to Himself and said, "You know that the rulers of the Gentiles lord it over them, and their great men exercise authority over them. It is not this way among you, but whoever wishes to become great among you shall be our servant, and whoever wishes to be first among you shall be your slave; just as the Son of Man did not come to be served, but to serve, and to give His life a ransom for many."
(Matthew 20:20-22, 25-28; NASB)

The world has struggled over the centuries to determine who was the greatest. Wars have been fought, families have struggled, nations have been divided, and lives have been lost, all for the desire to determine the person or persons who will rule over the others. Jesus' disciples were no different. They wanted the choice spots in leadership. The mother of James and John was so determined that she made a direct request for Jesus to place her sons as the two most important persons in His kingdom. Little did she understand that the drink Jesus mentioned was the drink of suffering which would be realized at the cross when He became the ransom for the sin of every person in the whole world.

Jesus explained that the truly great people are servants. They are those who choose to give themselves in service and love to those in need. True leadership is servant leadership. To be a follower of Jesus means we not only serve, but we do it with a cheerful heart and attitude. Someone has said, "How do you know if you have a servant heart? The answer is simple: how do you feel when you are treated like one?"

Who are you serving today? Are you giving yourself in service to those that God places in your pathway? The way of greatness is not in lording it over, or being the boss of scores of people. The true test of leadership is found in our attitude in serving them. The greatest person who ever lived was Jesus, and He served by giving His life as a ransom for many. Will you follow His example today? It will give your life real purpose.

~~

Talk to Yourself? June 16, 2011

My soul waits in silence for God only; From Him is my salvation.

He only is my rock and my salvation, My stronghold;
I shall not be greatly shaken. (Psalm 62:1-2, NASB)

My soul, wait in silence for God only, For my hope is from Him.
He only is my rock and my salvation, My stronghold; I shall not be shaken.
On God my salvation and my glory rest;
The rock of my strength, my refuge is in God.
Trust in Him at all times, O people;
Pour out your heart before Him; God is a refuge for us. (Psalm 62:5-8)

Ever talk to yourself? You might have heard that it is okay to talk to yourself as long as you don't answer yourself. Well, David not only talked to himself, but he did answer. His question would have been, "Where do I go when things around me seem to be falling apart?" His answer was, "To God."

His emotions, his thoughts, and his volition – his entire soul was struggling with a need for hope and protection. In verse 5, he spoke to his own soul and said, "Soul, wait in silence for God only." David knew that God was his hope and strength, but like us, David needed a reminder. Talk to yourself. Remind your soul that God is the answer. How easy it is to forget that in the past you found your salvation, stronghold, rock, hope, strength, and refuge in God. Talk to yourself again and say, "Soul, God is what I need to meet my needs." The world, Satan, and your own flesh will tell you that something else will meet your needs. Just remember, it is God only who is everything.

Here is where you probably run into difficulty. The psalmist says, "WAIT" on the Lord. You may be like so many others, and find that waiting is hard. You may get impatient and reach to other sources of help. It is time to have a heart-to-heart talk with yourself. God alone is your rock and salvation. He alone is your strength and refuge. He alone is your hope.

Trust Him at all times. Verse 8 says, "Pour out your heart before Him; God is a refuge" for your soul. Tell God how you feel and what you are thinking, and determine to trust Him to meet your needs. He does not want to GIVE you hope or strength. He wants to BE your hope and strength. Trust Him right now to be for you whatever you are lacking. So, you may need to talk to yourself, as well as to God.

May He bless you this very moment as you have your little talk with yourself and God.

~~

Your Life

Without faith it is impossible to please Him. (Hebrews 11:6, NASB)

What does faith look like? Mark 10:46-52 and Matthew 20:29-34 describe faith in action. Matthew's account says there were two men; Mark's account only named one, Bartimaeus. It is possible that Jesus encountered these men both on his entry into Jericho and on the way out of Jericho. They were both blind. But how did Bartimaeus express his faith?

1. He expressed a need. "A blind beggar named Bartimaeus ...was sitting by the road. When he heard that it was Jesus the Nazarene, he began to cry out and say, 'Jesus, Son of David, have mercy on me!' " (Mark 10:46-47).
2. He saw Jesus as the answer to his need and was persistent. "Son of David, have mercy on me!" (vs. 48). He repeated the cry of his heart to the One he knew could make a difference.
3. He responded to the call of Jesus. "And Jesus stopped and said, 'Call him here.' " (vs. 49). Jesus had interest in this man who expressed faith. He called to him to come to the Source of the answer to his need.
4. He jumped at the opportunity for an answer. "Throwing aside his cloak, he jumped up and came to Jesus" (vs. 50). It appears that he was enthusiastic about expressing his faith.
5. He told Jesus what was needed. "What do you want Me to do for you?" "Rabboni, I want to regain my sight!" (vs. 51). He didn't just ask Jesus to be with him or guide him or bless him. He went to the heart of the matter. He was blind - he wanted to see. Faith gets specific.
6. He received the answer to his need. " 'Go; your faith has made you well.' Immediately he regained his sight and began following Him on the road" (vs. 52). Your part of faith is to receive. As you believe, you also receive.
7. He followed Jesus. Your ultimate expression of faith is a daily life of following Jesus Christ as your Savior, Lord, and Life. He was following down a road. The phrase means more than just a dirt path or a well-traveled road. It is your life. It is God's plan. It means you are traveling down your personal road of life in the hands of God.

Do you walk by faith? Follow the example of blind Bartimaeus. Let faith be your daily walk down the road of life.

~~

Carrying a Burden

They said to me, "The remnant there in the province who survived the captivity are in great distress and reproach, and the wall of Jerusalem is broken down and its gates are burned with fire." When I heard these words, I sat down and wept and mourned for days; and I was fasting and praying before the God of heaven. I said, "I beseech You, O Lord God of heaven, the great and awesome God, who preserves the covenant and lovingkindness for those who love Him and keep His commandments, let Your ear now be attentive and Your eyes open to hear the prayer of Your servant which I am praying before You now, day and night, on behalf of the sons of Israel Your servants." (Nehemiah 1:3-6a, NASB)

It is one thing to care about yourself and your own needs, but there is something special about having a burden for someone else. Nehemiah received information that the city of Jerusalem was in ruins and that the people were in distress and reproach. The walls of the city were broken down and burned. His response was similar to what your response might be if your friend, family, or loved one was hurting. He sat down and cried. His heart was broken over the sorrow of someone for whom he cared deeply. They were going through a difficult time and he was moved with compassion. The Bible says that he mourned for days, and sometimes problems do not end overnight. They often continue over a long period of time. Such was the case for Jerusalem.

Nehemiah went into action. He knew that the only permanent help would come from God. He called upon God with fasting and prayer. His intercession for his beloved city caused him to approach God as the great, awesome God who preserves the covenant and is filled with love for His people.

Do you have someone right now for whom you are especially burdened? The Bible says to bear one another's burdens. You can do that right now by bringing your concern to God, who is full of lovingkindness. You can pray for the person or persons that you know need God's love and grace. God answered Nehemiah's prayer and He will answer yours, too.

More than likely, you have someone right now who is depending on your prayers and concern. Why not be the person who brings their needs in prayer to God?

~~

A Lesson for the Religious

July 7, 2011

"Two men went up to the temple complex to pray, one a Pharisee and the other a tax collector. The Pharisee took his stand and was praying like this: 'God, I thank You that I'm not like other people - greedy, unrighteous, adulterers, or even like this tax collector. I fast twice a week; I give a tenth of everything I get.' But the tax collector, standing far off, would not even raise his eyes to heaven but kept striking his chest and saying, 'God, turn Your wrath from me - a sinner!' I tell you, this one went down to his house justified rather than the other; because everyone who exalts himself will be humbled, but the one who humbles himself will be exalted." (Luke 18:10-14, HCSB)

Do you ever get the "look-down-your-nose syndrome"? Simply put, do you sometimes think you are better than someone else? Jesus was very hard on people whose attitude was like that of the Pharisee.

In this parable, Jesus illustrates two people. One person was pious in his own mind. He gave examples that would have been appropriate for a religious person of his day. He was a pray-er. He prayed to himself, by himself. He saw himself as absent of greed, unrighteousness, adultery, or of being even remotely like the tax collector. He fasted twice a week and was a faithful tither. Many churches would give anything to have a church full of people like this man. *Maybe we do.*

In the same room but far away (likely because of shame), stood the dreaded tax collector. He saw his sin but could do nothing about it. He was broken by his sin and recognized that he deserved punishment. He cried out for mercy. Jesus' conclusion: the tax collector was justified before God, made right, accepted, and received God's love and forgiveness. The Pharisee, on the other hand, was not. Jesus then said that if we exalt ourselves, we will be humbled. If we humble ourselves, God will exalt us.

What a great lesson for religious people! Our acceptance by God is based on our broken and humbled hearts. Put one on today. God will exalt you.

~~

Just a Touch

July 14, 2011

> *And they were bringing children to Him so that He might touch them; but the disciples rebuked them. But when Jesus saw this, He was indignant and said to them, "Permit the children to come to Me; do not hinder them; for the kingdom of God belongs to such as these. Truly I say to you, whoever does not receive the kingdom of God like a child will not enter it at all." And He took them in His arms and began blessing them, laying His hands upon them.* (Mark 10:13-16, NASB)

Do you need a fresh touch from God? Do you need to be embraced, loved, accepted? Do you need power in your life? Would you like for someone to say good things about you? Then come to Jesus.

The mothers of the little children wanted Jesus to touch their children. To touch was to make a connection. The desire of the mothers was for their children to be blessed by connecting with Jesus. Jesus is the same yesterday, today, and forever.

Do you need to connect or reconnect with God? Many in the Bible knew how special it would be if they could only connect with Jesus. The woman with the issue of blood believed that if she could just touch the hem of Jesus' garment, then things would be different. "For she thought, 'If I just touch His garments, I will get well' " (Mark 5:28).

Jesus touched the leper and he was healed. He touched Peter's mother-in-law who had a high fever and it was gone. He touched the eyes of two blind men and they could see.

Although the disciples of Jesus tried to stand in the way, Jesus made sure even the children could come to Him.

He is speaking to you today:
> *"Come to Me, all who are weary and heavy-laden, and I will give you rest. Take My yoke upon you and learn from Me, for I am gentle and humble in heart; and you will find rest for your souls. For My yoke is easy, and My burden is light."*
> (Matthew 11:28-30)

Would you ask Jesus to give you a fresh touch? Humble yourself as a little child and come to Jesus. He is ready to give refreshing to your life.

~~

I, MY, ME! July 21, 2011

> *So it will be that when the Lord has completed all His work on Mount Zion and on Jerusalem, He will say, "I will punish the fruit of the arrogant heart of the king of Assyria and the pomp of his haughtiness." For He has said,*
> > *"By the power of my hand and by my wisdom I did this, For I have understanding; And I removed the boundaries of the peoples,*
> > *And plundered their treasures, And like a mighty man I brought down their inhabitants, And my hand reached to the riches of the peoples like a nest, And as one gathers abandoned eggs, I gathered all the earth; And there was not one that flapped its wing or opened its beak or chirped."*
> *Is the axe to boast itself over the one who chops with it? Is the saw to exalt itself over the one who wields it? That would be like a club wielding those who lift it, Or like a rod lifting him who is not wood.*
> *Therefore the Lord, the God of hosts, will send a wasting disease among his stout warriors; And under his glory a fire will be kindled like a burning flame.*
> (Isaiah 10:12-16, NASB)

What does God think about pride, arrogance, and haughtiness? It is fairly obvious from the Bible that He is strongly opposed to that type of attitude.
> *God opposes the proud, but gives grace to the humble.* (James 4:6, NLT)

The King of Assyria was being used of God to punish Zion and Jerusalem. God then promised the king that he would in turn be punished because of his pride and arrogance. The characteristic of an arrogant, prideful person is the use of the pronouns "I" and "my" or "me." The king used the pronoun nine times in three sentences. He declared that he had accomplished everything by his own strength. Someone has said, "I was conceited until I found out that I was better than I thought I was." That was the king's evaluation of himself. Therefore, God would bring judgment against him.

God is the One who works in our lives to accomplish the works He desires. "The ax does not raise itself against the one who swings it" simply means that we are instruments in God's hand, not the other way around. Everything we accomplish can be attributed to God and others.

Humility, the opposite of pride, gives credit where credit is due. "Therefore humble yourselves under the mighty hand of God, that He may exalt you at the proper time" (1 Peter 5:6, NASB).

God will deal in judgment on an arrogant and prideful life. Give God glory in all things and humble yourself. He will reward your attitude.

~~

Don't Forget

July 28, 2011

> *And Gideon the son of Joash died at a ripe old age and was buried in the tomb of his father Joash, in Ophrah of the Abiezrites. Then it came about, as soon as Gideon was dead, that the sons of Israel again played the harlot with the Baals, and made Baal-berith their god. Thus the sons of Israel did not remember the Lord their God, who had delivered them from the hands of all their enemies on every side; nor did they show kindness to the household of Jerubbaal (that is, Gideon) in accord with all the good that he had done to Israel.* (Judges 8:32-35, NASB)

How easy it is to forget. Maybe you couldn't find your keys this morning, or remember where you parked your car at the mall, or whether you finished that project or assignment. No matter what you forget, it is usually not a big deal. But when you forget what God has done for you in the past, it is a big deal.

Gideon had been used of God to rid the Israelites of their arch-enemies, the Midianites. He had led them to an abundance of spoil, and positioned them as the leaders of their world. Gideon died at a ripe old age and as soon as he was gone, the sons of Israel again began to worship Baal. The Bible says they did not remember the Lord their God. We can forget lots of things, people, or events; but we cannot afford to forget God and all He has accomplished in our lives.

God had miraculously delivered Israel from the Midianites, even though they were greatly outnumbered. God intervened and gave three hundred men the victory over an entire army. You might wonder, "How could they forget that?"

But how many times do we worry, fret, stew, and become discouraged because we forget what God has done for us in the past? The great thing about God is that what He has done before, He can do again. Trusting in Him for what He has done should lead us to trust Him for what He is about to do.

Our faith is based on the God who does not change. Remember what He has done before and trust Him to do it again. Don't allow yourself the choice of forgetting the greatness of God and His past watch-care over you.

Remembering is the wonderful experience of reliving God's hand on your life in the past and making sure it is applied to the present. Remember how great God is!

~~

What Ministry?   August 4, 2011

> *Therefore, since God in His mercy has given us this new way, we never give up. We reject all shameful deeds and underhanded methods. We don't try to trick anyone or distort the word of God. We tell the truth before God, and all who are honest know this. If the Good News we preach is hidden behind a veil, it is hidden only from people who are perishing.* **Satan, who is the god of this world, has blinded the minds of those who don't believe. They are unable to see the glorious light of the Good News. They don't understand this message about the glory of Christ, who is the exact likeness of God.** *You see, we don't go around preaching about ourselves. We preach that Jesus Christ is Lord, and we ourselves are your servants for Jesus' sake. For God, who said, "Let there be light in the darkness," has made this light shine in our hearts so we could know the glory of God that is seen in the face of Jesus Christ. We now have this light shining in our hearts, but we ourselves are like fragile clay jars containing this great treasure. This makes it clear that our great power is from God, not from ourselves.* (2 Corinthians 4:1-7, NLT)

"I don't have any spiritual gifts. I don't have a ministry." Is that your attitude? God has gifted you to serve Him and others. You may say, "I don't know what to do." The problem is that you may be thinking in terms of ministry to children, prayer, missions, etc. What you need to be thinking of is a ministry of the New Covenant.

The Old Covenant was a covenant of laws regulating behavior and requiring conformity in order to have a relationship with God. The Old Covenant was contained in the Hebrew Bible and demanded that the followers not break the laws. Moses brought the Law down from Mount Sinai on tablets of stone. In order to have a righteous relationship with a Holy God, it was necessary to obey each and every law. The people failed miserably at keeping the laws. Thus condemnation, guilt, and death followed.

Jesus introduced a New Covenant. It is a covenant of grace and mercy. It recognizes that breaking the Law is sin. It recognizes that death follows the breaking of the Law but gives an opportunity for hope, forgiveness, life, and a relationship with God through Jesus' death and resurrection.

The ministry of the New Covenant is the proclamation of that hope. It is not an age-group ministry, a food distribution center, or a ministry to a specific need. It is a ministry of hope to all. It is a ministry of new life through Jesus Christ. It comes about as you serve the needs of people for eternal life. No matter what you do, you have this ministry. For that reason, Paul, in his second letter to the Corinthians, reminds us that this ministry is of God's Spirit. It brings life. It is with glory.

~~

~ Note from Sandy ~

Coffee and coffee shops were part of Dennis' life since 1968 when he began meeting in a coffee shop with fellow seminary students every morning before class. Each city we moved to, Dennis always found a coffee shop - and people always seemed to find him.

He loved hot, strong, bold coffee. So when Starbucks arrived in Tempe, Dennis found a place he knew was made just for him. He went to Starbucks every morning, with few exceptions. Even when we traveled, he would find the closest Starbucks and visit the next morning. Of course, "his" Starbucks was the best!

I remember one morning he arrived early before the store was open. So he reclined the front seat of his car and took a little nap. After the workers arrived and the coffee was made, he awoke to a tapping on his window. A manager came carrying his coffee personally to his car. He liked to say he was the only person that received both curbside service and a morning wake-up call from Starbucks.

Starbucks was more than coffee to Dennis. It was about people. He loved and cared for everyone he met on that corner. He knew almost everyone who came into the store - if not by name, by face. There at Starbucks, he talked to doctors, lawyers, business people, teachers, police officers, managers, baristas, family, friends, students, and strangers. The conversations were much the same. He talked about life and the struggles we all seem to have. He talked about his cancer, and about God and his Savior, Jesus Christ. Then he would share a funny story or two, and he seemed to breathe hope in every word he shared.

~ Sandy

~~

Be Prepared   August 11, 2011

> *Consider it all joy, my brethren, when you encounter various trials, knowing that the testing of your faith produces endurance. And let endurance have its perfect result, so that you may be perfect and complete, lacking in nothing.* (James 1:2-4, NASB)

What's happening in your life right now? Are you facing a trial, a tribulation, a difficult time, or an overwhelming struggle? Well, there is hope. God has a purpose for everything. His purpose is to bring us to a place in life that is more like Jesus.

> *And we know that God causes all things to work together for good to those who love God, to those who are called according to His purpose. For those whom He foreknew, He also predestined to become conformed to the image of His Son, so that He would be the firstborn among many brethren;* (Romans 8:28-29)

God allows the trial in our lives to make us like Jesus. Thus we can "count it as," "reckon it so," and "accept it as" true joy. Our faith is being tested. Throughout scripture, God allows His followers' testing to grow them. The testing of our faith grows us in endurance and patience. The testing will have a perfect result. That result is that we develop the life that can stand up under anything. We will be mature (Christ-like) and the finished product God desires. We will lack nothing.

None of this will happen without the experience of trials and tribulations. So whether it is the current trial, or the next one to come your way, you will be prepared. God will grow you into the Christ-like person He desires. Fight the good fight of faith as you experience the trials of life.

~~

Are You in the Pits?

August 18, 2011

> *The faithful love of the Lord never ends! His mercies never cease.*
> *Great is His faithfulness; His mercies begin afresh each morning.*
> *I say to myself, "The Lord is my inheritance; therefore, I will hope in Him!"*
> *The Lord is good to those who depend on Him, to those who search for Him.*
> *So it is good to wait quietly for salvation from the Lord.*
> (Lamentations 3:22-26, NLT)

Is there hope? That would have been the cry of Jeremiah as he faced the overwhelming scene of the city of Zion. The city was in rubble, the people had been taken into captivity, and he himself was in the depths of despair. It was not a pretty scene. The once-magnificent city of David was broken, and its people destroyed. In the first twenty-one verses of chapter 3, Jeremiah described his personal feelings. He had experienced the wrath of God. He was broken. The very body in which he dwelt was feeling old. He felt trapped with no escape.

He felt deserted by God. His prayers were of no avail. The people mocked him. He cried for help, but no one did anything. Inner peace had eluded him. The wealth he once enjoyed was no more. Only poverty surrounded him. He was bitter and downcast. Maybe the worst thing of all is that HE HAD NO HOPE of anything ever getting better. He was overcome with the feelings of hopelessness. Ever been there?

Jeremiah found hope. His only hope was in God. It was in God whose love never ends, whose mercy is new every morning, and whose faithfulness is great. The conclusion of Jeremiah was that there really is hope. Hope was not in the circumstances or the troubles or sorrows, but his hope was in the Lord. Thus he decided, "I will depend on Him."

Maybe you are in the pit with Jeremiah today. Look to your only real hope: it is in the Almighty God, the Lord of your life. He is full of mercy and love for you today. Depend on Him with all your heart. HE IS FAITHFUL!!

~~

Lawbreakers' Salvation

September 1, 2011

> *Obviously, the Law applies to those to whom it was given, for its purpose is to keep people from having excuses, and to show that the entire world is guilty before God. For no one can ever be made right with God by doing what the Law commands. The Law simply shows us how sinful we are. But now God has shown us a way to be made right with Him without keeping the requirements of the Law, as was promised in the*

writings of Moses and the prophets long ago. We are made right with God by placing our faith in Jesus Christ. And this is true for everyone who believes, no matter who we are. (Romans 3:19-22, NLT)

Aren't you glad that God gives us His plan for our lives in ways that we can not only understand but also apply to our lives? In this passage from Romans, the Bible gives us the contrast between our feeble attempts at keeping the Law, and God's provision for all of us who are lawbreakers.

The purpose of the Law was to show us our total inability to live a righteous life. The Law points out our sins, and leaves us with no excuse and no option except to admit we do not live up to its demands. It is then impossible for us to be right with God because we are sinners. He is holy and just; but thank God, He is also merciful and full of grace.

God, knowing full well that we are unable to keep the Law, provided in Jesus Christ the way to salvation by grace through faith. Our attempts at being right with God by the works of the Law either lead us to failure or to self-righteousness - neither of which can save us.

We do not obey the Law, and for that reason, God has shown a different way of being made righteous - that is by faith in Jesus Christ. He is our atonement for sin. He is the One who did keep the Law perfectly.

He made Him who knew no sin to be sin on our behalf, so that we might become the righteousness of God in Him. (2 Corinthians 5:21, NASB)

Would you admit your inability to keep the Law, and trust Jesus to save you?

~~

A Look at Your Heart
September 8, 2011

But the Lord said to Samuel, "Do not look on his appearance or on the height of his stature, because I have rejected him. For the Lord sees not as man sees: man looks on the outward appearance, but the Lord looks on the heart."
(1 Samuel 16:7, ESV)

We live in a culture where outward appearance means so much. We determine a person's value and worth by their height, weight, hair color, physical beauty, clothing, and on and on the list goes. God sent Samuel to the house of Jesse to find a new king to replace Saul. When Samuel approached the house, Jesse immediately brought his most handsome son, expecting him to be chosen. Samuel quickly said, "This is not the one."

How quickly do we make choices based on physical appearance? Do we determine a person's worth based on the outward appearance? The Bible says that God said to Samuel that he should not make a decision based on the outward appearance but on the heart. God looks on the heart. God looks inward to see what is in a person's character. What are the intentions and motives of the heart? What are the values, the purities and impurities? Jesus once said that the thing that defiles a person, comes from the heart.

In order to find a new king, God was concerned about the heart condition. He desired a "man after God's own heart." He found that in David. God's choice was not based on the outward appearance but on the heart.

How do you think of yourself, or others? Do you decide as you look in the mirror, or at someone's physical appearance? You are not capable of looking into the heart as God is, but you can look beyond the outward appearance to make your decision about someone's value, or maybe your own.

~~

Be There
September 15, 2011

When three of Job's friends heard of the tragedy he had suffered, they got together and traveled from their homes to comfort and console him. Their names were Eliphaz the Temanite, Bildad the Shuhite, and Zophar the Naamathite. When they saw Job from a distance, they scarcely recognized him. Wailing loudly, they tore their robes and threw dust into the air over their heads to show their grief. Then they sat on the ground with him for seven days and nights. No one said a word to Job, for they saw that his suffering was too great for words. (Job 2:11-13, NLT)

Barbara Chesser, in her book *Because You Care*, begins chapter 1 with the simple admonition: "Be There." Although Job's friends are often criticized for their lack of theological understanding, their bad advice, and their outright misrepresentation of God, at least they cared.

How much do you care when you see a friend struggling, suffering, going through a rough time, or just needing some encouragement? Job's friends, after having heard of Job's plight, immediately got together and went to see him. They took serious the task of "being there." The purpose of their visit was to comfort, console, encourage, and give hope.

Upon seeing Job (the Bible says he looked so bad that they scarcely recognized him), they began wailing loudly, tore their robes, and threw dust into the air. It was a sign of their personal grief over the struggles of their friend. They sympathized with his sufferings, and expressed it.

An interesting response was their silence. Instead of trying to answer all the questions at once or comfort with words, they simply sat in silence. Have you ever stayed away because you didn't know what to say? Maybe silence says more than your words. His suffering was too great for words. Just "being there" may be the best comfort you could give.

Find someone today who is hurting and just be there for them. It might just be what they need the most.

~~

Miles Mean Nothing to God — September 22, 2011

> *When Jesus returned to Capernaum, a Roman officer came and pleaded with Him, "Lord, my young servant lies in bed, paralyzed and in terrible pain." Jesus said, "I will come and heal him." But the officer said, "Lord, I am not worthy to have You come into my home. Just say the word from where You are, and my servant will be healed. I know this because I am under the authority of my superior officers, and I have authority over my soldiers. I only need to say, 'Go,' and they go, or 'Come,' and they come. And if I say to my slaves, 'Do this,' they do it." When Jesus heard this, He was amazed. Turning to those who were following Him, He said, "I tell you the truth, I haven't seen faith like this in all Israel!"*
> *Then Jesus said to the Roman officer, "Go back home. Because you believed, it has happened." And the young servant was healed that same hour.*
> (Matthew 8:5-10, 13; NLT)

Ever say to yourself, "I can't help - I am so far away"? It seems we have a belief that we have to be present in order to be of assistance or help to someone in need.

A centurion approached Jesus with a need and a request. (A centurion was a soldier with one hundred soldiers serving at his command.) One of the servants of this centurion was critically ill, and the officer asked for help. Jesus replied that He would come to the man's home and heal him. The response from the centurion was, "No, I am not worthy for You to come to my home."

Distance made no difference. In faith, the centurion spoke, "Say the word and my servant will be healed." You may not be near the need or the burden you have, but the power of Christ can reach beyond the miles and your own ability to be physically near, and care for your burden. The centurion saw that Jesus was a man of authority as he himself was. "Just speak the word, and my servant will be healed," showed his understanding of the power of Jesus even across distances.

Jesus responded by healing the servant and declaring that the centurion's faith was great. What do you believe God for right now that requires God to meet your need at a distance away from your present locale?

Distance means nothing to God. Pray and expect God to answer. Remember, you don't have to be present to call upon the ever-present God that you worship. He reaches beyond the miles.

~~

Will It Happen?
September 29, 2011

> *But he himself [Elijah] went a day's journey into the wilderness, and came and sat down under a juniper tree; and he requested for himself that he might die, and said, "It is enough; now, O Lord, take my life, for I am not better than my fathers." He lay down and slept under a juniper tree; and behold, there was an angel touching him, and he said to him, "Arise, eat." Then he looked and behold, there was at his head a bread cake baked on hot stones, and a jar of water. So he ate and drank and lay down again. The angel of the Lord came again a second time and touched him and said, "Arise, eat, because the journey is too great for you." So he arose and ate and drank, and went in the strength of that food forty days and forty nights to Horeb, the mountain of God.*
> *Then he came there to a cave and lodged there; and behold, the word of the Lord came to him, and He said to him, "What are you doing here, Elijah?" He said, "I have been very zealous for the Lord, the God of hosts; for the sons of Israel have forsaken Your covenant, torn down Your altars and killed Your prophets with the sword. And I alone am left; and they seek my life, to take it away."* (1 Kings 19:4-10, NASB)

In chapter 18 of 1st Kings, Elijah faced the prophets of Baal. He challenged them to a duel of fire in the desert. The Baal worshippers built an altar and called on their god to produce fire to consume the sacrifice. They cried, cut themselves, screamed and yelled - all to no avail. The fire did not fall.

Elijah rebuilt the altar, put on the wood, and then poured water all over the sacrifice and the wood. He then called on the name of God, and prayed for God to come and consume the sacrifice. God not only accepted the sacrifice by providing fire but also dried up the water, and the wood was burned. Victory was his - but also HIS.

Jezebel, the wife of Ahab the king, declared that by the next day, Elijah would be dead. He ran a day's journey from the area to save his life. He then declared to God that he wanted to die. Totally defeated, discouraged, depressed, and wishing to die, God met him. But what was he expecting in his state of mind? Maybe he was hoping for Ahab to change, or all Israel to fall before God in worship. Neither happened.

What do you expect in your situation or circumstance? It may not happen. What *will* happen is that God will meet you and meet your needs. He loves you and cares about you. Just trust that He is for you; and "if God is for us, who can ever be against us?" (Romans 8:31, NLT)

~~

Tasks to Complete   October 13, 2011

> *"For which one of you, when he wants to build a tower, does not first sit down and calculate the cost to see if he has enough to complete it? Otherwise, when he has laid a foundation and is not able to finish, all who observe it begin to ridicule him, saying, 'This man began to build and was not able to finish.'"* (Luke 14:28-30, NASB)

No one likes to be ridiculed, even if it is deserved. Jesus warned His disciples to be cautious of deciding to be His follower without first counting the cost. It is easy to sign on a dotted line and join up to all kinds of ventures. To become a disciple of Jesus is a lot more serious than building a house or buying a car.

The cost for a disciple is surrendering everything to the Lord. In Luke 5:11, the Bible says of the first disciples, "They left everything and followed Him." Jesus used an example of what it means to be His disciple by describing someone who decides to build a tower but does not sit down first and calculate the cost. Can you imagine building a house without knowing the final cost? When the money runs out, the builder would simply quit building, only to leave a partially finished house. That leaves him open to ridicule.

A professional baseball player was asked what was the most important part of hitting the baseball. His answer was simply, "Follow through." Books have been written with the theme of "finishing well" referring to life itself. To finish a job is maybe the most important part. Buildings, movies, projects, books, music, and a host of other things have been started and never finished. Many things have been started. Few things are finished.

To be a follower of Jesus and not finish, brings ridicule and failure. Don't begin the tower until you count the cost. In some cultures and countries, to become a disciple of Jesus could cost you family, job, status, and maybe even life itself.

When it comes to being His disciple, Jesus desires us to follow Him all of our lives. To commit to being His disciple is a life-changing experience in which there is no turning back. Are you considering becoming His disciple? First count the cost. You will find a life of challenge. Plan now to finish what you start, especially when it comes to being a disciple of Jesus.

~~

Just Be You

October 20, 2011

As each one has received a special gift, employ it in serving one another as good stewards of the manifold grace of God. (1 Peter 4:10, NASB)

God, in His graciousness, has given to every believer a spiritual gift. The gifts are given for the benefit of the Church and for the glory of God. The gifts are given in order to best serve one another. To receive a gift, is to become responsible for its management and use. No one can say they have not received a gift, for the grace of God has made sure each one has a gift.

Every person becomes a servant through the use of his or her gifts. A good manager is someone who uses his or her gift for its intended purpose. Our purpose in life is to use our various gifts to serve. As a pen is made to write, we are made to use our gift. If it were possible for a pen to experience fulfillment, it would happen as it would write, or accomplish its purpose. So we are meant to achieve fulfillment as we serve by using our spiritual gifts. Our personal sense of value and worth is enhanced and proven as we serve through the use of our giftedness.

Romans 12, 1st Corinthians 12-14, Ephesians 4, and 1st Peter 4 all reveal the names and uses of the gifts given by God's Holy Spirit to be used for His glory and the needs of others. You are unique. No one is given a gift mix quite like yours. Combine your personality, life experiences, and gifts; and you become a special instrument in the hands of God.

Our responsibility is the stewardship of all that God has given us. We will be fulfilled and our lives will count for His glory as we just "be who we were meant to be." Discover and use your gifts. Study the passages of scripture that relate to gifts. Begin by serving others, and you will likely find your gift as you serve.

Praise God for all things, but never forget to praise Him and thank Him for making you special. You are special to God and to all those you serve in His name. Use your gifts wisely and use them often.

~~

Let Go of Your Load

November 3, 2011

Cast your burden upon the Lord and He will sustain you; He will never allow the righteous to be shaken. (Psalm 55:22, NASB)

Ever pick up something too heavy for you to carry by yourself? No matter how hard you tried, groaned, or grunted - you just couldn't pick it up. Some things are too big to budge. It is not necessary to make attempt after attempt and continue to fail. You need victory. God has an answer: "cast your burden" on Him.

The word picture in this Psalm is a person carrying a burden too heavy to bear alone. The psalmist reminds us that God is able to receive our load, bear it, and to carry our burden. As in most things, there is a prerequisite. Something has to happen first - you have to cast your burden off of yourself.

We may attempt to convince ourselves that we can do it alone. We can try to convince friends and family that we can go it alone. We may try to convince God that we don't need His help, but think again. You need help. Be encouraged that God will sustain you. "He will never allow the righteous to be shaken."

So when we attempt to handle life's burdens and be in control of the outcome, we are merely fooling ourselves. God's desire is for the righteous, His children, to never be shaken or to become unstable or fearful. We will be shaken unless we learn to cast all our burdens on the Lord.

The promise of never being shaken is for you. What are you carrying around right now that has you "shook"? Give it up! Let Jesus have your load, by first letting go of your struggle, and then by "casting all your anxiety on Him, because He cares for you" (1 Peter 5:7). Find encouragement today by letting go, and letting God.

~~

Victory Is Ours

November 10, 2011

David inquired of the Lord, saying, "Shall I pursue this band? Shall I overtake them?" And He said to him, "Pursue, for you will surely overtake them, and you will surely rescue all." (1 Samuel 30:8, NASB)

When David's family was attacked, and his wives and daughters and sons were carried away into captivity by the Amalekites, David and all of Israel wept until they could weep no more. Then, when he had no strength left, David inquired of

God who told him not only to pursue the enemy but that he would have victory and all of the captives would be rescued.

The Amalekites were the descendants of Esau. When Moses brought the nation of Israel out of Egypt, they were attacked from the rear by the Amalekites at Rephidim. By approaching from the rear, they killed the weakest of all the people. A battle ensued and Israel prevailed. Moses then declared to Israel that the Amalekites would always be their enemy. Later, Saul was called to battle the Amalekites with the instruction to kill everyone. Saul disobeyed and brought back the King of the Amalekites, Agag.

Some have compared the Hebrews' battles against the Amalekites to the Christians' battles with their own flesh. The flesh is not the physical body but the selfish desires and lustful ways, as seen in the fruit it produces:

> Now the deeds of the flesh are evident, which are: immorality, impurity, sensuality, idolatry, sorcery, enmities, strife, jealousy, outbursts of anger, disputes, dissensions, factions, envying, drunkenness, carousing, and things like these, of which I forewarn you, just as I have forewarned you, that those who practice such things will not inherit the kingdom of God. (Galatians 5:19-21)

> But the fruit of the Spirit is love, joy, peace, patience, kindness, goodness, faithfulness, gentleness, self-control; against such things there is no law. (Galatians 5:22-23)

As Christians, we can have victory over the flesh by walking in the Spirit. The battle between the flesh and the Spirit is ongoing, and will be all of your life. The Christian is never free from the battle but can be victorious over the flesh. "But I say, walk by the Spirit, and you will not carry out the desire of the flesh" (Galatians 5:16). The battle will always be raging, but the victory is ours through God's Holy Spirit.

~~

Are You Chained to the Chariot? November 17, 2011

> But thank God! He has made us His captives and continues to lead us along in Christ's triumphal procession. Now He uses us to spread the knowledge of Christ everywhere, like a sweet perfume. Our lives are a Christ-like fragrance rising up to God. But this fragrance is perceived differently by those who are being saved and by those who are perishing. To those who are perishing, we are a dreadful smell of death and doom. But to those who are being saved, we are a life-giving perfume. And who is adequate for such a task as this? (2 Corinthians 2:14-16, NLT)

Picture in your mind an army general riding through the center of the city. He has just won a great victory. Behind him is the conquered general of the opposing army, tied to the chariot and led through the city. Often you may think of yourself as the conquering general riding in the beautiful chariot or on the back of a white horse, when in fact, the Scripture says you are the captive. The conqueror is King Jesus. He leads you in His triumph.

It is not your victory - it is His. The apostle Paul wrote that he was thankful, full of gratitude, to be led in Christ's triumph. He saw himself as being carried through the city as a spectacle. Although Paul discovered that an open door for the Gospel was available in Troas, he had no peace about staying there. Instead, grateful to be led in Christ's triumph, he ended up in Macedonia. He was committed to finding Titus. That was God's leadership for his ministry.

Remember when you find no rest for your spirit, and you are staring at an open door for ministry, that you are chained to the chariot of Christ. He is your Leader and He leads you in His triumph. The open door at Troas closed, but a new door opened. Paul understood the change of ministry assignment, as a result of being chained to the chariot.

How utterly impossible it is for you to accomplish the ministry of the Gospel in your own strength and power. Christ is our sufficiency and our adequacy. Be glad that you are chained to His chariot. Your life and ministry will, to some, be a fragrant aroma - to others, the stench of death. Some will see the life of Christ in you, as you are led in His triumph. Others will not understand, will reject Christ, and will see your life as wasted. Be grateful that you are chained to His chariot. You will be led in victory.

~~

Are You Facing the Lions?   November 24, 2011

> *But when Daniel learned that the law had been signed, he went home and knelt down as usual in his upstairs room, with its windows open toward Jerusalem. He prayed three times a day, just as he had always done, giving thanks to his God.*
> (Daniel 6:10, NLT)

> *Be thankful in all circumstances, for this is God's will for you who belong to Christ Jesus.* (1 Thessalonians 5:18)

> *Don't worry about anything; instead, pray about everything. Tell God what you need, and thank Him for all He has done.* (Philippians 4:6)

Daniel found himself between the proverbial rock and a hard place. The administrators, officials, high officers, advisers, and governors told King Darius, king of the Medes and the Persians, that he should make a law that would be strictly enforced. The orders said that for the next thirty days, any person who prayed to anyone, divine or human - other than Darius - would be thrown into the den of lions. Daniel, of course, could not follow that law. He knew that if he did not follow the law, the result would conclude with him becoming lion food.

Daniel did his usual thing - he prayed. He went to his room with its windows open toward Jerusalem and prayed. His normal custom was to pray to the Lord three times a day. This day, with a den of lions awaiting him, he still prayed. HE GAVE THANKS. What a time to give thanks! Circumstances say he should have been praying for rescue, intervention, and protection. Instead, he gave thanks to God.

What are you facing today that feels like a hungry lion, lying in wait to attack you? What is your response? Is it giving thanks in all circumstances? Is it your choice to not worry? Is it your choice to pray about everything?

When we experience life's difficulties, it is easy to complain, worry, fret, and give up. God's encouragement to us is to give thanks in all things. How can we do that? We can pray and give thanks because, no matter what we are facing, we know that we are in Christ. Here the Bible does not say to give thanks FOR all things but IN all things. God loves you and cares about everything you face. Give thanks in all things.

~~

Is Your Christmas Merry?
December 1, 2011

> *After the wise men were gone, an angel of the Lord appeared to Joseph in a dream. "Get up! Flee to Egypt with the Child and his mother," the angel said. "Stay there until I tell you to return, because Herod is going to search for the Child to kill him." That night Joseph left for Egypt with the Child and Mary, his mother, and they stayed there until Herod's death. This fulfilled what the Lord had spoken through the prophet: "I called my Son out of Egypt." Herod was furious when he realized that the wise men had outwitted him. He sent soldiers to kill all the boys in and around Bethlehem who were two years old and under, based on the wise men's report of the star's first appearance. Herod's brutal action fulfilled what God had spoken through the prophet Jeremiah:*
> "A cry was heard in Ramah - weeping and great mourning.
> Rachel weeps for her children, refusing to be comforted, for they are dead."
> (Matthew 2:13-18, NLT)

Christmas is not always the joyous, merry experience that the media or even the church portrays it. For many, and maybe you, Christmas is anything but a wonderful time of the year. For Mary and Joseph, Christmas was a time of running for their child's life. Herod heard rumors that a new king was born. His fear of losing power caused a chain of events that endangered the very life of this newborn baby boy named Jesus, who was God in human flesh. Joseph received a dream in which he was told to escape to Egypt with Mary and the Baby.

Herod, in order to make sure he remained in power, ordered his soldiers to kill all boys two years and younger. The cry was heard throughout the town of Bethlehem because of the sorrow. What a difficult time of the year to celebrate. It may be the same for you. Memories of Christmas may not be pleasant. Your family, your church, or your own personal life may be overflowing with sad thoughts of the season that is supposed to be filled with joy.

Remember that Herod himself died.

> *And they stayed there until Herod's death. This fulfilled what the Lord had spoken through the prophet: "I called my Son out of Egypt."* (Matthew 2:15)

Mary and Joseph, along with Jesus, returned to Israel. The "Merry Christmas" we share is because of the victory of Jesus. He lived, He died, He arose, and someday He is coming again. Although you may have experienced sad times at Christmas, remember so did Mary and Joseph. In the end, they found victory. We are also victorious. Celebrate a VERY MERRY CHRISTMAS no matter what the past or the present, because Jesus is our victory.

~~

Take a Break! December 8, 2011

> *"Come to Me, all who are weary and heavy-laden, and I will give you rest. Take My yoke upon you and learn from Me, for I am gentle and humble in heart, and you will find rest for your souls. For My yoke is easy and My burden is light."*
> (Matthew 11:28-30, NASB)

"Wow! I am so tired." The words of the season seem to be expressed in those five poignant words. Do those words express the way you feel also? Work, school, family, holidays; pressure from finances, travel, and a fast paced life style all lend themselves to a tired, discouraged, and burdened-down person. Jesus lived in a very different time, yet His observation of the people of His day concluded that they were also weary and burdened, and needed rest.

Biblical lifestyle may seem laid back to us, but maybe the pressures were much the same. Jesus knew that people needed to eat, have shelter, support family, and care for the needs of all; and yet He saw a hurting people.

Jesus explained to the crowds that His concern allowed them to come to Him and find a gentle and humble heart, and a place of rest. The demands of life were shrouded in the pressure to perform religiously. How often do you find yourself burdened with your faith instead of freed from weariness and the burden of living up to the demands of religion and religious leaders? Take a break! Come to Jesus.

Jesus was surrounded with people who were overwhelmed with the rules and pressures of meeting religious expectations. He came to bring something different. He came to give "life, and life more abundant." John 10:10 says it is the "life" He offers you. The yoke Jesus brings is easy, and His burden is light.

What a great time of year to learn to give your struggles to God! Let Him be your burden-bearer. Let Him be your Lord and Savior, and your very Life. Jesus says, "Learn from Me." Undoubtedly, Jesus exemplified a life that was filled with peace, joy, love, and patience in the midst of a chaotic world. Why not let Jesus have your burdens and weariness? Remember, His yoke is easy and His burden is light.

~~

Life for Christmas
December 15, 2011

For to me, to live is Christ and to die is gain. (Philippians 1:21, NASB)

I can do everything God asks me to with the help of Christ who gives me the strength and power. (Philippians 4:13, TLB)

Do you ever seem to accomplish getting between a rock and a hard place without even trying? What if the rock and the hard place was the choice between life and death? You might make that choice quickly because you like living. You might believe that you can accomplish more alive than dead, but for the apostle Paul, it was much easier. For to him, whether he was alive or dead, his whole life was Jesus. His life was more than the space of a few years between birth and death. His life was for eternity, and he saw eternal life as Christ's life. In order to call death a gain, we need to have an eternal perspective.

Paul also saw life as Jesus' life. Jesus is the Life that everyone desires. His life is full and abundant. It is not a life free from trials and tribulations but truly living in the midst of whatever would come your way.

The apostle Paul saw not only that Christ was life but also that He was the strength and the power to face all conditions. Another translation says, "I can do all things through Him who strengthens me" (ESV). Life was never meant to be experienced apart from His life. Anything and everything else falls short.

The Christmas season is a wonderful time to find a meaningful and full life. The Baby born in a manger was the One who came to give us His life. He lived a perfect sinless life, died on a cross for our forgiveness, and arose from the dead to give us a way to have a relationship with God. Jesus Himself was God in human flesh. He came to earth to give you life. Real purpose in life is having an eternal perspective on life and death through Jesus Christ.

~~

A Christmas Newsletter December 22, 2011

> *As to all my affairs, Tychicus, our beloved brother and faithful servant and fellow bond-servant in the Lord, will bring you information. For I have sent him to you for this very purpose, that you may know about our circumstances and that he may encourage your hearts; and with him Onesimus, our faithful and beloved brother, who is one of your number. They will inform you about the whole situation here.*
> (Colossians 4:7-9, NASB)

Do you get Christmas newsletters from friends, family members, and even those you hardly know? Paul wrote, at the end of the Colossian letter, a series of statements and questions that read much like a Christmas newsletter.

Newsletters contain universal elements. The first element is the latest information. Tychicus was the deliverer of the letter from Paul. His job was to inform the Colossians as to the wellbeing of the apostle, which hopefully would lead to great encouragement. Paul, after all, was a prisoner. Paul said that Tychicus would inform them of the whole situation. Paul continued the letter stating that Tychicus and Onesimus would be bringing encouraging words. They would accomplish that by sharing the latest news. Good news is always encouraging.

> *Aristarchus, my fellow prisoner, sends you his greetings; and also Barnabas' cousin Mark (about whom you received instructions; if he comes to you, welcome him); and also Jesus who is called Justus; these are the only fellow workers for the kingdom of God who are from the circumcision, and they have proved to be an encouragement to me.* (Colossians 4:10-11)

Paul also sent greetings from the others who were with him. A good newsletter almost always has a line that says something like, "Everyone here says hi."

> *Epaphras, who is one of your number, a bondslave of Jesus Christ, sends you his greetings, always laboring earnestly for you in his prayers, that you may stand perfect and fully assured in all the will of God.* (Colossians 4:12)

"By the way, we are praying for you." There is nothing as assuring and encouraging as the knowledge that we are being prayed for. Epaphras, a pastor, was a prayer warrior. He labored in prayer, and everyone must have known that he prayed for them. His prayers were specific: "That you may stand perfect and fully assured in all the will of God."

> *I, Paul, write this greeting with my own hand. Remember my imprisonment. Grace be with you.* (Colossians 4:18)

Ministry is not done without support. Prayer, encouragement, love, concern, and finances were all needed to fulfill the ministry God had called Paul to accomplish. He was a prisoner spreading the Gospel through verbal witness, a lifestyle, and the written Word. "Remember me" was Paul's reminder.

Send out your newsletter. Read the ones you get. Remember to encourage everyone with the latest information, a sincere greeting, prayer, and whatever support is needed. Merry Christmas!!

~~

With My Whole Heart

December 29, 2011

> *Let all that I am praise the Lord;*
> *with my whole heart, I will praise His holy name.*
> *Let all that I am praise the Lord;*
> *may I never forget the good things He does for me.*
> *He forgives all my sins and heals all my diseases.*
> *He redeems me from death and crowns me with love and tender mercies.*
> *He fills my life with good things. My youth is renewed like the eagle's!*
> (Psalm 103:1-5, NLT)

David the psalmist wrote this Psalm in his later years. He was deeply moved with the thought of all that God had done for him. He used the word "Lord," the personal name of God. He did so with much endearment.

Have you ever stopped to reflect on all the Lord has done for you? David did, so he had a little talk with himself. His words were spoken to his inner being. "His whole heart" is a translation of the word for soul. He reminded his own soul, his whole heart, to praise the Lord. He told his own heart to never forget what the Lord had done.

David then remembered his own sin and the need he had for forgiveness. David was called a man after God's own heart and yet he sinned deeply. He lied, and committed adultery and murder. Needless to say, as he reflected on his own sin and his forgiveness, he had a reason to praise the Lord. His mind also went to the great healing power of God, and again praised the Lord.

David then, with his eyes on the future, remembered the promises of eternal life. His life would not be over when he closed his eyes in death. There was a future life to anticipate because he had been redeemed. He quickly reminded himself that was only possible because of the love and mercy of God. He was not worthy, but God is a God of forgiveness.

He was rejuvenated and felt his youth return to his thoughts. No wonder he could say to himself, "Praise the Lord." Have you praised the Lord today? I am sure if you reflected on your life, you would realize that the mercy and grace of God have sustained and guided you during this past year, and you would have no response except to PRAISE THE LORD.

~~

The Real Marathon
January 5, 2012

> *Therefore, since we are surrounded by such a huge crowd of witnesses to the life of faith, let us strip off every weight that slows us down, especially the sin that so easily trips us up. And let us run with endurance the race God has set before us.*
> (Hebrews 12:1, NLT)

Witnesses surround us. They are a large crowd. Who are they? To what do they witness? In the book of Hebrews, chapter 12 begins with the word "therefore" which refers to what was written before. Chapter 11 is about the great people of faith who were witnesses to a life of faith.

This verse obviously does not refer to people looking over the edge of heaven and watching all who are currently living. If that were the case, then heaven would cease to be heaven. For in heaven there are no tears or sorrow. If people in heaven could see what was happening on earth, it would no longer be heaven. The witness is the life of faith that they lived.

Two qualities are observed in their lives. The first is faith itself. The examples in chapter 11 tell of the heroic deeds of faith lived by these witnesses. The second quality is endurance. They were not only people with great faith, but they endured hardship and ridicule. They never received the promises of God and yet they continued to believe.

The writer of Hebrews encourages us to a life of faith by admonishing us to remove any encumbrance that would hinder our walk of faith. The analogy is used of a runner who wears only the bare necessities of clothing in order to not slow down his speed and endurance. The author reminds us to lay aside anything that hinders us, and especially the sin that so easily entangles us. You likely have something that continually bogs you down and becomes a stumbling block to your faith - it interrupts your endurance. Set it aside. Remove it from your life. The fight of faith is not easy. It takes continual dependence upon the Holy Spirit to give us the power and discipline to live by faith, and to endure life and its difficulties.

You have a great crowd of witnesses whose lives were an example of faith and endurance. Run your race realizing there are those who have gone before you.

~~

Dead Is Good! January 12, 2012

> *Without becoming weak in faith he contemplated his own body, now as good as dead since he was about a hundred years old, and the deadness of Sarah's womb; yet, with respect to the promise of God, he did not waver in unbelief but grew strong in faith, giving glory to God, and being fully assured that what God had promised, He was able also to perform.* (Romans 4:19-21, NASB)

Faith is almost always tested. Has your faith been tested? Can you imagine how Abraham must have felt after moving from Ur to the land of Canaan, having been given the promise of a child and to be the father of many nations; and then have no child, a wife that is ninety years old, and he was one hundred? Now that is a real test of faith! It could also be called the "death of a vision." Let me assure you that if God is in something, the death of a vision may occur in order for God to bring about fulfillment of the vision in His way. He likes to do the miraculous in order to bring glory to Himself.

It is then that we need to learn to face whatever comes our way but also to not lose sight of the promise that God gave. Abraham, even though faced with the impossible, did not become weak in his faith. He did not give up. He did not waver in unbelief but instead grew even stronger - which gave God all the glory.

We don't have to hide the facts of a situation from our faith. Admit the impossibility. Recognize that the ultimate solution is God. True faith grows stronger when confronted with the impossibilities. Presumption gives up and gives in to it. Don't allow facts to intimidate your faith, or you will not believe.

Jesus said, "All things are possible to him who believes" (Mark 9:23). Your true faith is not in what you see but in a God who is faithful to fulfill His promises. His purpose for you is that you glorify Him. He does that through His faithfulness and your faith in Him.

~~

Where Do You Belong? January 19, 2012

> *But if we walk in the Light, as He Himself is in the Light, we have fellowship with one another, and the blood of Jesus His Son cleanses us from all sin.*
> (1 John 1:7, NASB)

One of the most popular names for a church in the twenty-first century is So-and-So Community Church. The word "community" seems to lend itself to the meaning and sense of belonging. One of the greatest needs of humanity is to belong. What does a church with authentic, genuine community look like? The biblical word that may best describe that kind of community is "fellowship."

As we walk in the light of God's revelation of Himself to us through His Son Jesus Christ, and we in turn relate to others with that same revelation, we have fellowship. We have authentic community. There are at least four characteristics of fellowship and authentic community:
1. We admit we cannot function effectively by ourselves.
2. We admit that we are not more or less important than anyone else.
3. We admit that it takes work to fulfill the unity we have in Christ.
4. We admit that we need to use our gifts in ministry to, and with, one another.

We all need a church where we can express our unity and community. We need to remember that real community is not people in close contact but people closely connected. Where are you connected with other believers? Where do you exercise your giftedness to serve others?

The Scripture is clear about our need to be together in unity. We are to accept one another as Christ has accepted us. We are to love one another, forgive one another, be devoted to one another, bear with one another, serve one another, submit to and admonish one another, and even confess our sins to one another.

It is not likely that these things will happen outside of an authentic, lifestyle community of believers. It is so vitally important to your own relationship with God to be involved in a church where these qualities exist.

If you are not a part of a church like this, or a church at all, why not find one this week? God desires our worship. We need God and we need one another.

> *Therefore if there is any encouragement in Christ, if there is any consolation of love, if there is any fellowship of the Spirit, if any affection and compassion, make my joy complete by being of the same mind, maintaining the same love, united in spirit, intent on one purpose. Do nothing from selfishness or empty conceit, but with humility of mind regard one another as more important than yourselves; do not merely look out for your own personal interests, but also for the interests of others.* (Philippians 2:1-4)

Become a part of an authentic biblical community now. You will be glad you did.

~~

Holy Attraction   January 26, 2012

> *And He said, "A man had two sons. The younger of them said to his father, 'Father, give me the share of the estate that falls to me.' So he divided his wealth between them. And not many days later, the younger son gathered everything together and went on a journey into a distant country, and there he squandered his estate with loose living."* (Luke 15:11-13, NASB)

In the story of the prodigal son, we find a young man who decided he wanted to "do his own thing," be his own boss, live his life apart from his loving father. A man by the name of Kenneth Bailey, a Presbyterian researcher and lecturer in the Middle East, for over forty years has asked people from Morocco to India and from Turkey to Sudan about the implications of a son requesting his inheritance while his father was still living. The answer has always been the same. His informal survey has gone something like this:

Q: "Has anyone ever made such a request in your village?"
A: "Never."
Q: "Could anyone ever make such a request?"
A: "Impossible!"
Q: "If anyone did, what would happen?"
A: "His father would beat him, of course!"
Q: "Why?"
A: "The request means that he wants his father dead."

Normally, after signing over his possessions to his son, the father still is entitled to live off the proceeds. Because the younger son in this parable demands and gets full use of the inheritance before the father's death, the implication is as though the boy said, "Father, I would rather you were dead."

The father could have shamed his son, beat him, or physically restrained him from leaving. But very matter-of-factly, the father divided his property and gave it to the son.

Isn't this how we treat God? We demand what we think is owed to us and then we proceed to go our own way. In our own self-centered way, we communicate the message, "Father, I would rather You were dead."

But in this beautiful parable, we see a "God Moment" – a moment of holy attraction. That is exactly what the prodigal son had, when he found himself in the pigpen. Luke 15:17 says, "But when he came to his senses, he said, 'How many of my father's hired men have more than enough bread, but I am dying here with hunger!' " He had a "God Moment of Holy Attraction."

Every time we have avoided the trap of sin, every incidence in which we opted for high moral standards, every decision for purity, and every lovely thought is a God Moment of Holy Attraction.

To discover moments of Holy Attraction, you will need to take a look at those moments in which you resisted God's way the most - those times when you totally rebelled against your loving Father. The only way the prodigal son found his way home was because of an irresistible attraction to home!

How do you uncover your moments of holy attraction? Those times when you also "came to your senses"? Are you being attracted to HOME today? Why not come home to the Father?

~~

Money Down a Hole

February 2, 2012

... Holding fast the word of life, so that in the day of Christ I will have reason to glory because I did not run in vain nor toil in vain. (Philippians 2:16, NASB)

The apostle Paul wrote a letter to the church at Philippi and made a strange statement. It seems Paul was saying, "Please make sure I don't spend my life in ministry by wasting it on people who are not growing in their faith and commitment to Jesus."

Ever hear the phrase "throwing money down a hole"? It is usually used when you are wasting resources on something. You know the experience. The car starts breaking down on a regular basis. It begins to be not just oil changes and tires but also transmissions, motors, air conditioner condensers; and suddenly you have spent more in repairs in one year than it would have cost to buy a new car. That is throwing money down a hole. Everyone who owns a swimming pool knows the feeling of throwing money in a big hole in the back yard.

Paul says in Philippians 4:1, you are "my joy and crown." He meant that they were the product of his ministry. His prayer request to the Thessalonian church was:

> *Finally, brethren, pray for us that the word of the Lord will spread rapidly and be glorified, just as it did also with you; and that we will be rescued from perverse and evil men; for not all have faith.* (2 Thessalonians 3:1-2)

"Don't let me waste my ministry. Don't let me throw money down a hole." Paul had experienced the waste. He mentions in Colossians 4:14 to greet Demas. He later mentions him again: "... for Demas, having loved this present world, has deserted me and gone to Thessalonica" (2 Timothy 4:10).

Paul said to the Corinthian church, "We also urge you not to receive the grace of God in vain" (2 Corinthians 6:1). He indicated that what we receive from God, needs attention.

Paul had planted the church in Philippi and had heard of their struggles. He desired for them to mature in their faith. He wanted to see the fruit of the Spirit in their lives. God desires you to not throw away what you have received from Him. Salvation is a gift - use it wisely. Growing in grace and in the likeness of Jesus is the desire of God for your life, as you are "holding fast the word of life."

~~

Know Your Enemy

February 9, 2012

> *Finally, be strong in the Lord and in the strength of His might. Put on the full armor of God, so that you will be able to stand firm against the schemes of the devil. For our struggle is not against flesh and blood, but against the rulers, against the powers, against the world forces of this darkness, against the spiritual forces of wickedness in the heavenly places.* (Ephesians 6:10-12, NASB)

In the pictures of the American Revolution, the British and the Americans stood a few yards apart, loaded their weapons, and fired. When the smoke settled, some were wounded and others were dead. Then they reloaded and took a few steps forward and shot again. What a novel idea: you actually knew your enemy. In recent wars, often the enemy is unknown and sneaks up on you undetected.

What a similarity between that type of warfare and spiritual warfare. It is easy to misunderstand the enemy. In spiritual warfare, the enemy appears to be the people, circumstances, or even one another. Instead, the enemy is none other than Satan and his host of demons. They are against God and God's people. Satan is not a fair enemy. He does not just line up against us and shoot it out. He is deceptive, aggressive, and attacks from every direction - often at the same time.

When the children of Israel first came out of Egypt, God did not lead them by the way of the Philistines but through the wilderness because they were not ready for war. They would have gone back to Egypt. God led them another way. Later, they were prepared to fight for the land God had promised them. It was their land - it was just occupied by someone else. God was leading them to victory. The enemy was there. It is vital that in order to win the war, we must recognize the real enemy and put on the full armor of God.

~~

What's Your Excuse?

February 16, 2012

As they were going along the road, someone said to Him, "I will follow You wherever You go." And Jesus said to him, "The foxes have holes and the birds of the air have nests, but the Son of Man has nowhere to lay His head." And He said to another, "Follow Me." But he said, "Lord, permit me first to go and bury my father." But He said to him, "Allow the dead to bury their own dead; but as for you, go and proclaim everywhere the kingdom of God." Another also said, "I will follow You, Lord; but first permit me to say good-bye to those at home." But Jesus said to him, "No one, after putting his hand to the plow and looking back, is fit for the kingdom of God." (Luke 9:57-62, NASB)

Excuses ultimately have little influence on God. When Jesus extended a call for someone to follow Him, many responded with various excuses and reasons why the timing was off, or the task was too difficult, or other needs were more pressing.

One person suggested he needed to first go home and say goodbye to his family. It seemed like a legitimate excuse, but it was answered by Jesus with a proverb. He said, "No one, after putting his hand to the plow and looking back, is fit for the kingdom of God." Jesus understood that in order to plow straight and to finish the task, you could not turn around and look behind.

Excuse-makers look backwards to see where they have been, how they are doing, and forget that the future is ahead. To plow a straight furrow, it is always necessary to look ahead. Make no excuses for following Christ. Simply look forward to where He is guiding, and follow Him.

~~

Content or Selfish?　　　　　　　　　　　　　March 1, 2012

For the mind set on the flesh [self] is death, but the mind set on the Spirit is life and peace. (Romans 8:6, NASB)

And He said to all, "If anyone would come after Me, let him deny himself and take up his cross daily and follow Me." (Luke 9:23, ESV)

If you try to hang on to your life, you will lose it. But if you give up your life for My sake and for the sake of the Good News, you will save it. (Mark 8:35, NLT)

Are you selfish? From the March 28, 1995, issue of the Arizona Republic newspaper: "Civilization was created to constrain egoism, to teach people to deny themselves for the common good."

It appears the most common qualities of most people are found in two very selfish expressions - one is greed, and the other is envy. Poles apart, and yet, so similar are both of these lifestyles. Both are extremely selfish.

Two quotes, apart from the Scripture, give a good perspective of selfishness: "Selfishness is that detestable vice which no one will forgive in others, and no one is without in himself." ~ Henry Ward Beecher
"He who lives only to benefit himself confers on the world a benefit when he dies." ~ Tertullian

The Bible gives great insight into living life to its fullest. Never is selfishness listed as an avenue to the wonderful life. In fact, Jesus made it clear that to find life, you have to lose your life. To truly be a follower of Jesus would be to deny yourself (the opposite of selfishness), take up your cross, and follow Him.

The apostle Paul reminds us in the book of Romans that a life set on the flesh or the self brings about death. It is as the mind is set on the Spirit that true life and peace will be found.

In the book of Philippians, the apostle Paul gives the secret of living with much or with little. That secret is contentment - the opposite of selfishness. TRY IT!!

~~

What Pleases Him? March 8, 2012

For we walk by faith, not by sight.
Therefore we also have as our ambition, whether at home or absent, to be pleasing to
Him. (2 Corinthians 5:7, 9; NASB)

Are you the ambitious type? Are you always looking for a new challenge - something exciting, something in which there is a risk involved? The apostle Paul shared with the Corinthians a rather ambitious goal. The goal was that whether dead or alive (maybe better put, "alive here on earth or alive in heaven"), to always be pleasing to God.

There are so many ideas about how to please God: acting religious, church attendance, good family relations, Bible study, giving of our material blessings, and so on and so on. No doubt, God is pleased with all these things, but the Bible says that in order to really please Him, it takes faith. We are to walk by faith. Not by our ambitious goals but by faith. The Bible says "Without faith it is impossible to please Him" (Hebrews 11:6).

Living by faith is a moment-by-moment dependence upon God. Faith believes He can and will direct your life, and protect and provide for your wellbeing. He is all-knowing, thus He is aware of what is coming next in our lives. And He is sovereign, so we can rest in Him through faith. What a relief to no longer live in fear! What a privilege to be loved by the Creator who knows our every need!

The ambition of the Christian life is to please God. The primary way we accomplish that goal in life is to walk by faith. It is not a life where "once in a while" we trust and have faith in God when things are difficult, but constantly having faith in the One who is Lord of all.

Do you worry? Are you filled with anxiety about the present or the future? Do you doubt that God really loves and cares for you? Are you overrun by the cares of this world? Let me assure you that God is able and willing to meet your life's struggles.

We need not live in denial of our struggles and needs. We just need to have faith that God is in charge. God not only knows of your difficulties, but He is all-powerful, and able to reach into your life and make the difference. He is waiting on you to have faith in Him.

Remember, we live by faith and not by sight. What you see happening around you is sight. What you don't see but believe, is faith.

~~

That Still, Small Voice

March 15, 2012

> *And the Lord said to Paul in the night by a vision, "Do not be afraid any longer, but go on speaking and do not be silent; for I am with you, and no man will attack you in order to harm you, for I have many people in this city." And he settled there a year and six months, teaching the word of God among them.*
> (Acts 18:9-11, NASB)

Great confidence comes when we receive a confirmation from the Word of the Lord. God is a revealing God and delights in giving to His children encouragement and hope. He speaks to us through the Bible, the circumstances of life, the indwelling Holy Spirit, prayer, and the counsel of godly people.

The apostle Paul was experienced in ministry that often included difficulties and trials. He could easily anticipate that at any time a new struggle was coming. For him to anticipate something coming next would have been normal. The majority of his struggles came at the hands of those to whom he ministered. He never knew what would come next. He could expect a beating, or an imprisonment, or both.

This time it was different. God spoke clearly to Paul about His protection. God gave him a vision that contained the hope and encouragement needed to carry on his ministry in Corinth. God's word was simply, "Do not be afraid." Paul's instruction from God was to continue his ministry with the assurance that he would be safe.

Paul was renewed in his mission. He was empowered to continue sharing the Gospel and teaching God's Scripture to the Corinthians. Paul's normal length of stay at any place was from a few days to maybe a few months, but this time he stayed a year and six months making disciples by teaching the Scriptures. The word from God was accompanied with the promise that many would respond to his message of salvation through Jesus.

Do you need a fresh word from God or a renewal of your calling to serve the Lord right where you are? Listen as God speaks to you through the Bible, prayer, godly counsel, and the still, small voice of God's Spirit speaking to your heart. Go forward with a sense of hope and encouragement to fulfill His calling in your life.

~~

Road Kill

March 29, 2012

> *Now they found an Egyptian in the field and brought him to David, and gave him bread and he ate, and they provided him water to drink. They gave him a piece of fig cake and two clusters of raisins, and he ate; then his spirit revived. For he had not eaten bread or drunk water for three days and three nights. David said to him, "To whom do you belong? And where are you from?" And he said, "I am a young man of Egypt, a servant of an Amalekite; and my master left me behind when I fell sick three days ago."* (1 Samuel 30:11-13, NASB)

Left for dead on the side of the road, or in this case in a field - that is the condition of the Egyptian, the servant of the Amalekites, that David found dying. The Amalekites were not only the enemy of David but of their own servants. The Amalekites represent the flesh in all of us. We have three basic spiritual enemies: the world, the devil, and the flesh.

The Amalekites had captured David's family. David, in hot pursuit of them, found one of the enemy's servants in a field, dying from lack of nourishment. As they gave him water, bread, fig cake, and raisins, he revived.

When David asked him, "To whom do you belong?" he answered that he was an Egyptian and a servant of an Amalekite. He also said that the Amalekite left him behind when he was sick. As in all of us, the flesh makes great promises but never fulfills them. The Amalekites (the flesh) took care of the servant as long as he was useful. After that, they left him to die.

The flesh promises prosperity, peace, excitement, popularity, and fun. The problem is that the flesh delivers death. The flesh is at war with the Spirit of God within every believer, and the flesh is a destroyer much like Satan is a destroyer. Never trust the flesh to give you anything except to leave you dying in the field. Only God gives life.

> *For the flesh sets its desire against the Spirit, and the Spirit against the flesh; for these are in opposition to one another, so that you may not do the things that you please.* (Galatians 5:17)

~~

Touching and Believing

April 5, 2012

> *But Thomas, one of the twelve, called Didymus, was not with them when Jesus came. So the other disciples were saying to him, "We have seen the Lord!" But he said to them, "Unless I see in His hands the imprint of the nails, and put my finger into the place of the nails, and put my hand into His side, I will not believe." After eight days His disciples were again inside, and Thomas with them. Jesus came, the doors having been shut, and stood in their midst and said, "Peace be with you." Then He said to Thomas, "Reach here with your finger, and see My hands; and reach here your hand and put it into My side; and do not be unbelieving, but believing." Thomas answered and said to Him, "My Lord and my God!"* (John 20:24-28, NASB)

Thomas had a story - a story of doubt, fear, and faith. He was for sure a faithful follower of Jesus. He even said he was willing to die for Jesus. He knew Jesus as his Savior and Lord, yet he doubted the Life Giver.

He was not present when the disciples gathered on that first Sunday night after Jesus' resurrection. He declared to the other disciples that he just could not believe unless he could see and touch Jesus for himself. For that reason, he is nicknamed "Doubting Thomas." His doubts were not a rejection of Jesus as his Savior and Lord. He was still waiting on "the power of His resurrected life" described in Philippians 3:10: "That I may know Him and the power of His resurrection." It was not until he reached out and touched Jesus that the resurrection became real to him.

Do you believe in Jesus? If yes, then do you believe He died on the cross for your sins? Do you believe He forgives you? If yes, then are you experiencing His resurrected life in you? Thomas was uncertain of the abundant life until Jesus revealed that He was alive and could give that life to Thomas.

You may have a story of Jesus saving you, forgiving you of your sins, and becoming the Lord of your life but have yet to grasp the "life-changing life" He offers you. "I came that they may have life, and have it abundantly" (John 10:10). To know Jesus and His resurrected life, is to know abundant life.

~~

Do You Know Jesus?

April 12, 2012

> *These things I have written to you who believe in the name of the Son of God, so that you may know that you have eternal life.* (1 John 5:13, NASB)

Are you sure today that you have eternal life? To be sure of anything, brings hope. Assurance gives peace, joy, and freedom. What a comfort and encouragement it is to know something for sure! If you knew that today you would have a great day with no problems or struggles, would that not give you hope? It is also true with eternal life. Do you desire an abundant life with meaning and purpose? Would you like to know that when you leave this earth in death, you will spend eternity with God in heaven? You can know for sure.

You may be one of those people who say, "Well, I hope so," or "I guess I'll know one of these days," or maybe you are so unsure as to just shrug your shoulders when asked that question. Well, here is good news for you: the Bible, God's Word, tells us that we can know. If we believe in the Lord Jesus Christ, we can know for sure. The assurance of our salvation and the hope of eternity are based on faith - the faithfulness of God and our faith in Him. We can know we have eternal life because God's Word says it. John has written to Christians to assure them that if they believe in the name of the Son of God, they will KNOW they are saved from hell and they have been given eternal life.

The lack of fear for the future, the peace of the present, and the hope of eternity are all the result of Jesus' death and resurrection, and our faith in Him. We can know we have eternal life. We don't have to live in fear or doubt about God's love and salvation because it is not determined by how we feel or think but according to what God says.

What God says in His Word is that if you will believe in Jesus Christ, the Son of God, you will not only have eternal life, but you can know you have it. You know this is true because God's Word says it. You can trust God and His Word. Would you place your faith in Jesus today?

~~

Freedom That Lasts April 19, 2012

> *It was for freedom that Christ set us free; therefore keep standing firm and do not be subject again to a yoke of slavery.* (Galatians 5:1, NASB)

One of the deepest needs of every person is to be free. Throughout history, mankind has fought wars, engaged in treaties, and defended their homes and countries to be free. Our founding fathers knew the importance of freedom as they wrote the Declaration of Independence and the Bill of Rights. They understood that only in the context of personal freedom could a nation thrive.

Strangely enough, God also knew that freedom was important to the individual. He sent His Son to set us free from the bondage of the Law and the slavery to sin. Jesus died and rose again to give true freedom to all who would trust Him by faith. The Bible declares it was for the purpose of freedom that Christ set us free. To be free to choose life in Christ is one of our greatest privileges. When we have the Son, we are free indeed.

How important is freedom to you? You may take for granted many of your freedoms: the freedom to move about, to make choices, to speak, to engage in business, to have relationships, to worship, to not be controlled by freedom-stealers. The apostle Paul wrote to the people of the Galatian church, who were in danger of losing their freedom in Christ, to not allow the subjugation of sin and the Mosaic Law to enslave them. His encouragement to them was to stand firm. "Do not allow yourself to be swayed by those who would remove your freedom."

It is through truth that we find freedom. "And you will know the truth, and the truth will set you free" (John 8:32, NLT). "So if the Son sets you free, you will be free indeed" (John 8:36, ESV). God's purpose through Christ was to set us free from whatever enslaves us. He replaces our bondage with true freedom.

What is controlling your life? Is whatever that is in control of your life, bringing you freedom - or enslaving you? If you are free, who or what is attempting to remove your freedom? What are you doing about it? Stand firm in your freedom, and do not allow anyone or anything to take it away from you.

It was for freedom that Christ has set you free. Rejoice in, and thank God for, your freedom!

~~

Who Let the Dogs Out?   April 26, 2012

> *Watch out for those dogs, those people who do evil, those mutilators who say you must be circumcised to be saved.* (Philippians 3:2, NLT)

What an unusual word to describe evil people: DOGS. It wasn't so unusual in the Middle East in biblical days. Unlike in the United States where dogs are domesticated, groomed, pampered and cared for like humans; in other parts of the world, dogs often run in packs in the streets. They are dirty, scavengers, dangerous, and frightening. To be called a "dog" is a great insult, and yet, this is the word chosen to describe these people.

The people described were perverting the Gospel of grace and mercy. They were adding to the work of Jesus Christ on the cross, where He died for sin. They were adding to the Gospel the demands of the Mosaic Law. Anything added to the finished work of Christ adds good works and deeds to the requirements of the Gospel. The response to the Gospel is faith. "For by grace you have been saved through faith; and that not of yourselves, it is the gift of God; not as a result of works, so that no one may boast" (Ephesians 2:8-9, NASB).

The warning of the Bible is to watch out for dogs - people who add to the Gospel and require more than God's grace for salvation. In this case, the Judaizers were requiring all those who believed in Christ for salvation to be circumcised in accordance with Jewish law, in addition to their faith in Christ. The Judaizers were true freedom-killers. The Bible identifies these people as evil.

You may have listened to the freedom-killers, the dogs, the evil ones, telling you that in order to be saved, you had to adhere to certain rules, regulations, and laws. The Bible is quite clear: these are in opposition to the grace and mercy of God. Faith is all that is needed. "He saved us, not on the basis of deeds which we have done in righteousness, but according to His mercy, by the washing of regeneration and renewing by the Holy Spirit" (Titus 3:5).

Do not allow the dogs to take away from you the freedom you have found in Christ, by adding the Law to your faith. God desires all His children to be free. You can walk by faith, and experience God's grace and mercy. Watch out for the dogs.

~~

Body Building

May 3, 2012

> ... *From whom the whole body, being fitted and held together by what every joint supplies, according to the proper working of each individual part, causes the growth of the body for the building up of itself in love.* (Ephesians 4:16, NASB)

How did God make you? What is your personality? Do you have a passion for something? What kind of things do you do well? Do you know your spiritual gift? How do you fit into the body of Christ? Your fit is determined by how God made you.

The Bible uses the word "body" as an analogy of the Church. The gathered Church functions as each part functions in the way God made each of them. As we have arms, legs, eyes, ears, and even toes, each part has to function properly in order for our body to operate at its greatest potential. The Church, the Body of Christ, has many parts. You are one of them.

We are each unique and thus we each have a function in the Church that is different from anyone else's. God's plan for the Church is to glorify Him as it grows numerically, in spiritual depth, in unity, and in love. In order for the Church to grow and to be built up in love, each part needs to function properly. That means you are important to the body.

It is not the "part" that causes the building up of the body but "the proper working" of each part that causes it to grow. It is also the proper working of your part that brings glory to God. Literally, as each part does its part, the body grows. If the Church has the need to grow in maturity, or needs more people, or more love, then your part needs to be functioning as God created you to function.

What are you doing to build up your church? Your personality, passion, gifts, experiences, and abilities will give you the answer as to how you are to function. The Scripture makes it clear that it is the functioning of the parts, and not just being one of the parts, that causes the body to be built up in love.

Your participation in the body of Christ is essential for the sake of the body itself. Find your place of service and do your part.

~~

Principles for Life   May 17, 2012

> *He revealed His character to Moses and His deeds to the people of Israel.*
> (Psalm 103:7, NLT)

> *"For My thoughts are not your thoughts, Nor are your ways My ways," declares the Lord.* (Isaiah 55:8, NASB)

God obviously has far loftier thoughts than we do, but often His thoughts as recorded in the Scripture seem senseless, logically unacceptable, or self-contradictory. Yet, Bible-believing people understand that God's thoughts are not our thoughts.

A few examples could possibly help you understand. These would be considered biblical principles:
> *Humble yourselves in the presence of the Lord, and He will exalt you.*
> (James 4:10)

Do not judge, or you too will be judged. For in the same way you judge others, you will be judged, and with the measure you use, it will be measured to you.
(Matthew 7:1-2, NIV)

If you try to hang on to your life, you will lose it. But if you give up your life for My sake, you will save it. (Matthew 16:25, NLT)

For the Scripture says, "You must not muzzle an ox to keep it from eating as it treads out the grain." And in another place, "Those who work deserve their pay!"
(1 Timothy 5:18)

One of the most profound of all principles is found in 2nd Corinthians 12:9-10.
And He has said to me, "My grace is sufficient for you, for power is perfected in weakness." Most gladly, therefore, I will rather boast about my weaknesses, so that the power of Christ may dwell in me… for when I am weak, then I am strong. (NASB)

See how many principles you can find in God's Word. Learn and live by God's principles.

~~

A New Name

June 1, 2012

And he brought him to Jesus. Jesus looked at him and said, "You are Simon son of John. You will be called Cephas" (which, when translated, is Peter).
(John 1:42, NIV)

He said, "Your name shall no longer be Jacob, but Israel; for you have striven with God and with men and have prevailed." (Genesis 32:28, NASB)

Then Saul, who was also called Paul, … (Acts 13:9, NIV)

Joseph, a Levite from Cyprus, whom the apostles called Barnabas (which means "son of encouragement"), … (Acts 4:36)

To the church of God which is at Corinth, to those who have been sanctified in Christ Jesus, saints by calling, with all who in every place call on the name of our Lord Jesus Christ, their Lord and ours: … (1 Corinthians 1:2, NASB)

Of all the name changes, the one that encourages believers the most is in this verse - 1st Corinthians 1:2. Before the ultimate change that God brought into your life, you could be described by the name "sinner." Now in Christ, you are a new person. As others in scripture had their names changed to describe them better, it is also true with you. In Christ, you have a new nature and a new name. You are sanctified, set apart, and made holy. You are a saint, a holy one, by calling. What an awesome thought! Someone who was condemned by sin, now has a new name. You are a new creation - created by God with a new life and a new name. You are a child of God!

"See how great a love the father has bestowed on us, that we would be called children of God; and such we are." (1 John 3:1)

Throughout history, people have changed their names. Agnes Gonxha Bojaxhiu became known as Mother Teresa. Martha Burk became known as Calamity Jane. John Chapman became known as Johnny Appleseed. Their new names reflected their character and persona.

Your new name, "saint," describes what Jesus has done for you. You are no longer sinner but saint. Your character and persona come from your relationship with Him. You are in Christ. "Therefore, if anyone is in Christ, the new creation has come: The old has gone, the new is here!" (2 Corinthians 5:17, NIV).

May you rejoice in your name, your character, and your relationship with God; and may He bless you this very day.

~~

If Only
June 8, 2012

Joshua said, "Alas, O Lord God, why did You ever bring this people over the Jordan, only to deliver us into the hand of the Amorites, to destroy us? If only we had been willing to dwell beyond the Jordan!" (Joshua 7:7, NASB)

"If only we had been willing..." These were words of defeat, discouragement, and failure. The "if" means Joshua believed that their attempt at conquering the Promised Land seemed doomed.

They had experienced great victory over the formidable foe of Jericho, only to be defeated by the small and insignificant city of Ai. Their problem was not that God was delivering them into the hands of the enemy, but that they had sin in the camp. They had attempted to pursue Ai without God's directive. Then a man named Achan had stolen some of the articles banned by God, and taken them back and buried them under his tent.

Joshua's courage and faith staggered as the defeat of Ai became reality. Instead of looking forward in faith, he looked back in defeat. We can never look back with an "if only" and expect to walk in faith and victory. We are conquerors through Christ.

Temporary setbacks and defeat are not a reason for retreat to the old life. We are truly new creations in Christ with an upward call to be like Jesus. Do not allow a defeat to send you to the place of saying, "If only I had been willing to settle for something other than God's best." The children of Israel were defeated at Ai, but that was not an excuse to make the choice of not moving forward in faith.

Once the people of Israel faced their sin, they were ready to move forward in conquering the Promised Land. Paul wrote to the Roman church about their victory in Christ: "In all these things we are more than conquerors through Him who loved us" (Romans 8:37, NIV).

You need not look back and live in defeat, discouragement, and failure. You can live in victory through Christ. Don't catch yourself saying, "If only I had been willing…" Rejoice in your victory.

~~

Victory From Defeat June 15, 2012

One day, after Moses had grown up, he went out to where his own people were and watched them at their hard labor. He saw an Egyptian beating a Hebrew, one of his own people. Looking this way and that and seeing no one, he killed the Egyptian and hid him in the sand. The next day he went out and saw two Hebrews fighting. He asked the one in the wrong, "Why are you hitting your fellow Hebrew?" The man said, "Who made you ruler and judge over us? Are you thinking of killing me as you killed the Egyptian?" Then Moses was afraid and thought, "What I did must have become known." When Pharaoh heard of this, he tried to kill Moses, but Moses fled from Pharaoh and went to live in Midian, where he sat down by a well.
(Exodus 2:11-15, NIV)

How has God taught you the greatest lessons of life? Most likely you can point to some of your most difficult times and say, "That is when God was at work in my life."

Moses had been raised in the court of Pharaoh. He was the child of a Hebrew family but was raised as an Egyptian. One day he saw an Egyptian beating a Hebrew man. He immediately came to his defense and killed the Egyptian. He quickly buried him in the sand and thought all was well, until the next day when someone pointed out to him about the murder. Out of fear, Moses left his plush home, his childhood place, his wealth and all that goes with it, and fled to the desert of Midian.

Moses spent the next forty years of his life on the run. He struggled with his crime for those years but also grew into the man that God could use to deliver Israel from Egypt. He was broken, yet ready. That does sound wrong, but it is the way God works. He must get us out of the way in order to use us.

As Galatians 2:20 says it so clearly, "I have been crucified with Christ and I no longer live, but Christ lives in me. The life I now live in the body, I live by faith in the Son of God, who loved me and gave Himself for me."

God's school of preparation may just include getting you out of the way for Him to work through you. God may be working through your struggles right now to prepare you for what He has in store for you in the future.

~~

Self-Sufficient or God-Sufficient

June 21, 2012

> *"I am the vine; you are the branches. If you remain in Me and I in you, you will bear much fruit; apart from Me you can do nothing."* (John 15:5, NIV)

Can you be self-sufficient and still remain in Christ? Are you self-sufficient or God-sufficient? If we are honest, we would have to admit that those two concepts are contradictory. We are either remaining in Christ, dependent upon Him - or we are trying to live our life without Him.

Self-sufficiency may be the greatest detriment to a victorious Christian life. Jesus came to give us His life in exchange for our self-sufficient life. When we take charge of our own life, we produce the fruit of the flesh - such things as immorality, hatred, disunity, selfish ambition, and envy. When we are yielded to God, we produce the fruit of the Spirit: love, joy, peace, patience, kindness, goodness, faithfulness, gentleness, and self-control – all as a result of remaining in Christ.

As a believer in Jesus, you have become a new creation, a new person, someone who is "in Christ." The Scripture simply says we are to remain in that position. Without remaining in Christ, the ability to produce fruit becomes impossible. We may strive, work at it, and try real hard, yet never produce the fruit of God's Spirit. This does not bring glory to God. As we remain in Him, He takes over our self-sufficiency and replaces it with God-sufficiency.

As believers, we will grow weary and defeated as we try to accomplish that which only God can do. You are in Christ - allow Him to live His life through you. You will never be inadequate, inferior, or disappointed. Your life will be a fulfilling and rewarding life, bringing glory to God.

God did not make us to be independent from Him but in total dependence upon Him. He came to give us life, and life more abundant, but that is only possible when we are yielded to Him and remain in Him.

God will bring into your life whatever is necessary to bring you to the end of self-sufficiency in order that you will remain in Him. He loves you and desires that you have His life.

~~

Old to New

> *I have been crucified with Christ; and it is no longer I who live, but Christ lives in me; and the life which I now live in the flesh I live by faith in the Son of God, who loved me and gave Himself up for me.* (Galatians 2:20, NASB)

Which "I" is good and which "I" is not? The Bible speaks in terms of an "I" which is needful of crucifixion and thus death, and another "I" that is the one by which we live in victory in Christ.

The Bible explains that the sinful nature, the selfish "I," needs to be dealt a deathblow. It happened when Jesus died on the cross and the old "I" died with Him. That is the meaning of "I have been crucified with Christ." The sin nature, the old "I," was crucified when Christ was crucified.

> *… knowing this, that our old self was crucified with Him, in order that our body of sin might be done away with, so that we would no longer be slaves to sin;* (Romans 6:6)

> *But God demonstrates His own love toward us, in that while we were yet sinners, Christ died for us.* (Romans 5:8)

The new person is the "not I, but Christ." The Bible sees that "I" as a new creation, made in the image of Christ, indwelt by the Holy Spirit, and alive to God. So the Bible says there is a good "I" and a bad "I."

But thanks be to God, the bad one was crucified and the new one lives by faith. The new person is made possible because Jesus not only died for the old person but also was raised from the dead, and delivered that old "I" from sin and death. Victory is in Christ. Purpose in life is found only in Him.

The new life you live is by faith in the Son of God, Jesus Christ. The new life is really His Life, lived in and through you. His victory in life is your victory because it is His life. Praise the Lord today for the death and life of Christ that brings death to your old "I" and life to your new "I."

~~

Why Did I Do That? July 5, 2012

> *For I do not understand my own actions. For I do not do what I want, but I do the very thing I hate. Now if I do what I do not want, I agree with the law, that it is good. So now it is no longer I who do it, but sin that dwells within me. For I know that nothing good dwells in me, that is, in my flesh. For I have the desire to do what is right, but not the ability to carry it out. For I do not do the good I want, but the evil I do not want is what I keep on doing. Now if I do what I do not want, it is no longer I who do it, but sin that dwells within me.* (Romans 7:15-20, ESV)

"Why did I do that?" "Why didn't I do the right thing?" "I feel like such a failure." "Every time I turn around, I am messing up again." "Is there any hope?" "What is the explanation for my actions, or lack of them?"

Are these thoughts ever churning through your mind? Do you feel defeated in your Christian life? Do you have a real desire to live in such a way that God gets glory and your life would be an example of the holiness that God has declared you to possess but it seems to elude you? Let me assure you of this: you are not alone. Even the apostle Paul wrote to the Roman church about his personal struggles. He was having a similar experience. He simply said, "What I want to do, I don't; and what I don't want to do, I do."

It is certainly frustrating to have the desire to live a life that is pleasing to God, and yet fail over and over. Paul says his inconsistency is really not the failure of the new person he is in Christ but the flesh that indwells him. It is the sin that is still present in the life of a believer.

You may not have difficulty admitting your struggles with the flesh, but maybe you do. Maybe to admit your struggle would be the most helpful decision you could make. By admitting your weakness, you can also find your strength. The Bible says in Romans 7:24-25, "Wretched man that I am! Who will deliver me from this body of death? Thanks be to God through Jesus Christ our Lord! So then, I myself serve the law of God with my mind, but with my flesh I serve the law of sin." Your dependence upon Christ within you is your only hope of victory.

~~

Real Intimacy

You did not choose Me but I chose you, and appointed you that you would go and bear fruit, and that your fruit would remain, so that whatever you ask of the Father in My name He may give to you. (John 15:16, NASB)

And He went up on the mountain and summoned those whom He Himself wanted, and they came to Him. And He appointed twelve, so that they would be with Him... (Mark 3:13-14)

No longer do I call you slaves, for the slave does not know what his master is doing; but I have called you friends, for all things that I have heard from My Father I have made known to you. (John 15:15)

What an incredible thought: God chose me. It seems today that maybe there is too much emphasis on the choosing, and not enough on the reason for God choosing us. The deep need of the human heart is a relationship with someone. By far the most important relationship is the one between the Creator and the created. God made us to glorify Him, to know Him, and enjoy Him. That is a relationship.

The longing of the human heart is to engage in relationships with family, friends, neighbors, church, and especially God. Jesus was so emphatic about His relationship with us that He chose us for that intimacy. He called His disciples, and us, to be "with" Him.

He told His followers that the new relationship was not one of slave to master but one of friendship. He calls you to be His friend, and you are.
There is no greater love than to lay down one's life for one's friends.
(John 15:13, NLT)

He did that for you. Thank God that He not only chose you, but He chose you for an intimate relationship.

~~

Christ Alone

July 19, 2012

> *But suppose we seek to be made right with God through faith in Christ and then we are found guilty because we have abandoned the law. Would that mean Christ has led us into sin? Absolutely not! Rather, I am a sinner if I rebuild the old system of law I already tore down. For when I tried to keep the law, it condemned me. So I died to the law - I stopped trying to meet all its requirements - so that I might live for God. My old self has been crucified with Christ. It is no longer I who live, but Christ lives in me. So I live in this earthly body by trusting in the Son of God, who loved me and gave Himself for me. I do not treat the grace of God as meaningless. For if keeping the law could make us right with God, then there was no need for Christ to die.* (Galatians 2:17-21, NLT)

The apostle Paul was being accused of being soft on sin. He quickly admitted he was someone who still sinned, and then added that his readers did as well. No one is perfect except Jesus, and He is the One who justifies; He makes us right with God. Paul had attempted to keep the Jewish laws and rules, with the end in sight of being perfected. It didn't work. He not only was NOT perfected under the Law, but he was also not free.

Paul proposed that his attempts at perfection, such as pleasing his peers and keeping rules, had actually taken away the relationship he had with God. It was a relationship of freedom. His accusers would tell him that Christ was not enough - he needed to add laws, works, and rules. His response was that Christ was enough, and to think that Christ wasn't enough to bring him into a right relationship with God meant Christ died needlessly.

You likewise cannot be right with God by laws, rules, and works. It is only by Christ and through grace that you have true freedom. His grace is sufficient.

~~

Reflecting His Glory

July 26, 2012

> *But we all, with unveiled face, beholding as in a mirror the glory of the Lord, are being transformed into the same image from glory to glory, just as from the Lord, the Spirit.* (2 Corinthians 3:18, NASB)

> *So all of us who have had that veil removed can see and reflect the glory of the Lord. And the Lord - who is the Spirit - makes us more and more like Him as we are changed into His glorious image.* (2 Corinthians 3:18, NLT)

"All of us." I like that. The apostle Paul, writing to the believers in Corinth, was writing to remind them of what Christ had done in their lives. He reminded them that Christ removed the veil of the Old Covenant - the Law. The veil that deceives us into believing that the Christian life is accomplished by our own effort, is defused by the truth. The truth is that when Christ died on the cross, He removed the curse of the Law and gave us the New Covenant. His Holy Spirit came to live within us. The Holy Spirit brightly reflects the glory of God.

We can become more and more like Jesus as we allow the Holy Spirit to control our lives, and reflect God's character. It is as the Spirit works in us that we are changed. If we look into a mirror, we see ourselves. As we look into Christ, and the perfect law of liberty and freedom, we become like Him as the Holy Spirit works in us.

God desires that we glorify Him. We were created for that purpose. All things are created to glorify God. Your ministry as a Christian is to bring Him glory by reflecting His glory in your life - by being like Jesus.

Therefore, having this ministry by the mercy of God, we do not lose heart.
(2 Corinthians 4:1, ESV)

For that reason you never give up. No matter what you are facing, what challenges you are experiencing, what struggles you endure - just remember you are here for His glory. Never give up.

~~

Love Someone! August 2, 2012

And it is my prayer that your love may abound more and more, with knowledge and all discernment, so that you may approve what is excellent, and so be pure and blameless for the day of Christ, filled with the fruit of righteousness that comes through Jesus Christ, to the glory and praise of God. (Philippians 1:9-11, ESV)

The apostle Paul was always concerned about the love that people had toward one another. This is one of those passages where he interjects into the text a word of encouragement for us to love one another. He not only asks that we have love but that our love would grow – "abound more and more." This love is to be filled with knowledge and discernment.

In 1st Corinthians, chapter 13 (the Love Chapter), he says three things are important: faith, hope, and love; and that the greatest of these is love. It is in love that our lives are preserved pure and blameless at the return of Christ.

Other New Testament writers say it is love that covers a multitude of sins. And remember, "Love never fails" (1 Corinthians 13:8, NASB).

In his letter to the Thessalonian church, Paul said:

> Now as to the love of the brethren, you have no need for anyone to write to you, for you yourselves are taught by God to love one another; for indeed you do practice it toward all the brethren who are in all Macedonia. But we urge you, brethren, to excel still more. (1 Thessalonians 4:9-10)

Not only does the Bible say to love one another but to excel still more.

Love is not static; it is always dynamic. Constantly our love will grow or wane according to what we do about the power of the Holy Spirit in our lives. The Scripture says in Galatians 5:22, "The fruit of the Spirit is love..." As we allow the Holy Spirit to control and direct our lives, we will find that our love will grow.

Is there someone to whom you need to express your love or show affection in order for them to know that they are loved? Could you do something even today to make it happen? Love them. Care for them. Let them know by your actions that you love them. Paul's implication is that to be filled with love, is to be filled with the fruit of righteousness. In the end, your life will bring glory and praise to God. What a great idea!

~~

Between a Rock and a Hard Place   August 7, 2012

> Then Jonah prayed to the Lord his God from the stomach of the fish, and he said, "I called out of my distress to the Lord, and He answered me. I cried for help from the depth of Sheol; You heard my voice." (Jonah 2:1-2, NASB)

Ever felt like you were between a rock and a hard place? Probably no one has felt that any more than Jonah. He was aboard a ship that was sinking. The reason it was sinking was his fault. He was running from God and found he could not escape the call of God in his life. Once he admitted to the other seaman that he was the problem, they threw him overboard. He couldn't win, or so it seemed. Yet when he fell into the deep, it was part of God's plan.

God had a great fish ready to swallow Jonah. It was in the belly of the great fish that he came to the realization that there was still hope. Few of us have ever found ourselves in quite the predicament in which Jonah found himself. He was in the sea, in the belly of a great fish, and unable to save himself from the sea waters.

So what would you do? How would you find an answer in this situation? In his distress, Jonah called out to God in fervent prayer. You have likely been at the point of despair, when you felt you were surely not going to survive. It is then that we truly learn to pray. It is when there is no hope of survival, no word of encouragement, no way out, that we learn to call out to God.

It is strange that we might think of prayer as the last resort rather than the first choice, but it is usually as we get desperate that we will ask God to save us. It is then that we discover that God was all we ever really needed.

If you are looking for purpose and have a burden, why not call out to God? He loves you. Start with prayer, end with prayer, and pray in the meantime. God desires to bring you through your struggle into hope, encouragement, and victory. Call out to Him as Jonah did.

~~

Where's Your Wilderness? August 16, 2012

> But despite Jesus' instructions, the report of His power spread even faster, and vast crowds came to hear Him preach and to be healed of their diseases. But Jesus often withdrew to the wilderness for prayer. (Luke 5:15-16, NLT)

> One day soon afterward Jesus went up on a mountain to pray, and He prayed to God all night. (Luke 6:12)

Ever say to yourself, "I need some time off. I am tired. I just have to have a break"? I think Jesus did just that. He worked tirelessly caring for the needs of people. Sometimes He healed the sick, raised the dead, argued with the Pharisees, and attended weddings. Sometimes he walked miles to the next place of service. No matter what He was doing, it took a physical, emotional, and yes, even a spiritual toll. No wonder the Bible tells us of the crowds of people that gathered around Him to express their needs and then anticipated He would do something about them. The Bible wants us to understand the need He had to withdraw into the wilderness.

The wilderness was any place of solitude and quiet where He could be refreshed in body, soul, and spirit. We need a place like that. The hustle of life, the cares of our work, family, church, and people expose us to the need for some time alone with God. Jesus did not just go into the wilderness one time but repeatedly. The Bible says He would often slip into the wilderness to pray. Later, as He made the great choice of His disciples, He spent the whole night in prayer. It was a prayer for making right decisions.

Do you need a time for refreshing, or a time for decision-making? Maybe it is time to escape to a place of prayer. You may say, "I think I could if I had a place like the beach, the mountains, or the redwoods; then I could pray." You only need to find the closet Jesus mentions in Matthew 6:6 -

> *But thou, when thou prayest, enter into thy closet, and when thou hast shut thy door, pray to thy Father which is in secret; and thy Father which seeth in secret shall reward thee openly.* (KJV)

Find your place of solitude today, and pray to discover refreshing for your life.

~~

So You're Human?   August 23, 2012

> *"Simon, Simon, Satan has asked to sift each of you like wheat. But I have pleaded in prayer for you, Simon, that your faith should not fail. So when you have repented and turned to Me again, strengthen your brothers." Peter said, "Lord, I'm ready to go to prison with You, and even to die with You." But Jesus said, "Peter, let Me tell you something. Before the rooster crows tomorrow morning, you will deny three times that you even know Me."* (Luke 22:31-34, NLT)

Peter was so human, so filled with frailties, yet Jesus saw in him the potential for great leadership. No one is ever fit for leadership until they have first been tested. Peter was tested over and over, but in his greatest test, he failed.

Jesus knew Peter would deny Him three times. Peter went to the point of cursing in his adamant denial of Jesus, yet Jesus did not consider Peter's denial the end of Peter's value and worth. He saw Peter's denial as an opportunity for growth and learning. Once Peter turned again to Jesus, and acknowledged his sin and failure, he would actually be used to strengthen his brothers in Christ. Jesus did not even consider his denial a failure of faith because He prayed that his faith would not fail. Peter repented of his sin and found forgiveness, and became an even greater leader than ever.

How human are you? The basis of so much failure in our lives is based upon our humanness. Peter felt very self-sufficient as he told Jesus he would go to prison and even die for Him, but his lack of trusting God actually caused him to do the opposite of what he said. He not only denied Jesus but denied Him three times in the space of a few hours.

The result would have seemed like total defeat, but on the contrary, Peter's actions led him to repentance, and eventually he became the leader of the disciples. Jesus' words to him included, "So when you have repented and turned to Me again, strengthen your brothers." Don't give up when you fail. Repent and trust Jesus. You may discover that your response will help others.

~~

Who Do You Blame?   August 30, 2012

Through all this Job did not sin nor did he blame God. (Job 1:22, NASB)

A recent TV commercial showed various scenarios that always ended with the phrase: "LIFE COMES AT YOU FAST." Although the scenes were always humorous, the point came through loud and clear: "You never know what to expect." Job was definitely taken off guard when he heard the news. The news came in rapid fire and was not good news. Isn't that just the way things come at us sometimes? Someone has said that bad news comes in threes. Job had more than that.

Job 1:13-19 tells of the tragedies in the beginning of Job's struggles. First, while his children were feasting and drinking, a messenger came and told Job that the Sabeans had taken all his oxen and donkeys, and killed all his servants. Another messenger came and told him the fire of God fell on the sheep and the servants, and they were all burned to death. Then another messenger came and told him Chaldeans swept down on the camels and made off with them, and killed all his servants. Finally, the last messenger came with the news:

> *While he was still speaking, another messenger also came and said, "Your sons and daughters were eating and drinking wine in their oldest brother's house, and behold, a great wind came from across the wilderness and struck the four corners of the house, and it fell on the young people and they died, and I alone have escaped to tell you."* (Job 1:18-19)

The barrage of heartbreaking events, from the loss of his livelihood to the loss of his children, happened in a short period of time. Any one of those would have caused most anyone to blame God. Blaming is such a "fun sport." It seems that the easiest one to blame when life is hard, is God. Yet the Bible says "through all this," Job did not blame God.

The real culprit is Satan. He is the accuser of the brethren, the father of lies, the deceiver, the destroyer, and the killer. Job's friends tried to convince him that God was the cause, but Job knew God, so he knew that was not true.

Whatever you are facing, trust that the enemy is not God. The enemy is the same one that was tempting Adam and Eve in the Garden of Eden. He is still the one who causes you problems. Never blame God for that which is Satan's fault.

~~

First Things First   September 6, 2012

"But seek ye first the kingdom of God, and His righteousness; and all these things shall be added unto you." (Matthew 6:33, KJV)

Is God our first consideration - our first loyalty? Do we depend on Him to meet our needs and carry our load? Preeminence means first place. Jesus told the multitude on the Mount to quit worrying about their future, about clothing, food, and the necessities of life. Being anxious can never make us grow, nor meet our needs.

The apostle Paul said, "For to me, to live is Christ and to die is gain" (Philippians 1:21, NASB). Trusting Christ for everything can bring real peace in one's life. Jesus knew our make-up, and He knew that we would be seeking the wrong things first. It seems our human nature is to satisfy the selfish desires of our hearts rather than God's kingdom and His righteousness.

It is not that Jesus' desire would be for us to be miserable, empty, and longing for life. He is very aware of what it takes to really receive those "other things." He simply says, "And all these things shall be added unto you." Seek the kingdom of God and the righteousness of God, and He will take care of the rest.

What is really first in your life? Maybe right now you are struggling with "things," "stuff," longing for something to fill a hole, climbing the wrong pole, digging the wrong ditch, or desiring more in life than you currently have. It could just be you need a change of focus.

> *But whatever were gains to me I now consider loss for the sake of Christ. What is more, I consider everything a loss because of the surpassing worth of knowing Christ Jesus my Lord, for whose sake I have lost all things. I consider them garbage, that I may gain Christ.* (Philippians 3:7-8, NIV)

Just remember to "seek first" His kingdom and His righteousness, and all these other things will be added unto you.

~~

Your Will Be Done

Then Jesus left them a second time and prayed, "My Father! If this cup cannot be taken away unless I drink it, Your will be done." (Matthew 26:42, NLT)

The New Testament is replete with the prayers of Jesus. He prayed in front of people, with His disciples, and alone. It was His prayer life that so impressed the disciples that they asked Him to teach them to pray. Although Jesus was a great teacher, the disciples did not ask to be teachers. They asked to pray as Jesus prayed.

Have you ever had something to pray about that was hard? I am sure you have. You have struggled with decisions, with needs, with alternatives, and could not make a decision. Jesus had prayed many times, but no doubt, His most difficult and challenging prayer came in the Garden of Gethsemane. He was praying with the disciples who were having difficulty staying awake. After all, it was in the middle of the night that He had caught them asleep a second time. As He returned to His place of prayer in the garden, He prayed a most profound prayer.

His prayer was a result of His understanding what was coming next in His life, and that was death. He was headed to the cross to die for all of mankind. He also knew that He was going to suffer much. The cup he referred to was the "cup of suffering."

His suffering would be more than physical torture, rejection, and pain. He was to suffer the weight of the sin of the entire world upon Him as Savior. His suffering was the punishment for sin that He Himself would bear for all mankind from every tribe and nation. He prayed to God the Father to remove that suffering but then said, "But Your will be done." That is a hard prayer to pray. He was leaving into the hands of God the Father, His life and His death. He was willing to suffer in order to glorify God and bring forgiveness and salvation to all creation.

You are not being called upon to die for humanity, but you are being called upon to yield your will to His will - "not what I will, but what You will." God does know best. He loves you, and has His perfect will that is found in your surrender to His will and His Spirit. Let your prayer be as Jesus' prayer. Won't you say with Jesus, "Your will be done"?

~~

Teach Us to Pray September 20, 2012

"Pray, then, in this way: 'Our Father who is in heaven, Hallowed be Your name. Your kingdom come. Your will be done, On earth as it is in heaven.' "
(Matthew 6:9-10, NASB)

Jesus' disciples requested that He teach them to pray like John the Baptist had taught his disciples to pray. No doubt they had watched Jesus pray, and had also observed the results. It is no wonder that they wanted that kind of power. Their thinking was very simple, "If we pray like He prays, then the results will be the same."

How would Jesus respond to such a request? Would He give them some magical formula, or possibly the way to become spiritual enough to have their prayers answered? No, instead He responded with a simple model prayer that we call the Lord's Prayer. It was a model prayer that gave us a pattern for our prayers.

Our prayers are addressed to God, who is called "Our Father." His address is heaven, and His character is holy. His purpose for us is to do His will on earth as it is in heaven. So our prayers are directed to our Father, the Holy One, to answer our prayers with our desire for His will to be done. We cannot improve on a prayer that desires the will of our Heavenly Father to be done in our lives.

As we yield our lives to Christ more and more, and allow the Holy Spirit to be in control, we will find His will being done through us. We will find answers to our prayers.

Why not ask your Father in heaven to allow His will to be accomplished in your life? You may be afraid, lacking faith, not sure of the future, questioning God Himself as the Source of your life, or maybe just not desirous of God's will. The disciples learned about prayer, not by saying what we call "The Lord's Prayer" but by learning that prayer is about a Holy God, called Our Father, with the desire that His will be done in our lives.

Jesus knew that if the disciples wanted to learn to pray, they would need to begin with the basics of who God is, and whether it was their desire that His will be done in their lives. It is the same with you. Are you eager for the will of God, your Heavenly Father, to be accomplished in your life?

~~

Red-Letter Words September 27, 2012

"If anyone comes to Me and does not hate father and mother, wife and children, brothers and sisters - yes, even their own life - such a person cannot be My disciple. "And whoever does not carry their cross and follow Me cannot be My disciple." (Luke 14:26-27, NIV)

"Do to others as you would have them do to you." (Luke 6:31)

"And I will do whatever you ask in My name, so that the Father may be glorified in the Son. You may ask Me for anything in My name, and I will do it." (John 14:13-14)

Jesus called them together and said, "You know that the rulers of the Gentiles lord it over them, and their high officials exercise authority over them. Not so with you. Instead, whoever wants to become great among you must be your servant, and whoever wants to be first must be your slave - just as the Son of Man did not come to be served, but to serve, and to give His life as a ransom for many." (Matthew 20:25-28)

Great spiritual leaders are often known by their sayings. They are identified with and by their words. The Chinese spiritual leader is known primarily by the "sayings of Confucius." Buddha is known for the "eight-fold path of Buddha" that are the sayings of Buddha. Philosophers are also known by their verbal and written words: "I think, therefore I am" - Rene Descartes.

Jesus is likewise known for His famous sayings. All the scriptures above are words that Jesus spoke. Many Bible translations print the words of Jesus in red letters in order to emphasize the words that He Himself said. Often His words are hard or difficult sayings. To take His words and only give them shallow attention will leave us with a lack of understanding. Read through the words above again and allow God's Holy Spirit to speak to your spirit. The words are truth, spoken by God's only Son. They are words of life, and words to live by.

His words are not always easy to apply or to even absorb. They are words that challenge, encourage, admonish, and guide. Take some time and read through the red-letter parts of the gospels of Matthew, Mark, Luke, and John to get the message of Jesus through His words.

~~

Boasting Is Dangerous October 4, 2012

This is what the Lord says: "Don't let the wise boast in their wisdom, or the powerful boast in their power, or the rich boast in their riches. But those who wish to boast should boast in this alone: that they truly know Me and understand that I am the Lord who demonstrates unfailing love and who brings justice and righteousness to the earth, and that I delight in these things. I, the Lord, have spoken!" (Jeremiah 9:23-24, NLT)

Jim's claim to fame and reason for bragging was his experience of having survived the famous Johnstown, Pennsylvania flood. Everywhere he went, he talked to anyone who would listen about the flood. Eventually people avoided him to keep from hearing about his adventure. He eventually died, and in heaven, God sat everyone down in a big circle and announced that everyone was going to have all the time they needed to tell of the most interesting and exciting thing that happened in their life. Jim was thrilled for the opportunity to talk forever about his flood experience. God then looked straight at Jim and said, "You will be next to speak, right after Noah."

That might take the wind out of anyone's sails. It seems that there is something in everyone that awakens a desire to want to brag or boast. Jeremiah gave God's perspective about bragging. The prophets often used words equivalent to "Thus says the Lord." Here is one of those occasions when God says words that are powerful and pointed. Don't brag about certain things, like your wisdom, your power, or your riches. If you desire to boast, boast that you truly know God and understand that He is Lord. Brag about the Lord who has unfailing love. Brag to others that God is a God of justice and righteousness, and that you delight in God and His ways.

Always be cautious about bragging about anything other than God. Normally bragging is not received well by other people, nor is God honored and glorified by our self-aggrandizement. Talk about what a great God you know. Tell people how much He loves them and how powerful, wise, rich, and loving He is. Tell yourself and others that God is Good.

~~

Real Life   October 11, 2012

And do not get drunk with wine, for that is dissipation, but be filled with the Spirit, (Ephesians 5:18, NASB)

The writer of Ephesians, the apostle Paul, was very familiar with the Greek culture, including their religious beliefs. In this verse, he alludes to one of their gods named Bacchus, or Dionysius. He was a god of wine and revelry. Wikipedia describes him this way: "He was so named because of the frenzy he induces. He is also the Liberator, whose wine, music and ecstatic dance frees his followers from self-conscious fear and care, and subverts the oppressive restraints of the powerful. Those who partake of his mysteries are possessed and empowered by the god himself."

The ancient Greeks did not understand the chemical results of intoxication, but they did know that when wine was ingested, the person would act differently and talk differently. Their explanation was that a god took over their lives. In this case, the god of wine and revelry - Bacchus. Paul called this drunkenness "dissipation" or hypocrisy. It was not real life.

Paul's answer to the Greeks was God the Holy Spirit. The Holy Spirit also fills the believer. He also takes control of the recipient by possessing and empowering the believer. He is the true liberator who truly sets free the one filled with the Holy Spirit - the Christian is set free from self-conscious fear and care. The Holy Spirit is likewise the One who is in you "greater than he who is in the world" (1 John 4:4).

The Bible says we are not to be drunk with wine, or have anything to do with the false gods that try to duplicate life and freedom, but we are to be filled with God Himself. Be filled with the Holy Spirit. He is real life. It is the Holy Spirit that produces the fruit of the Spirit.

> *But the fruit of the Spirit is love, joy, peace, patience, kindness, goodness, faithfulness, gentleness, self-control;* (Galatians 5:22-23)

As you yield and submit your life to the Holy Spirit who lives within you, God will fill you with His Spirit. By faith, you can respond to the call of Ephesians 5:18 to be filled with the Spirit. The result is a life that makes you walk and talk differently. It is not dissipation or hypocrisy but real life. Why not ask God to fill you with His Spirit right now?

~~

What's Your Big Stone?   October 25, 2012

> *Saturday evening, when the Sabbath ended, Mary Magdalene, Mary the mother of James, and Salome went out and purchased burial spices so they could anoint Jesus' body. Very early on Sunday morning, just at sunrise, they went to the tomb. On the way they were asking each other, "Who will roll away the stone for us from the entrance to the tomb?" But as they arrived, they looked up and saw that the stone, which was very large, had already been rolled aside.* (Mark 16:1-4, NLT)

The three women made their way to the tomb of Jesus early on Sunday morning. The plan was to anoint the body of Jesus for proper burial. They expressed to one another a worry or concern: "Who will roll away the stone for us from the entrance to the tomb?" They undoubtedly had observed the soldiers blocking the entrance to the tomb with an extremely large stone. The women knew it was too large for them to move by themselves.

Have you ever felt discouraged because it seemed a BIG STONE was in the way of your accomplishing your goals? Worry is ineffective at moving stones. I heard someone say, "Worry must work because what I was worrying about, never happened." Strange explanation.

The women approached the tomb with questions. They were not only concerned about how to remove the stone but what they would find inside. They had watched Jesus as He was crucified. They were aware of the crown of thorns, the spear-pierced side, and the piercing caused by the nails.

Their goal was to prepare Jesus for burial as was required by their faith, and for the honor they desired to give to their departed Leader. As they approached the tomb, they observed the stone had already been rolled away. The worry of moving a stone was gone. God had rolled away the stone. Maybe it is time you begin to realize that God will roll away your stone? He can move the obstacles in your life.

More than the stone that the angels rolled away, was the miracle the women found inside. Jesus was not there, either. He had risen from the dead. He was alive! Worry and fretting mean nothing to a living Savior. You can have more than just a stone removed from your pathway. You can have life through Jesus' death and resurrection. You need not worry about eternity. He arose to give you eternal life.

~~

Simple Truths   November 1, 2012

> *I am amazed that you are so quickly deserting Him who called you by the grace of Christ, for a different gospel; which is really not another; only there are some who are disturbing you and want to distort the gospel of Christ. But even if we, or an angel from heaven, should preach to you a gospel contrary to what we have preached to you, he is to be accursed!* (Galatians 1:6-8, NASB)

If we lose sight of the Gospel, the good news of Jesus Christ's all-sufficiency and preeminence, then most everything else we do or say is of no value. To have faith in Jesus PLUS anything else for our faith and life, is a diminishing of the finished work of Christ in His life, death, resurrection, and second coming. The author of Galatians was facing a church that heard the Gospel, received it, and then began to see its message erode in the culture and philosophies of the day.

The message of the Gospel was simple: Jesus Christ was God come to earth, born in a physical body, lived sinless in that body, and died on the cross. He arose in a physical body, and told His disciples that He would return to earth so that every eye could see His body. His incarnation was a miracle of God. His death on the cross was sufficient to provide love, forgiveness of sin, and reconciliation of sinful man to a Holy God.

In the church there came an attack upon the Gospel. It was probably subtle at first but was beginning to take a foothold. The influence of a group known as the Judaizers brought into the church an emphasis on keeping the Mosaic Law as a means to forgiveness, holiness, and justification. Jesus was no longer seen as adequate to bring humans into a reconciled relationship with God.

Paul wrote to the church that the need for reconciliation was necessary because humans are sinners by nature and by choice. It is sin that separates God and humans. It is the cross and the resurrection that bring God and humans together. The finished work of God the Son, Jesus, is enough.

~~

Pleasing God   November 8, 2012

> *Now faith is the assurance of things hoped for, the conviction of things not seen.* (Hebrews 11:1, NASB)

> *And without faith it is impossible to please Him, for he who comes to God must believe that He is and that He is a rewarder of those who seek Him.* (Hebrews 11:6)

Is it your desire to please God? The Bible is filled with references to pleasing God. It seems that it is not only the desire of God's creation to please Him, but it is God's desire that you please Him. The way of pleasing God begins with faith. It is impossible to please God without faith.

The beginning of faith is simply to believe that He is. God calls Himself the "I AM." That means He is. He exists. He is being. Your first step to pleasing Him is to accept the truth and reality that God is. Believing that He is, gives you the assurance of things hoped for, and conviction of things not seen. Those two things define and identify faith. Faith is the assurance and the conviction, or confidence.

What are you facing in your life right now that requires faith? It would be easy to say, "Everything." All of life is to be lived by faith - by believing not only that God is, but that He is the rewarder of those who seek Him. It pleases God that you seek Him, His ways, His will, and a relationship with Him. God loves you and wants to reward your life as you place your faith in Him.

No matter what you are experiencing in your personal life, the life of your family, your church, community, or friends - God desires to reward you because of your faith. Faith means you are believing God, trusting Him, depending on Him, and pleasing Him.

It also means you are loving God, listening to Him, obeying Him, and walking with Him, as you are seeking first His kingdom and His righteousness, and following His principles and priorities.

Faith affects every aspect of your life. It begins by believing that He is, and is followed by a life of faith. Why not place your faith in God today? He does love you, sent Jesus to die on the cross for you, raised Jesus from the dead, and offers you eternal life by faith in Him.

~~

Remember to Be Thankful   November 22, 2012

Every time I think of you, I give thanks to my God. (Philippians 1:3, NLT)

"And remember, I am with you always, to the end of the age."
(Matthew 28:20, HCSB)

Remember the wonders He has performed, His miracles, and the rulings He has given, (Psalm 105:5, NLT)

What do you remember that brings thanks to your heart? As you look back over the blessings of God, you can thank God. The apostle Paul said to the church at Philippi that he gave thanks for them every time he thought of them. Jesus told the disciples that they should remember that He would be with them day by day, all the way to the end of the age or world. The psalmist reminded his readers that they should be thankful as they remembered the wonders and miracles God had performed.

Our memories are the triggers to bring our minds to "thankfulness." Throughout the Bible, the word "remember" is used over two hundred and thirty times. It is used as a way of motivating God's people to "thanks-giving." Moses reminded the nation of Israel that God had blessed them with freedom from slavery:

> Moses said to the people, "Remember this day in which you came out from Egypt, out of the house of slavery; for by a powerful hand the Lord brought you out from this place." (Exodus 13:3, NASB)

God reminds us throughout the Bible to remember Him, His blessings, His provisions, His mercy and grace, His protection, and His love. The thief who was crucified next to Jesus said, "Jesus, remember me when You come into Your Kingdom" (Luke 23:42, NLT).

We are to remember what God is to us, and has done for us, in order to be thankful. Remember this: God remembers you! For that, you should be very thankful. Celebrate Thanksgiving by remembering.

~~

A Longing of Your Heart   November 29, 2012

> Instead, use your freedom to serve one another in love. (Galatians 5:13, NLT)

> Instead, be kind to each other, tenderhearted, forgiving one another, just as God through Christ has forgiven you. (Ephesians 4:32)

> Therefore, accept each other just as Christ has accepted you so that God will be given glory. (Romans 15:7)

When was the last time you reached out to love, forgive, and accept someone? Maybe the question could be, "When was the last time you felt loved, forgiven, and accepted?" There is a longing of the human heart to experience the unconditional love, forgiveness, and acceptance of others.

The Bible tells us that God extends to all His love, His forgiveness, and His acceptance. As God in Christ has met the needs of our own lives, we are to express that same expression of God's grace to others. The people God places in our lives long for the same things we do. They may seem self-sufficient, confident, lacking in struggles and trials; but the basic needs are much in evidence in the depth of their being. God has placed us in relationship with them for a reason.

Whether they are a family member, a person we work with, or someone from our church or neighborhood; they still need love, forgiveness, and acceptance. In all likelihood, you may be the very person God has given the opportunity to make a difference in that individual's life.

On the other side of the coin, God has placed in your life those He will use to show you the unconditional love of Christ, the forgiveness of God, and the acceptance you so desperately need. The Bible tells us to "give and it shall be given unto you." Why not reach out and be the conduit of God's unconditional love, forgiveness, and acceptance to someone God has placed in your pathway?

The world is in incredible need for real community. God has put humans together in unique relationships in order to meet those needs. Become an observer of needs, a responder to needs, and a receiver of God's grace to you. The TV commercial said, "Reach out and touch someone." Why not try it?

~~

All Together for Good   December 5, 2012

> *And we know that God causes all things to work together for good to those who love God, to those who are called according to His purpose.* (Romans 8:28, NLT)

Do you love God? Have you been called to be his child? Does God have a purpose for your life? If your answer is "yes," then the good news of this verse belongs to you.

The good news is that "God causes all things to work together for good." It would be easy to question that truth unless we really take a look at its meaning. The first statement simply says, "God causes all things." At face value, we would assume the verse means that every tragedy, every evil, every pain, and every struggle is caused by God. That would make God into a very cruel God. Yet, if we believe that God is really God and that He is sovereign, it will cause a problem if we do not believe that statement. What a quandary: God is in charge, and yet terrible things happen.

Looking deeper into the verse, we will notice that God causes all things "to work together for good." The meaning is clear. It is not that God causes all things but that He causes all things to work out for good. Even that is clarified further by a choice word. That word is "together." It means that we cannot conceive of all the things God puts together to bring good - even out of a tragedy. He is truly sovereign - in charge. He joins all the things that happen, and makes good of them. We cannot see the beginning or the end. God can. He weaves a tapestry of life for each of us.

The verse further clarifies that all things work together for good "to those who love God and are called according to His purpose." The purpose of life is that we will be conformed to the image of His Son, as written in the next verse (vs.

29). He is using every experience of life to make us like Jesus. He may use our problems, our joys, our ancestors, our circumstances, our family, our job, and whatever He chooses to work for our good so that we may be "conformed to the image of His Son."

Instead of seeing a conflict in your understanding, you can find truth and clarity as you understand that the Sovereign Lord knows all, and allows any and every thing in your life. He uses everything for your good, if you love Him and are called according to His purpose. Don't bemoan your circumstance. Praise the God who is in charge and has your wellbeing in mind as He works the fabric of your life into the image of His Son.

~~

The Fullness of Time December 13, 2012

> *But when the fullness of the time came, God sent forth His Son, born of a woman, born under the Law, so that He might redeem those who were under the Law, that we might receive the adoption as sons. Because you are sons, God has sent forth the Spirit of His Son into our hearts, crying, "Abba! Father!" Therefore you are no longer a slave, but a son; and if a son, then an heir through God.* (Galatians 4:4-7, NASB)

The time of Jesus' birth was no accident. It was the plan of God that He would be born in the fullness of time. He came to set us free. The Gentiles were enslaved to the pagan practices of the day. The Jews were enslaved to the Law. The Bible declares that true freedom was paid for by Jesus' death and resurrection.

He was born of a woman. Although He was God in human flesh, He was equally God. His life began in a manger in Bethlehem. Mary gave birth to the Jewish Messiah who would bring salvation and freedom to all who believed. He was also born under the Law. As a Jewish child, He was subject to the Law of Moses. He was required to live by its rules. The Scripture compares the slavery under the Law to a child born in a wealthy home that was still treated as a slave until such time as the child reached maturity. At that time, the child was given freedom from the guardian and became the heir of the father.

So it is with Jesus. He was born of a woman, under the Law, in order to redeem or pay for the slaves' freedom. God sent Jesus to free us from the penalty of sin and the Law. As a result, we are no longer in slavery; we are free to live as children of God. Down in your heart, you can experience the freedom of abundant life. It is your privilege to no longer be enslaved to rules and regulations set forth in the Law.

We cannot live "good enough" to receive the status as a child of God through our efforts. But you can become a child who can cry out to God, "Abba" (an endearing term meaning "Dad" or "Father"). It is because His Spirit is now in your heart by faith and grace, that you are no longer a slave but a child of God.

Your new relationship is a cause for rejoicing. What a privilege! Rejoice this day for your freedom and life, and your new relationship with God.

~~

God With Us

December 20, 2012

> *"Behold, the virgin shall be with child and shall bear a Son, and they shall call His name Immanuel," which translated means, "God with us."*
> (Matthew 1:23, NASB)

> *For in Christ lives all the fullness of God in a human body.*
> (Colossians 2:9, NLT)

Jesus was far from just an ordinary baby born in the city of Bethlehem. His birth had been prophesied some 800 years before his birth. It was even prophesied that His birthplace would be Bethlehem and that He would be conceived by the Holy Spirit. It was also prophesied that He would be born of a virgin, and He was born to a virgin named Mary. His was no ordinary birth. His was no ordinary life. In Him, all the fullness of God dwelt in a human body. He was God the Son in human flesh. Even His name "Immanuel" means "God with us."

The miraculous birth of the Son of God in that stable in Bethlehem changed the world. His birth brought a Savior for all the people, in the whole world. His message was: "I came that [you] might have life and have it abundantly" (John 10:10, NASB).

Two thousand years since His birth has not changed His identity, His message, or His purpose. You can be sure that He is God. He is Savior. He did die on a cross for your salvation and arose from the dead to give you His life.

Jesus loves you. He left heaven, came to earth, and was born as a human in order to live a sinless life, die on a cross, and arise from the dead to give you eternal life. Have you discovered the life that He brings to all who place their faith in Him? Have you received Him?

> *But to all who did receive Him, who believed in His name, He gave the right to become children of God,* (John 1:12, ESV)

This would be a great day to place your faith in Him and receive Him into your life. The reward will be life, and life more abundantly (John 10:10).

~~

A Prayer for You   December 27, 2012

> *I keep asking that the God of our Lord Jesus Christ, the glorious Father, may give you the Spirit of wisdom and revelation, so that you may know Him better. I pray that the eyes of your heart may be enlightened in order that you may know the hope to which He has called you, the riches of His glorious inheritance in His holy people, and His incomparably great power for us who believe. That power is the same as the mighty strength He exerted when He raised Christ from the dead and seated Him at His right hand in the heavenly realms, far above all rule and authority, power and dominion, and every name that is invoked, not only in the present age but also in the one to come.*
> (Ephesians 1:17-21, NIV)

Have you ever picked a special verse for the New Year? Are you praying a prayer to support the verse? Consider these verses as the basis of your prayer for the coming year. The heart's desire of God is that we would grow to maturity in our faith. The apostle Paul speaks here of what that might look like.

First, Paul prayed that God would give the Spirit of wisdom and revelation to believers in order to know Him better. A theme throughout the Bible is God's desire that we know Him.

Next, Paul prayed that the eyes of our heart may be enlightened. It would seem strange to consider the heart as having eyes, and yet, God knows we need the light to come on so we would know three very important truths:
1. Paul wants our hearts to be enlightened to the HOPE we have in Christ.
2. He prayed that we would wake up to the realization of the RICHES of His glorious inheritance He has in us.
3. He prayed that we would know God's incomparable POWER. As believers, we have the power of God. He has given us the same power He gave to Christ when He raised Him from the dead and seated Him in the heavenly realm.

The power that raised Christ from the dead and seated Him in the heavenly realm is the most awesome power in the world. He wants you to know you have that power. Your New Year's verses and your prayer will give hope and encouragement. Use this prayer daily in the coming year.

~~

Less of Me and More of Him

> *"A bridegroom's friends rejoice with him. I am the Bridegroom's friend, and I am filled with joy at His success. He must become greater and greater, and I must become less and less."* (John 3:29-30, TLB)

The Jewish wedding was a great festive occasion with days of celebration and a year's preparation. The custom was to have a betrothal - a year's engagement - before the actual wedding ceremony. The betrothal was celebrated with a feast. The bride and groom were then separated for a year during which time the bride and groom did not communicate directly. The friend of the groom, or best man, became the intermediary for that year.

The bride-to-be was virtually considered as the wife of the groom. She was to remain faithful to the groom. If she was found to be unfaithful, she could be punished with death. When Mary was espoused to Joseph and was found to be with child, Joseph could have rejected her, and she could have been put to death. He could have gone through a divorce either publicly or privately. He chose instead to marry her.

John the Baptist considered himself the friend of the groom, Jesus. The bride is the Church, or the people of God. John the Baptist came to announce the coming of the groom. He was the friend who had been responsible for the preparation of the bride for the coming groom.

John the Baptist recognized that as the groom, Jesus, came to earth, his own purpose was completed. He thus spoke the words, "He must become more important while I become less important." What a great plan for you! Jesus must become more important and you must become less important. Instead of asserting your importance, you can bring glory to God by becoming less and allowing Jesus to become more.

The fulfillment of your purpose for life will be in your decision to allow Jesus to become first and foremost in your life. John commented, "This is my joy."

~~

My Shepherd

> *For you were continually straying like sheep, but now you have returned to the Shepherd and Guardian of your souls.* (1 Peter 2:25, NASB)

Have you ever had someone who really took good care of you? It may have been as a child that your parents watched over you and protected you. Maybe you have a best friend that you know is watching out for your wellbeing. What do you call that person? Do you refer to him or her as a caregiver, friend, parent, BFF, or some name that relays the meaning of someone special?

God calls himself the Shepherd. David the psalmist declares, "The Lord is my Shepherd." God often compares people to sheep, and those who care for the sheep as shepherds. You might call the person who cares for your church a Pastor or Elder or Shepherd. The apostle Peter called himself a fellow elder, and admonished fellow elders to "Be shepherds of God's flock that is under your care, watching over them" (1 Peter 5:2).

Peter, as an elder of the church and a shepherd of the flock, rejoiced with the returning of the people to the Shepherd and Guardian of their souls. Our soul is that part of us that wanders from the Lord through neglect and sin. It is that part of our lives that continually needs to be nourished and treated with constant care. As we return to the Lord, it is He who really cares for us. He is the only One who can adequately be our true Shepherd.

The book of Isaiah says in chapter 53, verse 6:
All of us like sheep have gone astray, each of us has turned to his own way;
But the Lord has caused the iniquity of us all to fall on Him.

We are sheep that not only need someone to watch over us, feed us, and care for us - we need someone to remove our sin. It was prophesied in Isaiah that One would come that would take away the iniquity of us all. That One was Jesus. Be thankful that God loved you so much that He provided you with a Savior, Jesus Christ.

Peter reminded the people that it is easy to go astray in sin and rebellion. He reminded them that they were constantly straying but had at last returned to the Shepherd and Guardian of their souls. Would you come to Jesus and allow Him to be the Shepherd and Guardian of your soul?

~~

Delivered From the Dark Side

January 24, 2013

For He rescued us from the domain of darkness, and transferred us to the kingdom of His beloved Son, in whom we have redemption, the forgiveness of sins.
(Colossians 1:13-14, NASB)

... who gave Himself for our sins so that He might rescue us from this present evil age, according to the will of our God and Father, to whom be the glory forevermore. Amen. (Galatians 1:4-5)

"Free at last" are famous words used by the late Dr. Martin Luther King Jr. in a well-known speech with that title. Few Christians understand the implications of what true freedom is. You may be one who desires to be secure, but you need to grasp that freedom must come before security. It was necessary for God to set us free from the domain of darkness and transfer us into the kingdom of His Son in order to make us secure.

It was necessary for God to deliver us from our sins and the present evil age in which we live, so that He could make us free. Once we are free, we can enjoy and experience the security of belonging to God and His kingdom. God, our Heavenly Father, has given true freedom and life to all who believe in Christ. That life is a brand new life of true freedom.

It is new because we have been delivered from a life controlled by the dark side - by Satan and his fallen angels. We have been moved from sin's control to the kingdom of Jesus, God the Father's only Son. We are in His kingdom because of our faith in the person of Jesus, His death, and His resurrection. The darkness of sin kept us under the dominion of Satan, but through Jesus, we have been redeemed. We have had our sins removed and have been forgiven of all sin - past, present, and future.

Deliverance is freedom to truly live as God intended. We are free from the penalty, the power, and the control of sin in our life. Someday in heaven, we will be free from the very presence of sin itself. Right now, we are free to live life in the kingdom of His beloved Son.

"Free at last" is more than a phrase. It is a truth that you can know. Stop seeking to just be secure, and make sure you are free. Once you are free, you will discover true security in relationship to God through His Son, Jesus Christ. Trust Him right now to give you His freedom, and He will make you secure.

~~

Badge of Honor?

February 7, 2013

Then He said, "Do not come near here; ... for the place on which you are standing is holy ground." (Exodus 3:5, NASB)

What is your badge of honor? Maybe when we are asked how we are doing or who we are, the answer is, "I'm busy" or "I'm tired." It appears that the measure of our worth may be determined by the amount of work, the achievements we have accomplished, or what our newest project is.

Gordon McDonald, in his book *Ordering Your Private World*, discusses the measurement of success not on our public life but on our private life. He differentiates between a person who is called, and one who is driven. People who are busy and tired often fit the driven personality. He also says this of driven people:

1. Driven people are most often only gratified by accomplishments and symbols of achievement.
2. Driven people are caught up in the uncontrolled pursuit of expansion.
3. Driven people often have a limited regard for integrity.
4. Driven people are not likely to bother themselves with the honing of people skills.
5. Driven people tend to be highly competitive. It's not enough to compete. Driven people have to win, no matter what it takes to do so.
6. Driven people often possess a volcanic force of anger.
7. Driven people are usually abnormally busy, are averse to play, and usually avoid spiritual worship.

It may be a badge of honor, but it is more likely a cause of conflict, broken relationships, inner turmoil, poor ethical choices, poor self-image, and a lackluster relationship with God. Do you find yourself driven for approval, acceptance, and recognition? It could just be you are more driven than called.

Are you tempted to find status or power in material success? Are you struggling with relationships because you are more concerned about your position than your caring for others? Is your relationship with God shallow because you are more concerned with your public life than your private one?

The temptations of Jesus in the wilderness took the form of finding public life more important than His personal life. "Who are you?" was the question Satan asked Jesus. "Since you are the Son of God, turn the stone to bread, jump from the temple, and just worship me for a minute. Turn aside from your real purpose of glorifying the Heavenly Father and setting up the kingdom of God, and find approval in men's applause."

Maybe it is time to take inventory of what is really important in life. What is your struggle? Maybe it is time to "order your private world."

~~

The Good Shepherd

February 14, 2013

The Lord is my shepherd, I shall not want.
He makes me lie down in green pastures; He leads me beside quiet waters.
He restores my soul; He guides me in the paths of righteousness
For His name's sake.
Even though I walk through the valley of the shadow of death,
I fear no evil, for You are with me; Your rod and Your staff, they comfort me.
You prepare a table before me in the presence of my enemies;
You have anointed my head with oil; My cup overflows.
Surely goodness and lovingkindness will follow me all the days of my life,
And I will dwell in the house of the Lord forever. (Psalm 23, NASB)

These are likely some of the first verses that you memorized. It is also likely the verses have become more meaningful as your life passes by. In the words you have found comfort, peace, hope, assurance, victory, joy, and most of all, your Savior.

The Lord truly is our Shepherd. He loves and cares for us, His sheep. Because He is our Shepherd, we will be provided for. We are without want. He guides our lives into right living. He leads us through the depths of the valley of death. For that reason, we need not fear.

He comforts us with His rod and His staff. His staff is used to pull us through the struggles and difficulties. It brings such comfort to know the Great Shepherd is leading. He comforts through the rod. The rod was a stick used to throw at the sheep to warn them, correct them, and assure them they were being watched over.

The Shepherd fills our life with joy. His presence overwhelms, and our cup overflows. The sheep know and understand that the Shepherd is an everlasting Shepherd. He is not only with us in this life but leads us to the next and is with us forever. The Everlasting Shepherd is the Great Alpha and Omega. Remember: He is a Good Shepherd and He loves you.

~~

Look to the Hills

February 21, 2013

I will lift up my eyes to the mountains; From where shall my help come?
My help comes from the Lord, Who made heaven and earth.
He will not allow your foot to slip; He who keeps you will not slumber.
Behold, He who keeps Israel will neither slumber nor sleep.

The Lord is your keeper; The Lord is your shade on your right hand.
The sun will not smite you by day, Nor the moon by night.
The Lord will protect you from all evil; He will keep your soul.
The Lord will guard your going out and your coming in
From this time forth and forever. (Psalm 121, NASB)

When you need help, where do you look for help? Do you look to friends, family, your bank account, your status, your influence, or your own inner strength? David the psalmist looked to the hills. The hills symbolized the ascent up to Jerusalem. It was there David could see the Mt. of Olives, Mt. Zion, and Mt. Moriah. Jerusalem, the Holy City, represented to David the very presence of God.

His help came from God. "My help comes from the Lord." It was not just any god. It was the God who made heaven and earth. The Creator knows all. He is capable of being the help David needed. He desires, as well, to meet your needs.

"Your Father knows what you need before you ask Him" (Matthew 6:8). He is a God who does not sleep. David knew that God is ever-aware of what needs are in our lives. God knows our needs and is not only aware of them but is eager to come to our aid. He will not allow us to stumble or fall.

David was speaking of spiritual life. It is God who keeps us. He is our defense against attacks from the evil one. He is the shade to protect us at all times. In the book of Romans, it says, "If God is for us, who can ever be against us?" (Romans 8:31, NLT)

You are protected. You are kept in the hand of God. He preserves you from evil. He preserves your soul from destruction and danger. God knows where you are, where you have been, and where you are going; and He is always with you. As a believer in Jesus Christ, He is also in you. It is Christ in you that is the Hope of Glory. Look to the hills. God is your strength.

~~

Slapped Up the Side of the Head   February 28, 2013

Are they servants of Christ? - I speak as if insane - I more so; in far more labors, in far more imprisonments, beaten times without number, often in danger of death. Five times I received from the Jews thirty-nine lashes. Three times I was beaten with rods, once I was stoned, three times I was shipwrecked, a night and a day I have spent in the deep. I have been on frequent journeys, in dangers from rivers, dangers from robbers, dangers from my countrymen, dangers from the Gentiles, dangers in the city, dangers in the wilderness, dangers on the sea, dangers among false brethren; I have been in labor and hardship, through many sleepless nights, in hunger and thirst, often without food, in cold and exposure. Apart from such external things, there is the daily pressure on me of concern for all the churches. Who is weak without my being weak? Who is led into sin without my intense concern? (2 Corinthians 11:23-29, NASB)

Ever been "slapped up the side of the head"? Not literally but in a figurative way? Something came at you quickly, unexpected, and you were unprepared. Those experiences are commonplace for all, but for some reason, few people are really ready. Maybe it was an unexpected report from your doctor. It could be the pink slip the boss hands you on a Friday afternoon. You could find yourself concerned with a close family member who is struggling.

The apostle Paul found himself with more than one of those slaps to the side of the head. He was in prison, beaten with rods, stoned, shipwrecked, and in danger from the unexpected robber. He spent sleepless nights in hunger and in thirst without food or water, and with cold and exposure.

Our struggles and pain may be more than what we are dealing with in our own physical life. In Paul's case, he tells of the struggles and pain he experienced in his concern for others. He had founded several churches, and taught and guided others. The issues, troubles, and sin of the people he loved caused him great concern also.

Maybe today you are experiencing a "slap up the side of the head." God will see you through it all. Trust Him. Depend on Him. Love Him. Serve Him. Thank Him. Seek Him and His righteousness, and all other things will be added to you (Matthew 6:33).

~~

LIFE!

March 7, 2013

Then He said to them all: "Whoever wants to be My disciple must deny themselves and take up their cross daily and follow Me. For whoever wants to save their life will lose it, but whoever loses their life for Me will save it." (Luke 9:23-24, NIV)

Do you consider yourself a follower or disciple of Jesus Christ? Just what does that mean to you? What does it mean to Jesus? Early in Jesus' ministry, He chose followers. His call to them was described in several of the gospels, like the one here in Luke's gospel. Did you notice that Jesus says, "Whoever wants to be My disciple [or follower] must..." and then the requirements follow? First of all, we must want to be a follower. Jesus never forces anyone to follow Him. On the other hand, if we want to be His disciple, then much is required.

We must deny ourselves. At first it would seem that a vow of poverty, a denial of happiness, a life of loneliness and suffering would be in order. The world in which we live is a selfish world. Whether it is the individual who wants their own way, or societal structures, governments, or academia that seeks selfish ends, it is truly a selfish world. It only takes a trip to the preschool to hear a two-year-old grab hold of a toy and cry out, "Mine!" to realize that something within every human is innately selfish. Jesus is saying that if we want to be His disciple, we must surrender our selfish life, lived for and by ourselves, for His will. To deny yourself is to deny your selfish will and yield yourself to the will of Jesus.

Jesus then makes it clear that the cross is a daily experience for a follower of His. Some say, "This is my cross to bear," meaning some burden or suffering. That is not what Jesus is talking about. He is emphasizing the need to die to our selfish life and again yield to Him each day. The cross was a place of death, not just a place of hurt. Yielding to Christ is necessary to be His disciple.

The result of losing your life for His sake is LIFE. His life, lived in and through you, is real life. The lie of Satan is to get you to believe that you can somehow gain life by selfish ambition. Life is found in losing your life to Christ. Save your life by losing it.

~~

The Race March 14, 2013

Therefore, since we have so great a cloud of witnesses surrounding us, let us also lay aside every encumbrance and the sin which so easily entangles us, and let us run with endurance the race that is set before us, fixing our eyes on Jesus, the author and perfecter of faith, who for the joy set before Him endured the cross, despising the shame, and has sat down at the right hand of the throne of God. For consider Him who has endured such hostility by sinners against Himself, so that you will not grow weary and lose heart. (Hebrews 12:1-3, NASB)

Ever felt like throwing in the towel and giving up? You, more than likely, have been to that point in a struggle or trial where there seemed to be no hope, no solution, and your answer was to give up. The writer of Hebrews says there is an answer "so that you will not grow weary and lose heart."

If you are there, or have been close to giving up, the Bible gives us some real help. That help is faith. After the writer spends the eleventh chapter talking of the great people of faith in the Bible, he then turns his attention to the "HOW TO." First, we need to realize that there are multitudes that have been where we are. They are a great cloud of witnesses. That doesn't mean they are looking down from heaven, but they themselves have endured during difficult times in order to give hope to us.

The writer also says that life is a race. It is not a hundred-yard dash but a marathon. The hope comes in realizing that most things "come to pass." He admonishes us to lay aside anything that is in the way of victory, especially the sin that entangles us. We are in a race. A race, to ancient Greeks, was anything that was a struggle or conflict. The needed element to win a race was endurance. We have a race ahead. Endure. That is not a passive word but one in which all energy is required. It refuses to be sidetracked.

That is not done without "fixing our eyes on Jesus" and "considering Jesus." You need Him to see you through. He endured the shame of the cross, and endured its pain and suffering, for you. Look to Him for your strength. Faith in Him is your answer.

~~

Eliminate the Negative   March 21, 2013

> *Paul, an apostle of Christ Jesus by the will of God,*
> *Blessed be the God and Father of our Lord Jesus Christ, who has blessed us with every spiritual blessing in the heavenly places in Christ, just as He chose us in Him before the foundation of the world, that we would be holy and blameless before Him. In love He predestined us to adoption as sons through Jesus Christ to Himself, according to the kind intention of His will, to the praise of the glory of His grace, which He freely bestowed on us in the Beloved. In Him we have redemption through His blood, the forgiveness of our trespasses, according to the riches of His grace which He lavished on us... In Him also we have obtained an inheritance, having been predestined according to His purpose who works all things after the counsel of His will, to the end that we who were the first to hope in Christ would be to the praise of His glory. In Him, you also, after listening to the message of truth, the gospel of your salvation - having also believed, you were sealed in Him with the Holy Spirit of promise, who is given as a pledge of our inheritance, with a view to the redemption of God's own possession, to the praise of His glory.* (Ephesians 1:1, 3-8, 11-14; NASB)

Do you have the disease "Negativitis"? It has symptoms like most diseases. And like other diseases, it gets worse unless something is done about it. Also, we may have it and not know it.

Do you find yourself complaining about your situation? How about being critical of people and the problems you encounter? Maybe you need to go to the Great Physician and thank Him for the cure He has already provided.

The book of Ephesians says we are blessed in Christ with every spiritual blessing in the heavenly places. We need to keep our eyes on the spiritual life, and not too much on the problems of the here and now. We have been saved, redeemed by Christ's blood - forgiven completely. We have been given God's stamp of approval and acceptance through the truth of the Gospel that we accepted. We were sealed for all of eternity in the Holy Spirit.

That doesn't leave much room for "Negativitis." Your life is for the praise of His glory, not your comfort or prosperity. Allow the presence of God's Holy Spirit to teach you that His Life is your life.

~~

Pray Anyway   April 4, 2013

> *When he had seized him, he put him in prison, delivering him to four squads of soldiers to guard him, intending after the Passover to bring him out before the people. So Peter was kept in the prison, but prayer for him was being made fervently by the church to God.* (Acts 12:4-5, NASB)

A pastor had a plaque on the wall behind his desk that read: "PRAYER CHANGES THINGS." Daily, he would start by reading the plaque and reminding himself that God does change things through prayer.

The apostle Peter never endeared himself to the religious people of his day. He more often irritated them. He had publicly accused them of crucifying Jesus. It was likewise normal for him to end up in jail. On one particular occasion, the Church met in the home of Mary to pray fervently for Peter. While they were praying, an angel released Peter from jail, and Peter went to Mary's home and was pounding on the door. A maid named Rhoda went to the door and was shocked to see Peter. She returned to the "praying" church, but they declared it could not be Peter because he was in jail.

Does it seem strange to you that they were praying fervently for Peter but when their prayers were answered, they couldn't believe it?
> *They said to her, "You are out of your mind!" But she kept insisting that it was so. They kept saying, "It is his angel." But Peter continued knocking; and when they had opened the door, they saw him and were amazed.* (Acts 12:15-16)

God does answer prayer - sometimes even when we lack the faith to believe He will. God responds to the corporate prayer of His Church. The desperate need of the Church today is to return to being God's prayer warriors. There is a need to pray even though the people of God may doubt that God will answer. Peter's life is one of ups and downs, but it is also a reminder of the Great God who answers the prayers of His people.

~~

You Can't Buy Grace

April 11, 2013

> *Now when the apostles in Jerusalem heard that Samaria had received the word of God, they sent them Peter and John, who came down and prayed for them that they might receive the Holy Spirit... Then they began laying their hands on them, and they were receiving the Holy Spirit. Now when Simon [the Sorcerer] saw that the Spirit was bestowed through the laying on of the apostles' hands, he offered them money, saying, "Give this authority to me as well, so that everyone on whom I lay my hands may receive the Holy Spirit." But Peter said to him, "May your silver perish with you, because you thought you could obtain the gift of God with money!"*
> (Acts 8:14-15, 17-20; NASB)

It is so easy to fall prey to the lie of Satan that somehow we can earn or buy God's grace. Simon the Sorcerer observed John and Peter as they laid hands on the believers in Samaria. He had been the man of great magic that had mystified Samaria with his abilities to the point he was called, "The Great Power of God." He now desired the gift of God to lay hands on someone who would then receive the Holy Spirit. He missed the truth that only by God's grace is His work accomplished. Somehow, he believed he could pay money to perform God's works.

Peter rebuked Simon and declared that he would perish because he thought he could buy God's gifts and favor. BEWARE: It is easy to forget that all we are, or all we do in God's work, is accomplished through grace. It is not you - it is God. He will share His glory with no one. Whether it is good works, hard work, money, personal power, or influence, we cannot receive God's gifts through our efforts. God gives His gifts to whomever He wishes. No purchasing power exists to diminish the grace of God.

How often are we deluded, as Simon was, into believing that we could somehow pay the right amount, accomplish the right "stuff," and somehow be endowed with God's power? God's miracles are brought about by God Himself, and not by our effort or money.

The next time you are tempted to ignore the grace of God in order to accomplish God's work, remind yourself of Simon the Sorcerer. Peter was prophetic with his words, "May your silver perish with you, because you thought you could obtain the gift of God with money."

~~

Drink the Water

> *"For My people have done two evil things: They have abandoned Me - the fountain of living water. And they have dug for themselves cracked cisterns that can hold no water at all!"* (Jeremiah 2:13, NLT)

Have you ever felt abandoned, rejected, forsaken, left all alone? Did you ever consider that God has feelings? God had chosen the nation of Israel as His own people. He had provided for them for centuries. He loved them with unconditional love. He led them from slavery to freedom. He fed them with manna in the wilderness. He had shown them that they were special to Him.

God was their fountain of living water. He was life itself. God is that to you, also. Jesus calls Himself the living water. He provides us with life. He declared that He is the way, the truth, and the life. To the Jews of Jeremiah's time, God had been their Strength, their Rock, their Provider, their Healer, and the One who loved them.

Jeremiah had watched as they committed two sins that he reminded them are evil. They had done the evil of abandoning the One who was their God. He was truly their fountain of living water. It was bad enough to abandon God, but on top of that, they had become idolaters. They abandoned God and dug cisterns for themselves.

They were trying to provide what they needed as living water by digging a hole that relied on runoff water to supply their needs. How easy it is to look to something or someone else to provide that which only God can provide. He is life. He provides us with life. Don't abandon the only true God just to find something or someone else that you think will fulfill your life. Only God can do that.

The Jewish people were soon to be captured by Babylon and carried into seventy years of captivity. Again they would be enslaved because they had abandoned God. They were searching for something apart from God that only God could provide.

What are you willing to trade for your relationship with God? What cistern are you digging that you believe is the answer to your own needs, and in the process you have abandoned God?

Return to God. Instead of abandoning God, turn your back on your cisterns that can only hold runoff water on a temporary basis. They are full of holes. They will not sustain true life. God provides you with living water. Drink from His endless supply.

~~

Is He Sifting You?

> *"Simon, Simon, [also called Peter] behold, Satan has demanded permission to sift you like wheat; but I have prayed for you, that your faith may not fail; and you, when once you have turned again, strengthen your brothers." But he said to Him, "Lord, with You I am ready to go both to prison and to death!" And He said, "I say to you, Peter, the rooster will not crow today until you have denied three times that you know Me."* (Luke 22:31-34, NASB)

Failure, for most people, comes as a result of pride. Simon Peter was no exception. He bragged to Jesus that he would be willing to go to prison or be martyred before he would ever turn his back on Jesus. He saw himself as a loyal, faithful, and strong follower of Jesus. In the deepest part of his heart, he was sure he would never fail. We are very aware that failure is a part of everyone's life. At some place, some time, or some situation, there is failure lurking in the darkness to pounce on us like an animal on its prey.

Our pride is the beginning of our failure, and yet, something else is in the background also. "Satan has demanded to sift you like wheat," were the words of Jesus to Peter. Satan is the author of failure. For some reason, Jesus allowed the request of Satan, and Peter was indeed tempted and fell into failure by denying three times that he even knew Jesus. In Peter's most vivid imagination, he could not have conceived that he would ever fail Jesus. He was the faithful follower, ready to die for his leader.

Have you ever failed? Have you ever considered you were the target of Satan's attack? Have you thought that your own pride was the open door for failure? Surely, you and everyone else struggles with temptation. The desire for success will often lead us to an inflated concept of our ability to overcome whatever comes our way. No amount of self-determination will overcome the temptations that we will face. Only God can provide that strength.

Jesus had a word of encouragement for Peter: "I have prayed for you." What a privilege and hope to know that Jesus is praying for you! His prayer was that Peter's faith would not fail, even in the face of failure. He also promised that "once you have turned" back to God, you still have a place in the work of the Kingdom to strengthen your fellow believers.

~~

A Strategy for Winning May 2, 2013

> *But I say, walk by the Spirit, and you will not carry out the desire of the flesh. For the flesh sets its desire against the Spirit, and the Spirit against the flesh; for these are in opposition to one another, so that you may not do the things that you please. But if you are led by the Spirit, you are not under the Law. Now the deeds of the flesh are evident, which are: immorality, impurity, sensuality, idolatry, sorcery, enmities, strife, jealousy, outbursts of anger, disputes, dissensions, factions, envying, drunkenness, carousing, and things like these, of which I forewarn you, just as I have forewarned you, that those who practice such things will not inherit the kingdom of God. But the fruit of the Spirit is love, joy, peace, patience, kindness, goodness, faithfulness, gentleness, self-control; against such things there is no law. Now those who belong to Christ Jesus have crucified the flesh with its passions and desires.* (Galatians 5:16-24, NASB)

Do you like to win? Whether it is a pick-up basketball game, a board game, a race, or a friendly game of poker, most people like to win. Someone has said the real issue is not that they like to win - they just hate losing. In your walk with God, it is easy to lose and not win. The Bible gives us insight to winning. In some ways, it is a strategy for spiritual life. It is simply this: "walk in the Spirit." That is winning. The opposite, "walking in the flesh," is losing. They are on opposite ends of life. One is pure self-effort, living for and in the flesh, while the other is a surrender of your life to the Spirit of God.

The flesh is losing because the life in the flesh ends in failure and deception, and eventually brings destruction. The Bible lists deeds of the flesh: immorality, impurity, sensuality, idolatry, sorcery, enmities, strife, jealousy, and on and on. All these deeds lead to death of spiritual wellbeing. On the other side is the spiritual life that leads to really winning. It is called the fruit of the Spirit. It is a life of love, joy, peace, patience, kindness, goodness, faithfulness, gentleness, and self-control. That is real life.

The strategy for winning is simply to walk in the Spirit - accomplished by belonging to Jesus and crucifying the flesh. Surely, you want to win. It may sound strange, but you win by surrendering your life to Jesus.

~~

Freed From the Curse
May 9, 2013

Christ redeemed us from the curse of the Law, having become a curse for us - for it is written, "Cursed is everyone who hangs on a tree" - in order that in Christ Jesus the blessing of Abraham might come to the Gentiles, so that we would receive the promise of the Spirit through faith. (Galatians 3:13-14, NASB)

When Christians are asked the question, "Why did Jesus come to earth?" the answer is most often, "To die for our sins." That is only part of the answer. Jesus, God in human flesh, did die on a cross for the sins of all mankind. He did suffer the cruel death on a cross. The writer of Galatians called the cross a "tree." The Bible says it is a curse to die on a cross. So in all reality, Jesus did die on a cross to forgive the sin of mankind by becoming a sin offering and taking the place of every sinner, and as a substitute, He died in our place also.

He did far more than that. His death was preparation. It was on the cross that Jesus provided a way to be forgiven. He vicariously took the place of sinners. The Bible says in 2nd Corinthians 5:21, "For God made Christ, who never sinned, to be the offering for our sin, so that we could be made right with God through Christ" (NLT).

It is because we are forgiven that God sent the Holy Spirit to live in every believer. In Galatians 3:14, the words "so that" connect the cross with the promise of the indwelling Holy Spirit. We receive the Holy Spirit through faith in Jesus Christ.

The Holy Spirit lives in us. He gives us the power to live the Christian life. So, not only does God forgive us through Christ's death on the cross, He then comes to live in us because we have been redeemed from the curse of the Law. The Law is only able to condemn us of our sin. The cross is able to free us from that curse. Then the Holy Spirit indwells us to give us abundant life. It is through the Holy Spirit who lives in us that we are able to call our Heavenly Father "Abba" or Daddy. The relationship is close. You are His child. You are special to Him.

If Jesus had not died for you, then you would be cursed because of sin. But now, because you have been forgiven and by faith received forgiveness, you are also able to receive the Spirit of promise, God's Holy Spirit, to live in you.

You are forgiven in order to be indwelt. Praise God for His two-fold blessing! Live in the Spirit and walk in the Spirit, and call upon your Daddy for life itself.

~~

Waiting Eagerly May 16, 2013

> *For we know that all creation has been groaning as in the pains of childbirth right up to the present time. And we believers also groan, even though we have the Holy Spirit within us as a foretaste of future glory, for we long for our bodies to be released from sin and suffering. We, too, wait with eager hope for the day when God will give us our full rights as His adopted children, including the new bodies He has promised us. We were given this hope when we were saved. (If we already have something, we don't need to hope for it. But if we look forward to something we don't yet have, we must wait patiently and confidently.)* (Romans 8:22-25, NLT)

Do you have something special in your future that you are eager to experience? Maybe you have a birthday or anniversary, or a graduation, or big vacation planned. You can hardly wait. The expectations of future events can bring great joy. Likely no other future event will bring greater joy and fulfillment than the day God takes us to our eternal home in heaven.

We are all aware of the struggles of this life. The Bible calls it "groaning." Something within us longs for some relief from the struggles of life. It does not mean all of life is one big GROAN, but it does mean we suffer in our present state, living in this body. We have peace within, at the same time, because God has placed His Holy Spirit in every believer as a foretaste of the future. As believers in Jesus Christ, God has given us hope. One day we will find release from the current body that enshrouds us. We will be released from sin and suffering.

Right now we are waiting eagerly for that day. That is hope - we don't have it yet. We were given this hope when we first trusted Jesus as our Savior, our Lord, and our Life. Our hope is based on God's promises of life eternal. For all of time, mankind has longed for immortality. In Jesus, that has become reality. Yet it is still not completed. We are waiting in hope.

In the meantime, the Holy Spirit guarantees the future with no pain, sorrow, suffering, or groaning. You can wait patiently and confidently in the promises of God and His indwelling presence. Someday you will have a brand new body. It will be one without corruption. It will be free indeed. You will be totally free.

~~

While We Wait May 25, 2013

> *Let us hold unswervingly to the hope we profess, for He who promised is faithful. And let us consider how we may spur one another on toward love and good deeds, not giving*

up meeting together, as some are in the habit of doing, but encouraging one another - and all the more as you see the Day approaching. (Hebrews 10:23-25, NIV)

The writer of Hebrews spoke of "the Day approaching." What day was he talking about? He was writing about the Day of the return of Jesus Christ to earth. He was writing about the coming of Jesus in the clouds to receive His Bride, the Church, into His presence for all eternity.

The writer then gave instructions concerning our preparation for the Day. First, he tells us to "hold unswervingly to the hope we profess." We have hope in Christ. It is the hope that when He comes, we will be caught up with Him. It is the hope that we are His children by faith. It is the hope that what He began in us, He will complete. As the hymn says, "My hope is built on nothing less than Jesus' blood and righteousness."

The writer then tells us to "spur one another on toward love and good deeds." The motivation to live the Christian life is affected by one another. We need to spur one another forward in our faith. The writer says we accomplish this motivation by meeting together. Do not forsake meeting together. The emphasis in the Scripture is the Body of Christ, the Church - the believers meeting with and for one another, in order to support one another in our faith.

The last thing the writer says is that we need to be "encouraging one another." We need encouragement on a daily basis. As you find a greater need in your life to be encouraged because of situations, circumstances, struggles, and trials, you will find that you need your fellow believers to encourage you.

The community of believers is designed to be a support system for each and every believer. There is no such thing as a "Lone Ranger" Christian. God has placed you in a community of believers in order to walk in Christ. As you look forward to the Day of His second coming, praise God for the fellowship you have with other believers.

~~

Tell Everyone

May 30, 2013

Those tending the pigs ran off and reported this in the town and countryside, and the people went out to see what had happened. When they came to Jesus, they saw the man who had been possessed by the legion of demons, sitting there, dressed and in his right mind; and they were afraid. Those who had seen it told the people what had happened to the demon-possessed man - and told about the pigs as well. Then the people began to plead with Jesus to leave their region.

As Jesus was getting into the boat, the man who had been demon-possessed begged to go with Him. Jesus did not let him, but said, "Go home to your own people and tell them how much the Lord has done for you, and how He has had mercy on you." So the man went away and began to tell in the Decapolis how much Jesus had done for him. And all the people were amazed. (Mark 5:14-20, NIV)

When was the last time you told someone what Jesus has done for you? The man called Legion (which means "for we are many," referring to the demons that possessed him) met another man called Jesus. It was that Man who cast the demons from Legion and sent them into a herd of pigs wandering on the hillside. The pigs were cast into a lake, and Legion was set free.

The local people observed that Legion was clothed and in his right mind - his demons had been cast out. The local people also observed what had happened and then watched as Jesus entered a boat to leave. The man who was now free from his demon possession followed Jesus and made a request of Him. He begged Jesus to allow him the honor of going with Him. He was basically requesting the privilege of being a close disciple. It seems strange that Jesus refused his pleading, but Jesus had another purpose for him…

Instead of opening His arms to another disciple, Jesus told the man, "Go home to your own people and tell them how much the Lord has done for you, and how He has had mercy on you." In total obedience to Jesus, the man went away and began to tell in Decapolis how much Jesus had done for him. The result was that all the people were totally amazed. Have you told your story to someone? They might be amazed as well.

~~

Use Your Resources
June 6, 2013

In this case, moreover, it is required of stewards that one be found trustworthy. (1 Corinthians 4:2, NASB)

"He who is faithful in a very little thing is faithful also in much; and he who is unrighteous in a very little thing is unrighteous also in much. Therefore if you have not been faithful in the use of unrighteous wealth, who will entrust the true riches to you? And if you have not been faithful in the use of that which is another's, who will give you that which is your own?" (Luke 16:10-12)

Who or what owns you? It has been said that if you cannot give away what you have, you don't own it - it owns you. There is a story of a man in the church that had a wealthy relative who died and left him a million dollars. About the same time, he had a severe heart attack and was in the hospital, in critical condition. No one wanted to tell him about the money for fear it would cause him to have another heart attack. Feeling he needed to know, the pastor of his church was selected to tell him. The pastor went into the room and talked of sports, weather, and whatever, until he finally placed this question to the man: "What would you do if someone gave you a million dollars?" Without hesitancy, the man said, "Pastor, I would give half of it to the church" - whereupon the pastor had a heart attack and died.

Remember this: God owns everything. We are given the honor and responsibility to be stewards of what He gives to us. To be a good steward of what God has entrusted to us, we can choose at least six things to do with it. We can give it away, we can save it, we can spend it, we can protect it, we can hoard it, or we can invest it.

God has promised to those who are faithful stewards of anything, that He will bless them. The blessing does not necessarily mean an accumulation of more. It can mean the blessing of seeing God use whatever has been given away to help others. It can mean protection provided by God of all you have.

It is a real joy to be a faithful steward. Use the resources God has entrusted to you to help others. Use those resources to know that God receives glory from the faithful steward. Your goal of bringing glory to God is accomplished as you express your faithfulness.

~~

Come and Dine

June 13, 2013

> *Jesus said to them, "Come and have breakfast." None of the disciples ventured to question Him, "Who are You?" knowing that it was the Lord. Jesus came and took the bread and gave it to them, and the fish likewise.* (John 21:12-13, NASB)

There is nothing quite like a fishing trip, a fish fry, and friends getting together for a meal. Peter had decided to return to his old life - fishing. He announced to the other disciples that he was going fishing. They, in unison, agreed to go along. Of course, as happens on many fishing trips, they caught nothing. You call that "getting skunked."

Jesus was on the shore waiting for them. After an all-night fishing trip, they were tired and hungry. Jesus called to them from the shore and teasingly said, "You have not caught any fish, have you?" Their answer was in the negative. Jesus then gave instructions to cast the net on the right side of the boat. They complied and filled their net with 153 large fish.

There were so many fish, they could not put them on the boat. So they dragged the net to shore, where they found Jesus with breakfast cooked and ready to eat. Fish and bread awaited the hungry disciples. Jesus merely said to them, "Come and have breakfast with Me." This was the third time they had seen Jesus alive after his resurrection. They knew that it was Him and yet they made no comments.

The disciples had eaten many meals with Jesus and it must have been a highlight for them. But this was special. It was with the resurrected Jesus. It was the climax of three years of ministry. He was alive and breaking bread with His friends. Do you break bread with Jesus? Do you dine with Him? Do you spend time soaking up His words from the Word of God? Do you talk with Him, fellowship with Him, and thank Him for His presence? Today spend some time with Jesus. Fellowship with Jesus is great!

It was during this encounter that Jesus asked Peter the BIG QUESTION: "Do you love Me?" It may be that as you commune with Christ and eat from His words that He will ask you that question. How will you answer? What would you say if Jesus asked you, "Do you love Me?" Spend some time with Jesus today and tell Him that you do love Him.

~~

~ A Personal Note ~

Over the 32 years that I had the pleasure of knowing Dennis, he was my pastor, my spiritual mentor, co-laborer, friend, and fishing buddy. Dennis' mention of the joys of friends, food, and fishing brings back many fond memories for me.

Dennis and I spent countless hours together casting a line in Wisconsin, Arizona, and Missouri lakes. During our times together, I noticed a somewhat competitive nature in Dennis. Dennis was always telling stories. Bragging really... bragging on his catch (or the one that got away), his church, or his family. He was so very proud of all of these. But mostly, Dennis was bragging on his Savior - telling what God was doing in his life, in the people that he came in contact with (some complete strangers), and how God was working in mighty ways in everyone. Dennis would say, "It's not bragging if it's true."

The other thing that was difficult to miss, was that Dennis had a tendency towards mishaps. It is hard to believe that Dennis even survived a part-time job at a knife store. When it came to fishing, a trip with Dennis often meant falling off of a trailer, lost or broken equipment, and spilled fish attractant (yes, the super-odorous fluorescent kind that never, ever comes out of the boat carpet).

On one fishing outing together, Dennis and I were fishing in the late evening into the night, thinking we would catch some tasty walleye for dinner the next day. Dennis was fishing with a spoon-bait on light tackle and latched onto a huge MUSKY! For those that have not fished in northern Wisconsin, a Muskellunge is a long fish (in Dennis' case, it was over 36") with long teeth and razor-like gills. After playing this fish for about 10 minutes, he got it close enough to the boat that I could get a net around it. As I lifted the net into the boat, the net succumbed to those teeth and gills, which sliced a gaping hole right through it. The musky went crashing into the center of the boat and Part 2 of the fight with this fish was on. The fish had the upper hand as it crashed and smashed everything in sight. Minnow buckets, coolers, rods and reels went flying everywhere. Finally, Dennis was able to hold the fish in place with his feet. Since everything in the boat needed at least some attention (or a trash can) we decided we were done for the day and went into our boat dock at the small fishing resort where we were staying. We hauled that musky and walked the shoreline to the main office of the resort where Dennis proudly and loudly rang the "Musky Bell" at about midnight - which brought a small crowd to check out the catch. That got the stories going, and going, and going.

The Musky Bell story is one of my favorites. I can still picture that fish in the bottom of the boat – but what I remember most is Dennis' big smile as he was holding up his musky next to the "Musky Bell."

I am sure that the countless people with whom Dennis came in contact would also have their stories. Most of them are held onto fondly – but all of them are precious. Which leads us into Dennis' next devotion...

~ Mark

~~

Precious Memories   June 20, 2013

His divine power has given us everything we need for a godly life through our knowledge of Him who called us by His own glory and goodness. Through these He has given us His very great and precious promises, so that through them you may participate in the divine nature, having escaped the corruption in the world caused by evil desires. But whoever does not have them is nearsighted and blind, forgetting that they have been cleansed from their past sins.
So I will always remind you of these things, even though you know them and are firmly established in the truth you now have. I think it is right to refresh your memory as long as I live in the tent of this body, because I know that I will soon put it aside, as

our Lord Jesus Christ has made clear to me. And I will make every effort to see that after my departure you will always be able to remember these things. (2 Peter 1:3-4, 9, 12-15; NIV)

How's your memory? There are likely many things we remember with joy and happiness. Some of our remembrances hold pain and sorrow. The apostle Peter reminds his readers that remembering is very important. In order to grow spiritually, it is necessary to remember. He reminds us that we have received, at salvation, everything we will need to live a godly life through God who called us.

"Remember," he says, "that you have received the great and precious promises of God through salvation. Remember that you have escaped the corruption of the world because you share in God's divine nature. Christ is in you and you are in Him. Don't forget it! Don't forget that your sins have been forgiven."

He calls his readers nearsighted and blind when they forget the blessings of God's redemption. You may not ever have thought of "remembering" as a spiritual discipline like prayer and Bible reading, but Peter's emphasis is upon remembering for the sake of becoming all that God desires of you.

Take time to reflect upon your salvation experience. Think about those times when God was most real to you. Remember the moments when God spoke to your heart and gave you direction. God does desire for you to grow spiritually and has given memories as one of the ways to accomplish His will for you.

~~

Roads Traveled

June 27, 2013

A highway shall be there, and a road,
And it shall be called the Highway of Holiness.
The unclean shall not pass over it, But it shall be for others.
Whoever walks the road, although a fool, Shall not go astray. (Isaiah 35:8, NKJV)

As they were going along the road, someone said to Him, "I will follow You wherever You go." (Luke 9:57, NASB)

"The sower went out to sow his seed; and as he sowed, some fell beside the road, and it was trampled under foot and the birds of the air ate it up." (Luke 8:5)

On the road, down the road, at the fork in the road, rocky road, road to nowhere, winding road, crooked road, rough road, road to recovery, roadblock, and on and on the road goes. Have you ever noticed how many ways we use the word "road"? Have you ever looked into God's Word, the Bible, and seen how many times a reference is made to a road? Like the road to Jericho, the road to Calvary, the road to Emmaus, the road that leads to Samaria.

Paul was saved and met the resurrected Jesus on the road to Damascus. Philip preached Jesus in the town of Samaria, and throngs came to faith in Jesus. As he left town, he met a man on the road who inquired about being baptized - because he saw water by the road. Philip said he could be baptized, if he believed in Jesus.

The path or road that Jesus walked as he approached the hill called Golgatha, or Mount Calvary, where he was crucified is called the Road of Suffering. It was on this road that led to His crucifixion, that He suffered much. In Spanish it is called the "Via Dolorosa."

What road are you on? Are you following Jesus down the road to holiness? Are you walking on the narrow road, or headed down the road to destruction? It would be a good time to choose to walk on the Highway of Holiness, the road to victory in Jesus.

> ...*Choose this day whom you will serve... But as for me and my house, we will serve the Lord.* (Joshua 24:15, ESV)

~~

Stand Firm in Grace   July 4, 2013

> ... *For he who has died is freed from sin.* (Romans 6:7, NASB)

> *But now having been freed from sin and enslaved to God, you derive your benefit, resulting in sanctification, and the outcome, eternal life. For the wages of sin is death, but the free gift of God is eternal life in Christ Jesus our Lord.* (Romans 6:22-23)

> *It was for freedom that Christ set us free; therefore keep standing firm and do not be subject again to a yoke of slavery.* (Galatians 5:1)

How important is freedom to you? Do you long to be free, not only from something but to something? Being free involves not being in bondage or slavery to any one or any thing. Free from sin, the entanglement of addictions, the fears that control your life - just a few of the enslavements from which God desires to set you free.

Freedom was the hallmark of the early American patriot, Patrick Henry, who said, "Give me liberty [freedom] or give me death." Freedom was also the message of the Bible throughout the New Testament. It proclaims freedom from the power and the penalty of sin, freedom from the legalism of the Law, and freedom from the flesh.

In order to be truly free, it is necessary to have a living, vital relationship with God in Christ. Jesus came to earth to give you life, and life more abundantly. In order to do that, He needed to take your sinful nature and nail it to a cross. When Jesus died, you died with Him. It is only as you accept your death and resurrection in Christ, and put your trust in Him, that you can truly be free.

We will be constantly bombarded with freedom killers - people and situations that want to take our freedom from us. No wonder the book of Galatians reminds us to stand firm in our freedom.

Sin can defeat you until you realize, believe, and embrace the freedom that Christ secured for you on the cross and with an empty tomb. Live life abundantly, in freedom by His grace.

~~

Are You a Survivor? July 11, 2013

> *Then Jesus was led up by the Spirit into the wilderness to be tempted by the devil. And after He had fasted forty days and forty nights, He then became hungry. And the tempter came and said to Him, "If You are the Son of God, command that these stones become bread." But He answered and said, "It is written, 'Man shall not live on bread alone, but on every word that proceeds out of the mouth of God.'"*
> (Matthew 4:1-4, NASB)

Is God really good? Ever wonder if Jesus questioned the goodness of the Father? The Scripture says that Jesus was tempted just as we are, yet did not sin. Suppose the conversation with the devil, or Satan, in this passage was increased by a few choice words from Satan that would make this temptation a little more real to us. What if Satan had added words like, "Jesus, you look awful. I thought God, the one you call Father, was good. If He is so good why are you so emaciated? You look downright gaunt. If your Father is so good, why hasn't He fed you these forty days? Most fathers would have provided their son with abundance. Yet look at you. If I were you, I would question whether He was a good God or good Father"?

Maybe your temptation is not about eating or even being hungry. Do you ever question the goodness of God when things get tough? When you are in need of more money, a job, better health, a more loving family, a relief from the depression or the struggles of just getting by, are you tempted to think that God must have a warped sense of humor, or that, even worse, He is just plain mean?

The world in which we live is shattered by war, hurricanes, tornadoes, fires, and floods. The children of the world are starving. We look at the situations we see even in our families and neighborhoods, and question God's goodness. Let me assure you that Jesus' temptation was just as real as ours. His answer was simply, "Man shall not live by bread alone, but by every word that proceeds from the mouth of God." Jesus fought the temptation with the Scripture. More than that, He found the true answer: God really is good. His Word declares Him so. He is there for you and loves you.

Don't allow the devil to remove from you the peace that only God can give. GOD IS GOOD!! He is full of grace and mercy. He wants you to know that you will survive whatever you face because He is good. He is desirous that you only trust Him. Without faith it is impossible to please Him. Jesus discovered in this temptation that God can provide, and that He will.

~~

Thank You July 18, 2013

> *Now on His way to Jerusalem, Jesus traveled along the border between Samaria and Galilee. As He was going into a village, ten men who had leprosy met Him. They stood at a distance and called out in a loud voice, "Jesus, Master, have pity on us!" When He saw them, He said, "Go, show yourselves to the priests." And as they went, they were cleansed. One of them, when he saw he was healed, came back, praising God in a loud voice. He threw himself at Jesus' feet and thanked Him - and he was a Samaritan. Jesus asked, "Were not all ten cleansed? Where are the other nine?"* (Luke 17:11-17, NIV)

Ray Boltz recorded a song a few years ago with these words: "Thank you for giving to the Lord. I am a life that was changed. Thank you for giving to the Lord. I am so glad you gave." The song reveals a person's gratitude for the many influential people in their life that brought them to the Lord.

The question is, to whom do you show your gratitude with a big "thank you" when you remember what they have done in your life? Maybe as the song says, we had a Sunday school teacher, a missionary, a parent, a friend, a co-worker, or maybe even a stranger that gave to us. They likely were not famous. The experience we had, as we received encouragement, growth, caring, and support from them may have seemed small to most, but to us it made all the difference in the world.

Have you said, "Thank you"? Jesus encountered ten extremely needy men. They all had the dreaded disease of leprosy. They were doomed to an extremely painful death. Jesus healed them all. Only one of them returned to say, "Thank you." It was at that point, Jesus asked the question, "Were not all ten cleansed? Where are the other nine?" What a tragedy to receive such an incredible blessing and not be grateful.

Who in your life today needs a word from you? Maybe a simple "thank you" would mean a lot. Try it today. Maybe an email, letter, card, phone call, or a one-to-one engagement would give encouragement to the one who "gave to the Lord."

~~

Whom Do You Trust? July 25, 2013

Commit your way to the Lord; trust in Him and He will do this:
(Psalm 37:5, NIV)

The Lord is good, a refuge in times of trouble.
He cares for those who trust in Him, (Nahum 1:7)

When I am afraid, I will put my trust in You.
In God, whose word I praise, In God I have put my trust;
I shall not be afraid. What can mere man do to me? (Psalm 56:3-4, NASB)

Though He slay me, yet will I trust in Him: (Job 13:15, KJV)

Someone said, "I have great faith in God, but sometimes I have difficulty TRUSTING HIM." How about you? Are you able to say that you have faith in God? You would agree that your faith is real, but sometimes it is hard to trust God for everyday things. Maybe you find it hard to TRUST God for your finances, your family, your job, your church, or your personal wellbeing. It is not unusual.

Although the two words "faith" and "trust" are different in the original languages of the Bible, they are very similar in meaning. Yet for you, they may mean something a little different. Trust, as defined by Webster, is: (1) a charge or duty imposed in faith or confidence or as a condition of some relationship, (2) something committed or entrusted to one, to be used or cared for in the interest of another. Your relationship with God is based on trusting Him with your very life - your total being, and everything related to you.

You may have had a time in your life when trusting anyone or anything was really hard. Maybe you experienced someone close to you who let you down, turned on you, or betrayed you. That experience may have caused you to not only distrust people but also God.

The only alternative to trusting God is to trust in yourself. That means you can determine for yourself what you believe can be trustworthy, and then place your trust in your predetermined set of criteria for trusting anyone or anything. It is not the best idea.

God is always worthy of your trust. Why not today make a commitment to trust Him?

~~

What Is Your Motive?   August 1, 2013

> *Jesus, therefore, six days before the Passover, came to Bethany where Lazarus was, whom Jesus had raised from the dead. So they made Him a supper there, and Martha was serving; but Lazarus was one of those reclining at the table with Him. Mary then took a pound of very costly perfume of pure nard, and anointed the feet of Jesus and wiped His feet with her hair; and the house was filled with the fragrance of the perfume. But Judas Iscariot, one of His disciples, who was intending to betray Him, said, "Why was this perfume not sold for three hundred denarii and given to poor people?" Now he said this, not because he was concerned about the poor, but because he was a thief, and as he had the money box, he used to pilfer what was put into it. Therefore Jesus said, "Let her alone, so that she may keep it for the day of My burial. For you always have the poor with you, but you do not always have Me."*
> (John 12:1-8, NASB)

Jesus was back at the home of Lazarus, Martha, and Mary. He was again eating a meal in their home. This time, instead of Martha complaining about Mary's lack of service, we find her serving supper without complaint. Mary was again at Jesus' feet, this time with a pound of very costly perfume. On another occasion, Mary was at Jesus' feet listening to Him. She now broke open the perfume container and anointed the feet of Jesus, wiping His feet with her hair.

She had possibly purchased the perfume or saved it for the purpose of anointing Jesus' body for burial. Jesus told Judas to "leave her alone" because she was using it for burial. The fragrance of the perfume filled the house. It likely brought back the memory of the stench of Lazarus' body at his death. Such a contrast in smells.

But it was Judas, the apostle who betrayed Jesus, who complained of misusing the perfume. He complained that it could have been sold for 300 denarii - a year's salary - and given to the poor. His motive was not pure. He was the treasurer of the disciples, and the Scripture says he pilfered the treasury box. In other words, he was not only a betrayer but also a thief.

What are you doing with what you have? Are you remembering Jesus? Are you giving to Him? Jesus reminded them that there would always be needy people around. Mary was doing the right thing.

~~

A World Savior

> *Now there was a man in Jerusalem called Simeon, who was righteous and devout. He was waiting for the consolation of Israel, and the Holy Spirit was on him. It had been revealed to him by the Holy Spirit that he would not die before he had seen the Lord's Messiah. Moved by the Spirit, he went into the temple courts. When the parents brought in the child Jesus to do for Him what the custom of the Law required, Simeon took Him in his arms and praised God, saying:*
> *"Sovereign Lord, as You have promised,*
> *You may now dismiss Your servant in peace.*
> *For my eyes have seen Your salvation,*
> *which You have prepared in the sight of all nations:*
> *a light for revelation to the Gentiles,*
> *and the glory of Your people Israel."* (Luke 2:25-32, NIV)

Simeon was a watcher. He was constantly watching for the fulfillment of the Old Testament promise of the coming Messiah. He went into the Temple courts to observe parents who brought their sons to be dedicated to God. Simeon was an old man. He believed and was led by the Holy Spirit to wait for His coming. The Holy Spirit revealed to him that he would not die until the Messiah would be born. As he watched Joseph and Mary, and saw the Child, Jesus, he took Him in his arms and praised God.

He knew that he had truly seen the coming Messiah of God. As he praised God, he called God the "Sovereign Lord." He knew the God of Creation had fulfilled His promise. He told God that he was now ready to die: "Let your servant go in peace." He knew that, in Jesus, all the nations of the world would be saved. He saw the Messiah as not just the Promised One to Israel but as the Savior of the whole world.

Today, we know that Jesus is not just a Savior for a specific nationality or race. Jesus is the Savior of the world. By faith, everyone everywhere can receive Jesus as the Lord God; and be saved from their sin, the world, the devil, the Law, and their own flesh. Jesus was the answer to a lifetime of waiting for Simeon. He may be the answer for you today. This would be a wonderful time for you to receive Him as your Savior and Lord. Trust that His death and resurrection was for you.

~~

Introduce Jesus! August 15, 2013

> *One of the two who heard John speak and followed Him, was Andrew, Simon Peter's brother. He found first his own brother Simon and said to him, "We have found the Messiah" (which translated means Christ). He brought him to Jesus. Jesus looked at him and said, "You are Simon the son of John; you shall be called Cephas" (which is translated Peter).*
> *The next day He purposed to go into Galilee, and He found Philip. And Jesus said to him, "Follow Me." Now Philip was from Bethsaida, of the city of Andrew and Peter. Philip found Nathanael and said to him, "We have found Him of whom Moses in the Law and also the Prophets wrote - Jesus of Nazareth, the son of Joseph."*
> (John 1:40-45, NASB)

God uses people! Did you ever think that God could use you for His glory? Jesus called the first of His followers from a group of men that He later used to bring others into His flock. Andrew had been a disciple of John the Baptist when he met Jesus. The Bible says that he followed Jesus after meeting Him. His first action as a new disciple of Jesus was to introduce Jesus to his brother, Peter. God used Andrew as a spokesman for the man who was to become known as the Messiah. Since that day, many have come to know Jesus as the Messiah. Both the Bible and the Quran proclaim Him as the "Messiah."

Whenever believers call Jesus the "Christ," they are actually calling Him the "Messiah." God has used many people, and maybe even you, to tell brothers and sisters and friends and family about the Messiah. Faith in Jesus as the Messiah is the basis of being a true believer of God. Placing your faith in Him is the answer to eternal life. His death and resurrection satisfied the holiness of God, and through His death on the cross, He became our substitute and died for our sins. When the Messiah died and rose again, He made it possible for you to live forever in heaven.

You may think that God cannot use you, but He can. He can use your life, your story of salvation through Jesus, your faith, your joy, and your peace as a means of expressing your relationship with the Messiah, Jesus, who is also called the Christ.

Never sell short your opportunity to be used by God to introduce others to the Messiah. God desires for you to be an Andrew or a Philip, and use your life to proclaim to a needy world that there is a Savior - Jesus, the Messiah. Use this day as the opportune moment when God uses YOU!!

~~

God's Prerequisite

> *And this is His command: to believe in the name of His Son, Jesus Christ, and to love one another as He commanded us. The one who keeps God's commands lives in Him, and He in them. And this is how we know that He lives in us: We know it by the Spirit He gave us.* (1 John 3:23-24, NIV)

Did you ever attempt to take a class in school and then discover you couldn't because you had not taken the prerequisite? That meant that before you took chemistry, you had to take biology; or before you took calculus you had to take geometry and algebra.

Life has a lot of prerequisites. *The New Oxford American Dictionary* defines prerequisite as "a thing that is required as a prior condition for something else to happen or exist."

The Bible is likewise filled with prerequisites. In order for God to live in you and you to live in Him, it is necessary to meet the criteria. The prerequisite for that to happen is to keep His commandments. It seems rather harsh of God to require that you keep the commandments in order to have God in you and for you to be in God. Maybe it is the greatest prerequisite in the world.

It is necessary to ask the question, "What commandments?" Jesus said that His commandments are not burdensome. He undoubtedly was not speaking of the Mosaic Law or commandments, because not only were they a burden, but they were impossible to keep and brought death for breaking them. This passage in 1st John tells us that the commandments of Jesus are two-fold. The first commandment is to believe in the name of His Son, Jesus Christ. The second is to love one another.

And how do you know that He lives in you? You know because the Holy Spirit of God lives in you. He gave you the Holy Spirit to live within you in order that you will know you belong to Him. "For His Spirit joins with our spirit to affirm that we are God's children" (Romans 8:16, NLT).

~~

How's Your Soil?

And He was saying, "He who has ears to hear, let him hear [or listen]." As soon as He was alone, His followers, along with the twelve, began asking Him about the parables. And He was saying to them, "To you has been given the mystery of the kingdom of God, but those who are outside get everything in parables, so that while seeing, they may see and not perceive, and while hearing, they may hear and not understand, otherwise they might return and be forgiven." (Mark 4:9-12, NASB)

But prove yourselves doers of the word, and not merely hearers who delude themselves. (James 1:22)

Jesus was the Teacher of all teachers. He often taught in what we call parables. A parable is an earthly story with a heavenly meaning. It is a simple story taken from life and life experiences that conveys a deeper spiritual or moral teaching. Jesus was a master at telling these parables. One of His most famous parables was the parable of the sower or the soils. In it, He taught the principle of listening. It has been called the "Parable of Parables."

Jesus spoke many words. The Gospel of John says the world could not contain the words Jesus spoke. Through the use of simple stories, Jesus conveyed deep messages. The parable of the sower told of the scattering of the Word of God, using seeds to represent the Word. The places where the seed fell determined its effectiveness. Some died, some grew quickly then died, some were strangled by the weeds, and some produced a crop.

The difference in how the seed developed was in the kind of soil on which it fell. It is much like that with you. When you are ready to listen and apply the Word of God, you will hear a different message - a spiritual one that you can apply to your life. Listen with spiritual ears to hear spiritual messages.

~~

What's Your Aim in Life?

However, I consider my life worth nothing to me; my only aim is to finish the race and complete the task the Lord Jesus has given me - the task of testifying to the good news of God's grace. (Acts 20:24, NIV)

What are your goals, aims, objectives, and desires for your life? Are you ambitious about where you are headed? Do you see a future that will give you a sense of accomplishment and success? Your life may be lived with no goals or aims. It could be you are merely living in an existence with no real purpose. Over the past few years, much has been said about finding purpose for life. No doubt you have thought about your own life and your desires to find real meaning.

Life is filled with ups and downs, and curves and frustrations. Without an anchor that holds you fast, there is a good chance you are not getting much out of life, or maybe you would just like to find more.

The aim of the apostle Paul, as he shared with the elders at Ephesus, was to finish the race and complete the task that the Lord Jesus had given him. Let me assure you that God has a task for you, also. You may not be a missionary or a preacher or an apostle like Paul, but you still have a purpose - an aim in life.

Paul said his aim was to finish the task of testifying to the good news of God's grace. He was not only speaking of his personal experience of meeting Jesus on the road to Damascus but also his task of testifying that all of life is achieved, lived by, and finished with God's grace. His grace is sufficient, saving, serving, fulfilling, finishing, and final.

You have an aim in life also. No matter what your vocation, your family, your lot in life - you still have been put on earth to glorify God and tell of His amazing grace. It is simply to testify (tell) what the Lord has done for you. Tell someone today of your testimony of God's grace.

~~

Relief From Depression

September 19, 2013

> *How blessed is he whose transgression is forgiven, Whose sin is covered!*
> *How blessed is the man to whom the Lord does not impute iniquity,*
> *And in whose spirit there is no deceit!*
> *When I kept silent about my sin, my body wasted away*
> *Through my groaning all day long.*
> *For day and night Your hand was heavy upon me;*
> *My vitality was drained away as with the fever heat of summer.*
> *I acknowledged my sin to You, And my iniquity I did not hide;*
> *I said, "I will confess my transgressions to the Lord";*
> *And You forgave the guilt of my sin. (Psalm 32:1-5, NASB)*

David the psalmist consistently declared that people are blessed. Here he speaks to his own soul and instructs his soul to bless God. The thirty-second Psalm reminds the readers that they are blessed. Are you blessed? David's recollection of his own sins reminded him how blessed he was to be forgiven. As believers in Jesus Christ, we have already been forgiven through the death and resurrection of Jesus, and our faith in Him. David said that everyone who has been forgiven is blessed. The Old Testament idea of atonement says that the sins are covered, referring to the blood of the lamb sacrificed on the Day of Atonement.

David also declared a blessing on all whose iniquity God does not charge to their account, and in whose spirit there is no deceit. David then gave personal testimony to his own blessings. Before his confession of sin, his transparency, and his acknowledgment of his sins, he was physically sick. He described a person in deep depression. He was losing weight through his groaning all day long. He felt the guilt as if the heavy hand of God was on him.

It so affected his physical body that even his energy was gone. His vitality was drained like he had been out in the sunshine in the heat of summer. He was drained of his ability to function. He found the answer. He acknowledged his sin, and the guilt of his sin was gone. It is the feelings of guilt, which accompany your sin, that deprive you of your strength. Repent of your sin and find the refreshing that comes from God's forgiveness.

~~

Love as Jesus Loved
September 26, 2013

> *This is My commandment: Love each other in the same way I have loved you. There is no greater love than to lay down one's life for one's friends.*
> (John 15:12-13, NLT)

Whom do you love? Who loves you? How much do you love them? Jesus was near the end of His life and He gathered the disciples together for the last discourse. He was giving to them the instructions for being a true disciple. The primary emphasis of Jesus is "love." To this very day, the emphasis of those who are true disciples of Jesus is to love not only one another but to love our enemies as well.

The commandments of Jesus are not a burden to us. The commandments of Jesus can be summarized as "loving one another and believing in Him." Jesus reminded the disciples of the kind of love He wanted them to have. Jesus explained how His followers are to love, "as I have loved you." No doubt after following Jesus all over Palestine, they knew that He loved them. This close relationship is seen throughout the gospels. Jesus had placed the welfare of the disciples above His own. He has done that for you, too.

Within hours of this time of teaching, Jesus was arrested and later crucified. The reason was because of His love. John 3:16 tells us clearly, "For God so loved the world, that He gave His only begotten Son, that whoever believes in Him shall not perish, but have eternal life" (NASB). Jesus then reminded the disciples, using Himself as the example, there is no greater love than to lay down your life for your friends.

How valuable are people to you? You would probably give your life without question for your family and your close friends. One of the ways you are like Jesus is your willingness to sacrifice whatever it takes to express your unconditional love. Why not tell someone today that you love them? Why not show in your actions that you love someone? Do something for a family member or friend that they don't expect. Direct your love to someone and do something specific. Remember as you do, that Jesus did something very specific for you - He died for you on the cross. He died for you, His friend.

~~

You Have the Power October 3, 2013

Bear one another's burdens, and thereby fulfill the law of Christ.
(Galatians 6:2, NASB)

We who are strong ought to bear with the failings of the weak and not to please ourselves. (Romans 15:1, NIV)

For the entire law is fulfilled in keeping this one command: "Love your neighbor as yourself." (Galatians 5:14)

For you were called to freedom, brethren; only do not turn your freedom into an opportunity for the flesh, but through love serve one another. For the whole Law is fulfilled in one word, in the statement, "You shall love your neighbor as yourself." (Galatians 5:13-14, NASB)

The Bible is filled with admonitions to love one another. Through the love you give to others, you are bearing their burdens. To love someone, as Jesus loved us, is the fulfillment of the Law. Although it is impossible to keep the Law of Moses, the Scripture clearly teaches we are to allow the Holy Spirit to live His life through us, which is the fulfillment of the Law through love.

Render to all what is due them: tax to whom tax is due; custom to whom custom; fear to whom fear; honor to whom honor. Owe nothing to anyone except to love one another; for he who loves his neighbor has fulfilled the law. For this, "You shall not commit adultery, you shall not murder, you shall not steal, you shall not covet," and if there is any other commandment, it is summed up in this saying, "You shall love your neighbor as yourself." Love does no wrong to a neighbor; therefore love is the fulfillment of the law. (Romans 13:7-10)

Paul wrote in Galatians about freedom. There is no suggestion in Galatians that freedom means "freedom to do what we want" or "freedom to indulge in any kind of behavior" or "freedom from rules." It is the freedom to come to God by faith, unhindered by the knowledge that we are unable to conform to the Law. It is the freedom to accept Christ's sacrifice on the cross by faith, and in so doing, receive His mercy.

Paul never declared that believers are now allowed to do the things that the Law said were sin. On the contrary, he expects exemplary behavior from believers, and often defined that behavior in terms of the moral requirements of the Law. The Bible does not grant license to act as one pleases without accountability. Christ's death did not legitimize sinful behavior but rather, through the indwelling Holy Spirit, He gave believers the power to live righteously before God by faith.

~~

Who's Got the Power? October 10, 2013

> *For this reason I bow my knees before the Father, from whom every family in heaven and on earth derives its name, that He would grant you, according to the riches of His glory, to be strengthened with power through His Spirit in the inner man, so that Christ may dwell in your hearts through faith; and that you, being rooted and grounded in love, may be able to comprehend with all the saints what is the breadth and length and height and depth, and to know the love of Christ which surpasses knowledge, that you may be filled up to all the fullness of God. Now to Him who is able to do far more abundantly beyond all that we ask or think, according to the power that works within us, to Him be the glory in the church and in Christ Jesus to all generations forever and ever. Amen.* (Ephesians 3:14-21, NASB)

The Bible is rich with illustrations of prayer. Often these are the recorded prayers of God's greatest leaders and servants. In this case, the apostle Paul was writing to the Ephesian church and expressed his prayer for them. As in all our prayers, he appealed to the "Father" as the father of all mankind. Paul's prayer was specific. He prayed for the Ephesian church to be strengthened with God's power. The source of the power is God the Holy Spirit. The place of the power is in their inner being.

Paul also prayed they would be aware that Christ dwelt in their hearts by faith. The need to be rooted and grounded in love permeated his prayer. So much so, that he called for their deepest understanding of God's love for them - its breadth, length, height, and depth - the love that transcends the ability to even know completely.

The last part of Paul's prayer was that they be filled with the fullness of God. It is the power in the inner being, where the Holy Spirit dwells, that became Paul's main emphasis for prayer.

He finished with praise to the God who provides the power, strength, and love. Ultimately, his desire was that God be glorified.

Paul's prayer is also a prayer for you. You need the power, strength, and love of God in your life. Whether it is your individual life, the life of your family, or your church, you need a renewal of your dependence on the God who provides all things. Ask and you shall receive.

~~

Shut My Mouth

October 17, 2013

> *Then the Lord said to Job, "Do you still want to argue with the Almighty? You are God's critic, but do you have the answers?" Then Job replied to the Lord, "I am nothing - how could I ever find the answers? I will cover my mouth with my hand. I have said too much already. I have nothing more to say."* (Job 40:1-5, NLT)

Have you ever argued with God? If you have ever experienced a crisis in your life or the life of your family then you likely have. Job struggled with the loss of his family, his livelihood, and his possessions. As a result, he questioned God: "WHY ME?" Those were likely Job's constant words. He could not understand the reasons or the plans of God surrounding his troubles. You may have had a time when things made no sense to you. You were beside yourself and began to argue with God, and expressed your own, "WHY ME?"

God spoke to Job and asked him if he still wanted to argue and be God's critic. Job had questioned God for most of the book of Job. Finally near the end, God spoke to Job with some very pointed questions. The main gist of His questions dealt with the finiteness of Job and the opposing infiniteness of God. "Where were you?" was the question God asked Job in relationship to creation, and His control of the earth and its people.

> *Then the Lord spoke to Job out of the storm. He said: "Who is this that obscures My plans with words without knowledge? Brace yourself like a man; I will question you, and you shall answer Me. Where were you when I laid the earth's foundation? Tell Me, if you understand."* (Job 38:1-4, NIV)

After all of chapters 38 and 39, Job found that he was not God. He discovered that God has plans, and none of them can be thwarted. Job saw life from God's perspective and had a new answer. "I am nothing - how could I ever find the answers?" God alone knows why things happen. Job realized that in his finite wisdom he would never understand the ways of God. In response he simply said, "I will put my hand over my mouth and shut up." His recognition was that he had already said too much: "I will say no more."

Have you argued with God, only to realize in the end that God is in control and in charge of your life? To argue with God is futile. To trust Him is wisdom and strength.

~~

A Future and a Hope October 24, 2013

> *"For I know the plans I have for you," says the Lord. "They are plans for good and not for disaster, to give you a future and a hope."* (Jeremiah 29:11, NLT)

Jeremiah was an encourager as he wrote to the exiles in Babylon about their future. They had been in captivity long enough to know this was not where they wanted to spend the rest of their history. The Jewish people had already spent four hundred years in slavery in Egypt and now, because of disobedience, God had allowed them to be captured and sent into a subservient position in Babylon. Likely, they were saying to themselves: "Why?!" Yet they knew why - they had worshiped idols and disobeyed God. Have you ever been in a place or a time in life when you felt no hope, no direction, no plans for the future? It is not unusual to feel like you are in exile - living in a new land, and unprepared for what that means.

Jeremiah gave hope and instructions:
> *This is what the Lord of Heaven's Armies, the God of Israel, says to all the captives He has exiled to Babylon from Jerusalem: "Build homes, and plan to stay. Plant gardens, and eat the food they produce. Marry and have children. Then find spouses for them so that you may have many grandchildren. Multiply! Do not dwindle away! And work for the peace and prosperity of the city where I sent you into exile. Pray to the Lord for it, for its welfare will determine your welfare."* (Jeremiah 29:4-7)

To summarize his words: "Live a normal life. Continue to have houses, gardens, and families." Whenever you find yourself in a difficult place or set of circumstances, it is usually good to continue living life as usual.

He also told them:

This is what the Lord says: "You will be in Babylon for seventy years. But then I will come and do for you all the good things I have promised, and I will bring you home again." (Jeremiah 29:10)

God promised to bless them. He promised a future and a hope. They would go home - not soon, but after seventy years. They would be taking their grandchildren with them. In the meantime: don't give up, don't stop being productive, continue life as normally as possible. If you need hope and encouragement today, just remember the words of Jeremiah.

~~

Truth Revealed

For to us God revealed them through the Spirit; for the Spirit searches all things, even the depths of God. For who among men knows the thoughts of a man except the spirit of the man, which is in him? Even so the thoughts of God no one knows except the Spirit of God. (1 Corinthians 2:10-11, NASB)

For who has known the mind of the Lord, that he will instruct Him? But we have the mind of Christ. (1 Corinthians 2:16)

The deep things of God are not known because of our abilities or knowledge. They are revealed to us by God's Spirit. To know and to understand the things of God, is to allow the Holy Spirit to be our teacher. God made it clear that His thoughts are not our thoughts and His ways are not our ways. True wisdom is to understand things from God's perspective, and the only way that can happen is if the Holy Spirit shows us. The Scripture is not understood by man's grasp but by illumination of the Word through God's Holy Spirit.

The apostle Peter was asked by Jesus, "Who do you say that I am?" Peter answered, "You are the Christ, the Son of the living God." Jesus then explained to Peter that his understanding did not come from human abilities or knowledge but by God revealing Himself. The only way we know the spiritual things of God is through God revealing the truth to us. God lives in every believer through the Holy Spirit.

The only one who really knows what is in your thoughts is you. It is your human spirit that knows what is in you. It is also true of your thoughts, and understanding and knowledge of God. It only comes from God's Spirit. You have the mind of Christ.

Trusting God to reveal truth to your life is dependent on you allowing the Holy Spirit to reveal truth to you. Be open to God's revelation of Himself, His work, His truth, and His ways in your life. Trust God. He does want you to know the deep things of God. Let Him be your teacher.

~~

True and Faithful   November 14, 2013

> *And the hand of the Lord was with them, and a large number who believed turned to the Lord.*
> *Then when he [Barnabas] had come and witnessed the grace of God, he rejoiced and began to encourage them all with resolute heart to remain true to the Lord;*
> (Acts 11:21, 23; NASB)

The believers from Cyprus and Cyrene went to Antioch to tell the good news that Jesus Christ had died for their sins and had arisen. The Good News, the Gospel, is found throughout the Bible, but as spelled out in 1st Corinthians:

> *Now I make known to you, brethren, the gospel which I preached to you, which also you received, in which also you stand, by which also you are saved, if you hold fast the word which I preached to you, unless you believed in vain. For I delivered to you as of first importance what I also received, that Christ died for our sins according to the Scriptures, and that He was buried, and that He was raised on the third day according to the Scriptures,* (1 Corinthians 15:1-4)

In the passage from Acts, we see that large numbers believed and were born again. That is what happens when the Gospel is preached. Then they sent for Barnabas, the encourager, who upon his arrival, witnessed the grace of God through the changed lives of the people. He observed their faith and the new life of these believers, and rejoiced.

The Bible makes it clear that we are saved by God's grace through faith, but it is through the faith we have in Jesus Christ as the Son of God that opens the door for God's grace to save us. What a joy it is to see people come to know Jesus as Lord and Savior, and Life!

Barnabas, who was known as the Encourager or Son of Consolation, immediately began to encourage the believers to remain true to the Lord, knowing that temptation would come their way.

Temptation comes in many forms and in many ways, but the real temptation is to turn from our faith, or not trust God. Barnabas reminded them that because of the truth of the Gospel, they needed to remain true and faithful to Jesus Christ. What or whom are you trusting right now? Remain faithful to Jesus.

~~

Not a Guessing Game   November 21, 2013

> ... *(As it is written, "A father of many nations have I made you") in the presence of Him whom he believed, even God, who gives life to the dead and calls into being that which does not exist. In hope against hope he believed, so that he might become a father of many nations according to that which had been spoken, "So shall your descendants be."* (Romans 4:17-18, NASB)

God's will was that Abraham would be the father of many nations. He said, "I have made you." Abraham responded in faith to that which was the will of God. Abraham believed "so that he might become..." It was God's will revealed to Him that he acted upon in faith.

When his faith became united with God's will, then God's purpose was fulfilled. God has a purpose for all of us. When our faith becomes united with His will, then His purpose is fulfilled. God is looking to our faith in order to fulfill His purpose in us. The great Bible teacher, Ron Dunn, used to say: "Faith operates only within the boundaries of God's will."

In other words, without the knowledge of God's will, there can be no real faith. We cannot ask in faith if we are guessing at the will of God. Faith based upon our wishes, guesses, or desires, is nothing more than presumption. The prayer of faith is the prayer offered in the sure knowledge of God's will - it is not shooting in the dark, or hoping we will be lucky and hit the target.

Faith is not man's way of getting his own will done in heaven - it is God's way of getting His will done on earth. We must understand that faith itself is a gift from God. It is not an emotion we stir up. It is not a way of thinking positively. It is not "hoping real hard" for something. Biblical faith is a gift from God, and He will not grant us faith to believe something that is contrary to His will.

When Abraham believed God that he would be the father of many nations, he was responding to God's purpose and will. Faith enables us to cooperate with God's will.

~~

Thanksgiving Doorway November 28, 2013

Enter His gates with thanksgiving and His courts with praise.
Give thanks to Him, bless His name. (Psalm 100:4, NASB)

Be thankful in all circumstances, for this is God's will for you who belong to Christ Jesus. (1 Thessalonians 5:18, NLT)

It is good to give thanks to the Lord, and to sing praises to Your name, O Most High; To declare Your lovingkindness in the morning, and Your faithfulness every night, (Psalm 92:1-2, NKJV)

Now when Daniel knew that the writing was signed, he went home. And in his upper room, with his windows open toward Jerusalem, he knelt down on his knees three times that day, and prayed and gave thanks before his God, as was his custom since early days. (Daniel 6:10)

Throughout the Bible, we are encouraged to give thanks to God. The thanksgiving is not just for the good things that come our way but everything. We are even to enter into God's presence, His gates and courts, with a thankful heart. Daniel found that he would be condemned by his action of praying to God, and yet, he still went to God in prayer three times a day. His prayer was a prayer of thanksgiving.

Being thankful shows we understand that God is good. No matter what is happening in your life, God is there for you. He responds to your praise and thankfulness.
Give thanks to the Lord, for He is good! His faithful love endures forever.
(Psalm 107:1, NLT)

"We pray for the big things and forget to give thanks for the ordinary, small (and yet really not small) gifts." - Dietrich Bonhoeffer

~~

~ A Personal Note ~

Over the last few years of his life, a bunch of guys would spend Friday mornings at Starbucks visiting with Dennis. His delight in spending time with us, and his love for us, were what captured our hearts. Our discussions touched on many topics from fishing and camping, to witnessing and growing in discipleship, and on to discussing apologetics and addressing many theological questions. We were brothers with a kindred spirit. Dennis always had good input and a gracious spirit.

Our boisterous laughter at times consumed Starbucks, causing many comments about this group of guys who were having just too much fun. But it was our joyful spirit that opened many opportunities to share our faith with others. We developed many friends with the regular guests at Starbucks.

What we remember most about Dennis was his great enthusiasm for life and his tremendous love for people. We greatly miss that, but spending those times with Dennis enriched all our lives, and I know that we'll carry that enrichment with us to the end of our days here on earth.

~ DeWayne

~~

Body Building

December 5, 2013

> *Therefore I, the prisoner of the Lord, implore you to walk in a manner worthy of the calling with which you have been called,* (Ephesians 4:1, NASB)

> *…until we all attain to the unity of the faith, and of the knowledge of the Son of God, to a mature man, to the measure of the stature which belongs to the fullness of Christ.* (Ephesians 4:13)

> *… causes the growth of the body for the building up of itself in love.* (Ephesians 4:16)

Do you know someone who is a "body builder"? They are usually bulging from muscles that are taut, over extended, and have a look of fullness. It appears from the Bible that the apostle Paul, who wrote the book of Ephesians, was a sports fan. Often in his writings, he referred to terms that indicate so. He talked of boxing, racing, and here in these verses of growing the body, or body-building.

Maybe we could learn a little body-building technique from these simple plans. First, he said that to build our spiritual bodies, we need to walk. This is not a physical walk but a walk worthy of our calling. We have been called to be Christ-like in our behavior. To walk would be to exercise our life in such a way as to grow up into that which God desires for us to become.

The second lesson is to embrace unity. The body of Christ is united through Jesus. Anyone we meet who is a believer in Christ, is our partner. The apostle would admonish us to walk in unity. Our unity is built upon a common faith and knowledge of Jesus Christ. As we grow in unity, we also grow into maturity. Although we are in unity, we also celebrate our diversity. God has gifted each of us differently than other brothers and sisters in Christ. He has given each of us a unique personality, and different abilities and passions that make us a special person in Christ.

In order to be mature in Christ, we will need equipping. To be equipped is to be prepared for use. Ready to allow God to use your life and ministry for His glory?

The result of your growth in maturity is that the whole Body of Christ grows and builds itself up in love. Allow God to build you into His design for your life.

~~

Stress! December 12, 2013

> *Consider it all joy, my brethren, when you encounter various trials, knowing that the testing of your faith produces endurance. And let endurance have its perfect result, so that you may be perfect and complete, lacking in nothing.* (James 1:2-4, NASB)

Ever have any "trials" or stress in your life, family, business, church, or neighborhood? Maybe the stress is just inside you. What are you dealing with in your life that you would attribute to stress?

The bigger question may be, "What is the source of the stress?" Could it be the fear of the unknown, or the fear of the known? Could you have taken on more than you are capable of producing? Is the pressure from other people's expectations placing an undo amount of stress on you?

No doubt there are special times of the year, or specific times in our lives, when stress seems to be greatly overblown. Whether it is a holiday, a change in living conditions, a move, a new job, or no job, an illness, a broken relationship, or a failure of some kind or another - it is then that the pressure mounts and life seems out of control.

It is at those moments we need God's answer to stress. The book of James was written to give advice to a group of people who were having all kinds of pressure and stress in their lives. The advice was, first, to count it all joy: "Consider it all joy, my brethren, when you encounter various trials" (James 1:2). Of course, as most things, it is easier said than done, but God is giving us counsel in order to overcome the stress of life. Why would we ever count it joy? The word for "consider" means to put it in the ledger as a joy instead of something bad. There is a positive outcome of stress as we consider or count it joy.

Then, "knowing that the testing of your faith produces endurance. And let endurance have its perfect result, so that you may be perfect and complete, lacking in nothing" (James 1:3-4). In order for your life to be mature and complete, God uses stress. As you sense stress coming your way, just count it joy. Thank God for what He is doing in your life to grow you and produce the great plans He has for your life.

~~

Jesus Has the Cure   December 19, 2013

> *That night there were shepherds staying in the fields nearby, guarding their flocks of sheep. Suddenly, an angel of the Lord appeared among them, and the radiance of the Lord's glory surrounded them. They were terrified, but the angel reassured them. "Don't be afraid!" he said. "I bring you good news that will bring great joy to all people. The Savior - yes, the Messiah, the Lord - has been born today in Bethlehem, the city of David! And you will recognize Him by this sign: You will find a baby wrapped snugly in strips of cloth, lying in a manger." (Luke 2:8-12, NLT)*

The message and hope of the Christmas story is found in the middle of the tenth verse of Luke, chapter 2: "I bring you good news that will bring great joy to all people." It continues into verse eleven: "The Savior – yes, the Messiah, the Lord - has been born today in Bethlehem, the city of David!"

"Good News": the Gospel has come in the form of a person - not an ordinary person but God in human flesh. God, in order to give salvation and life to every person who believes, sent His only Son to take on the bodily form of a man named Jesus. He also sent Jesus to die for our sins and arise from the dead to give all His life.

The Christmas Story is the story of the God of creation coming to earth to be the Messiah of all people. The Good News was proclaimed by the angel and fulfilled the prophesies of the Hebrew Bible concerning the coming Messiah. This God/Man - Jesus - brought hope, joy, peace, forgiveness, and undeserved and unconditional love.

Why was it GOOD news? First, because it was from God. Second, because it was for all the people. Can you imagine someone finding a cure for cancer but announcing that it only worked for people of a certain race? That would not be good news for everyone, only a select group. The Gospel good news is for all people. No matter your past or your present circumstances, no matter your place in society, or your economic situation - the Gospel is for you.

Jesus was announced by the angel as the Savior of the whole world. He was declared the "Messiah" and the hope for all who believe. There is no better time than right now to place your faith in Him.

~~

Celebration   December 25, 2013

> *When they had seen this, they made known the statement which had been told them about this Child. And all who heard it wondered at the things which were told them by the shepherds. But Mary treasured all these things, pondering them in her heart. The shepherds went back, glorifying and praising God for all that they had heard and seen, just as had been told them.* (Luke 2:17-20, NASB)

Have you been to a celebration lately? What did you celebrate? Was it an anniversary, a graduation, a birthday, a retirement, or maybe just an evening at home? Celebration has the meaning of being emotionally, socially, and mentally involved in something of excitement. While watching their sheep, the shepherds had been startled by the angel of God. The result was a time of ecstatic celebration. The angel had announced the birth of the long-awaited Messiah. They were the first to celebrate what we call Christmas. Outside of Mary and Joseph, we know of no one who knew what was happening in the manger in Bethlehem.

The shepherds, Mary and Joseph, and all who heard about the Savior being born, give us a beautiful picture of true "celebration." What are the elements of celebration? Four words describe the response to the birth of Jesus. The first is **Proclaim**. The Bible tells us the shepherds made known what had been told to them. They let others know of this Christ Child who was God in human flesh.

The second word is **Wonder**. The sense of awe at the prospect of the Messiah's birth caused all who heard to wonder what the shepherds were talking about. We need a sense of wonder as we consider Jesus.

The third word is **Ponder**. The Bible tells us that Mary pondered these things in her heart. She thought through all the things which had been told to her and to the shepherds, and allowed these amazing things to dwell in her mind.

And the fourth word is **Praise**. The shepherds went back glorifying and praising God. These four words give us a perfect way to celebrate Christmas: Proclaim, Wonder, Ponder, and Praise - all to the glory of God.

~~

A New Year's Resolution

> *Not that I have already reached the goal or am already fully mature, but I make every effort to take hold of it because I also have been taken hold of by Christ Jesus. Brothers, I do not consider myself to have taken hold of it. But one thing I do: Forgetting what is behind and reaching forward to what is ahead, I pursue as my goal the prize promised by God's heavenly call in Christ Jesus. Therefore, all who are mature should think this way. And if you think differently about anything, God will reveal this also to you. In any case, we should live up to whatever truth we have attained.*
> (Philippians 3:12-16, HCSB)

Do you make New Year's resolutions? You probably do but also realize that it doesn't mean anything. Here is a suggestion for this New Year: mature into the believer that you already are in Christ. You are, in Christ, a new creation - old things are passed away and all things have become new, as written in 2nd Corinthians 5:17.

The apostle Paul, the writer of the book of Philippians, was on a quest to become a mature believer. He was aware that in everyday life, he had not yet arrived at maturity or, as some translations say, "perfection." Yet Paul desired to continue to be all that God wanted him to be in Christ.

In order to reach the goal of Romans 8:29, "conformed" to the image of Christ, he realized some steps of action needed to be taken. First, he needed to forget "what is behind." The Christian life is a forward-looking experience. In a desire for maturity in Christ, Paul chose to forget the past with its failures and look forward to what lies ahead.

His goal was to reach the prize of spiritual maturity and the prize of God's heavenly calling in Christ. He admonished the believers at Philippi to think this way. In other words, he reminded them of who they were in Christ and the need to become, in daily life, who they already were in Christ. The Colossians received a word from Paul in Colossians 2:10, "In Him you have been made complete" (NASB). You are in Christ, complete in Him, and made new in Him; and yet there is a need for the daily life to become mature in Christ, as you are already complete in Him.

What a great New Year's resolution! "Therefore, all who are mature should think this way" (Philippians 3:15, HCSB). Live up to the maturity you have already attained in Him (vs. 16).

~~

The Memory of Victories
January 8, 2014

> *David said to Saul, "Let no man's heart fail on account of him; your servant will go and fight with this Philistine." Then Saul said to David, "You are not able to go against this Philistine to fight with him; for you are but a youth while he has been a warrior from his youth."* (1 Samuel 17:32-33, NASB)

Saul was not the most encouraging person in the world. The young teenager, David, volunteered to fight the giant Goliath. Saul's response was that David did not have a chance against this seasoned warrior. David heard, "You can't do this." Instead, David relied on his faith.

The question to ask is, "Where did he get such faith?" It would be easy to say that he just trusted God, or that God was in control, but maybe more importantly, David had vivid memories of his past experiences.

> *But David said to Saul, "Your servant was tending his father's sheep. When a lion or a bear came and took a lamb from the flock, I went out after him and attacked him, and rescued it from his mouth; and when he rose up against me, I seized him by his beard and struck him and killed him. Your servant has killed both the lion and the bear; and this uncircumcised Philistine will be like one of them, since he has taunted the armies of the living God."* (1 Samuel 17:34-36)

David's past experience told him that God would bring victory over Goliath. Do you remember past encounters with struggles, difficulties, and seemingly impossible situations? How did you make it? What happened? It could be that what happened in the past can happen again. David knew he had killed lions and bears with his bare hands. The thought of a giant was not a time for fear but for anticipating a new victory. Remembering our past can bring triumph in the present and the future.

The best way to defeat the giants and faith killers in our lives is with "God memories." Our greatest defense against attack is a remembrance of the God memories of yesterday. How we remember yesterday will determine how we live today and tomorrow.

As you discover how to bring good memories to the surface, you will find new strength to fight the giants. Remember, "What, then, shall we say in response to these things? If God is for us, who can be against us?" (Romans 8:31, NIV). "In all these things we are more than conquerors through Him who loved us" (Romans 8:37).

~~

Pride???

In the year of King Uzziah's death I saw the Lord sitting on a throne, lofty and exalted, with the train of His robe filling the temple. (Isaiah 6:1, NASB)

The words of Isaiah in this sixth chapter are some of the most quoted of all scripture. You likely have read it, heard a sermon taken from it, or maybe even memorized sections of chapter 6. Do you know how or why Uzziah died? Have you considered the importance of Isaiah entering the Temple? The Scripture says of Uzziah in 2nd Chronicles 26:4 –

He did right in the sight of the Lord according to all that his father Amaziah had done. He continued to seek God in the days of Zechariah, who had understanding through the vision of God; and as long as he sought the Lord, God prospered him.

From reading this passage, it seems that Uzziah was a great man of God. Yet the Bible gives us a different picture later in his life. It tells us of the real struggle of Uzziah in his relationship with God and in his character. He was a man with a severe pride issue. Pride is listed as one of the seven deadly sins. The book of Proverbs says that pride goes before a fall.

Uzziah was a great leader. He led Israel into victory in war. He improved their capacity in growing crops. He built towers and buildings. Through his leadership, the nation developed many wells to water the large herds of cattle. His elite army numbered over 307,500 warriors. Verse 15 says, "Hence his fame spread afar, for he was marvelously helped until he was strong."

Continuing in verse 16:

But when he became strong, his heart was so proud that he acted corruptly, and he was unfaithful to the Lord his God, for he entered the temple of the Lord to burn incense on the altar of incense.

His pride led to his fall. He decided to enter the Temple to burn incense as only the priest could do. He was warned not to follow his pride, but he did - and while being implored not to do it, he became very angry. It was at that point that leprosy broke out on his forehead. Verse 21:

King Uzziah was a leper to the day of his death; and he lived in a separate house, being a leper, for he was cut off from the house of the Lord.

What a horrible end to the life of a man who had followed the Lord! His downfall was his own pride. He forgot that all he was, and all he had, came from God. He took the glory rather than give the glory to God. Be cautious that pride does not destroy your walk with God. Give Him all the glory.

~~

Don't Be Discouraged

January 22, 2014

> *David rose to his feet and said: "My brothers and my people! It was my desire to build a Temple where the Ark of the Lord's Covenant, God's footstool, could rest permanently. I made the necessary preparations for building it, but God said to me, 'You must not build a Temple to honor My name, for you are a warrior and have shed much blood.'*
> *He said to me, 'Your son Solomon will build My Temple and its courtyards, for I have chosen him as My son, and I will be his Father.'"*
> *Then David continued, "Be strong and courageous, and do the work. Don't be afraid or discouraged, for the Lord God, my God, is with you. He will not fail you or forsake you. He will see to it that all the work related to the Temple of the Lord is finished correctly."* (1 Chronicles 28:2-3, 6, 20; NLT)

King David desired more than anything to build a temple for God in order to house the Ark of the Covenant. Because David had been a warring king, God brought an end to his dream. David's son, Solomon, was chosen to build the Temple instead of David. History tells us of the magnificent structure of the Temple of Solomon. It would have brought joy and fulfillment to any father.

The last instructions that David gave to Solomon are found in verse 20. He encourages him to not be afraid and to be full of courage, and promised him that God would be with him until the Temple was finished correctly.

The Bible, in the New Testament, compares our own lives and bodies to the Temple:

> *Don't you realize that your body is the temple of the Holy Spirit, who lives in you and was given to you by God? You do not belong to yourself, for God bought you with a high price. So you must honor God with your body.* (1 Corinthians 6:19-20)

Don't be discouraged or afraid - God is at work in you, also. He will not fail you or forsake you. He will see that all the work related to you is also completed correctly.

~~

~ Personal Message from Dennis ~

February 10, 2014

Greeting from THE HOSPITAL:

Sorry I have not been in contact with you in the last week, but as you see, I am in the hospital. I came in on February 4 with jaundice, sepsis and fever, and lots of pain. I went straight from the ER to the ICU.

Surgery was done on the 6th to clean out the stent in the bile duct. On the 7th, the doctors added an additional stent. As of today, my bile duct is still not draining and the bilirubin is still above 5. Not sure what comes next, just praying for the liver to again function properly.

While here, I have developed a blood clot in the jugular vein. They have also found nodules on my thyroid. I am writing this shortened version of The Encourager to just ask for prayer. Love you all and appreciate your concern.

~ Dennis

~~

~ Note from Sandy ~

As you can see, Dennis' health continued to decline. The medical issues seemed to come closer and closer together. In his writings, you can see spaces of time with no messages. His physical energy was used to fight the cancer, and moments to think and write took too much energy for him.

But God was not silent in his life. Although Dennis was too weak to write, God used his voice to pray and minister to others while he was in the hospital. He shared with doctors, nurses, staff, and visitors about the wonderful God whom he served and how God was sparing his life because of prayer.

With each hospital visit, Dennis' strength would seem to increase. The doctors would meet his needs and then would simply shake their heads in wonder when a few days later, he would be released. His professional hospital family knew that Dennis was praying for them - even as they wheeled him to a surgical procedure. Aware that his time was short, it was important to Dennis to make the most of every opportunity to tell others of his Savior, the Lord Jesus Christ.

~ Sandy

~~

Hope of Glory   February 18, 2014

... Which is Christ in you, the hope of glory. (Colossians 1:27, NASB)

I have been crucified with Christ; and it is no longer I who live, but Christ lives in me; and the life which I now live in the flesh I live by faith in the Son of God, who loved me and gave Himself up for me. (Galatians 2:20)

One of the most amazing truths in all of scripture is that Christ lives in the one who believes in Him as Lord, Savior, and Life. The victory, joy, hope, peace, and love we experience as believers are all because of the indwelling Christ. The hope we have of heaven and eternal life is a result of Christ living in us. When we come to faith in Jesus through death with Him on the cross, we no longer live, but He lives in us. You live your life because He is in you.

The fifth chapter of the book of Romans tells us: "For if while we were enemies we were reconciled to God through the death of His Son, much more, having been reconciled, we shall be saved by His life" (Romans 5:10). He saves us by His life, by dwelling in us, and living His life out through us. The Christian life is His life lived through us. That is only possible because He is in us.

We *were* saved from sin and forgiven by His death and the blood He shed on the cross, but we *are* saved by His life dwelling in us. The victory of life is allowing the indwelling Christ to live His life out through us. The Christian life is truly an inside-out life.

The blessings we receive are a result of Him and not us. Our hope of glory, both now and in eternity, is a result of Him and not us. How easy it is to think we can accomplish that which only God can achieve. His power, His grace, His mercy, His authority, and His love are not within our ability to fulfill. Only Christ in us is our real hope.

That hope is far beyond anything you can even imagine. It is a life of faith in the Christ who lives in you. You can try and try, but only as you die to your own strength and abilities, can you find that it is Christ in you who is the only real hope of glory. Yield your life to Him right now and find His presence in you.

~~

Get to Give   February 26, 2014

> *"Give, and you will receive. Your gift will return to you in full - pressed down, shaken together to make room for more, running over, and poured into your lap. The amount you give will determine the amount you get back."* (Luke 6:38, NLT)

> *"… Remembering the words the Lord Jesus Himself said: 'It is more blessed to give than to receive.' "* (Acts 20:35, NIV)

When was the last time you received a gift? Was it on Christmas, a birthday, anniversary, or maybe Valentine's Day? How did you feel? Did you appreciate and enjoy the love and thoughtfulness of the person who gave it to you? How about the reverse? When did you last give a gift to someone? Maybe it wasn't a present wrapped in a nice package but maybe your time, your service, your kindness, or an expression of love. How did you feel then?

According to the words of Jesus, we should have received a greater blessing by giving than we did from receiving. There is an interesting thing about giving that defies logic. That truth is: as we give, we in turn receive. Not only do we receive, but we receive what we gave in fullness.

The words of Jesus in Luke 6:38 are quite clear: "The amount you give will determine the amount you get back." Jesus makes it clear that the gift we give, no matter what it is, will return to us. It will be measured by the amount we gave. It will be pressed down, like putting something into a container to make room for more. It will be shaken to take up empty space, and it will be running over.

What are you giving right now that God will bless you with in return? What do you do with what you have received back as a result of giving? The answer is clear also: give some more! Keep God's plan of economy working.

You will never out-give God and you will bring about God's circle of giving, in order to receive, in order to give some more. Blessings to you as you give however God has blessed you.

~~

Facing Your Giants   March 5, 2014

> Then David said to the Philistine, "You come to me with a sword, a spear, and a javelin, but I come to you in the name of the Lord of hosts, the God of the armies of Israel, whom you have taunted. This day the Lord will deliver you up into my hands, and I will strike you down and remove your head from you. And I will give the dead bodies of the army of the Philistines this day to the birds of the sky and the wild beasts of the earth, that all the earth may know that there is a God in Israel, and that all this assembly may know that the Lord does not deliver by sword or by spear; for the battle is the Lord's and He will give you into our hands." (1 Samuel 17:45-47, NASB)

Do you have a giant taunting you? Are you discouraged and feeling defeated? Does the giant seem insurmountable? Take a good look at how God deals with giants. Your giant may be a spiritual issue - you feel God is far away, sin keeps knocking at your door and you see no victory, or faith eludes you. Maybe your giant is financial - there seems to be no end to the debts, the overdue bills, and the lack of provisions for your needs. It could be you are facing the giant of broken relationships - with family members, your spouse, or a friendship that has gone south; and reconciliation has evaded you. Are you facing a physical giant? Your health has failed, the pain and devastation to your body is unbearable, and you don't know where to turn.

David found himself facing the giant, Goliath. No one in Israel was willing to face Goliath. He had poked fun at the whole nation and the response was fear. David took the challenge to go head-to-head with him. David's answer was based upon the recognition that the battle was not between him and the giant but between the giant and God. Your giant may be frustrating, discouraging, and defeating you, but don't ever forget that God is on your side.

God defeated Goliath, but David's part was faith. Trust God with whatever giant you are facing today. "Faith is the victory!" (1 John 5:4, my paraphrase)

~~

You Cannot Lose

And when Christ, who is your life, is revealed to the whole world, you will share in all His glory. (Colossians 3:4, NLT)

For to me, to live is Christ and to die is gain. (Philippians 1:21, NASB)

I have been crucified with Christ and I no longer live, but Christ lives in me. The life I now live in the body, I live by faith in the Son of God, who loved me and gave Himself for me. (Galatians 2:20, NIV)

No doubt you have heard someone say, "We need to be living for Jesus." Let's look at what the Bible says about living: to live a Godly life apart from Christ is impossible. You really can't live for Christ. Christ lives for you.

The sinful nature, with which we were born, led us to follow with a choice of sinning. We were condemned for our sin by a Holy God. His standard of living is not only based upon the commandments but also on "Be holy as I am holy." Both are impossible for anyone to accomplish. So what do we do to live?

The apostle Paul, in his writings to the Colossians, Philippians, and Galatians, said it well. He came to understand, through God's revelation, that the impossible was possible with Jesus Christ living His life in and through him. He said, "FOR TO ME to live is Christ" and "Christ, who is your life." He did not say to live for Christ but to allow Christ to live in you. The real life of a Christian is not the effort, or energy, or trying that is attempted by human means. The Christian life is one in which Christ lives in you. He is your source of life.

The only way possible to allow Christ to live in you, is to accept your crucifixion with and in Him when He was crucified, and to receive His resurrected life in you. One of Paul's favorite terms was "in Christ." Your life is lived by faith in the Christ who lives in you. That life is lived by FAITH.

The Bible not only says that to live is Christ but to die is gain. When you are IN CHRIST, you cannot lose. Living is Christ and dying is gain. Eternal life is the Christ life. It is the joy of knowing that you can't but He already has. He lives in you and you are living in victory. Why not surrender to the Christ who lives in you, to live your life for you, instead of you living for Christ?

~~

How Can You Tell? March 26, 2014

> *And this is His command: to believe in the name of His Son, Jesus Christ, and to love one another as He commanded us. The one who keeps God's commands lives in Him, and He in them. And this is how we know that He lives in us: We know it by the Spirit He gave us.* (1 John 3:23-24, NIV)

> *"I will ask the Father, and He will give you another Helper [or Comforter or Advocate – Greek 'paraklete'], that He may be with you forever; that is the Spirit of truth, whom the world cannot receive, because it does not see Him or know Him, but you know Him because He abides with you and will be in you. I will not leave you as orphans; I will come to you. After a little while the world will no longer see Me, but you will see Me; because I live, you will live also. In that day you will know that I am in My Father, and you in Me, and I in you."* (John 14:16-20, NASB)

How can you tell that you are a born again Christian? How do you know that you are a child of God? What is your evidence that you are truly a believer? The apostle John wrote not only the Gospel according to John but also three letters that bear his name. He spoke often of the third person of the Godhead - the Holy Spirit. He said you can know you are a believer because the Holy Spirit lives in you. The very presence of God in your life is IN YOU. He is the Spirit of Christ, the Holy Spirit. He testifies that you are a child of God as He lives in you.

John also said, in the Gospel according to John, that the Holy Spirit is the Helper or the Comforter who will not only live in us but will be with us forever. Those who are not saved and have not received Jesus as their Savior, Lord, and Life, cannot receive the Holy Spirit. It is only those who believe or have faith in Jesus whom the Holy Spirit comes to live within. He will abide with you forever.

We cannot see the Spirit of God. Jesus said of the Spirit that He is like the wind. We cannot see the wind, only the results. So it is with the Holy Spirit. You do not see Him, but you will see the results of His presence in you. The Holy Spirit brings to your life the fruit of the Holy Spirit, which includes love, joy, peace, patience, kindness, goodness, faithfulness, gentleness, and self-control. You see the Holy Spirit working in your life by what He does through you.

~~

No More! No More! April 8, 2014

> *Therefore there is now no condemnation for those who are in Christ Jesus. For the law of the Spirit of life in Christ Jesus has set you free from the law of sin and of death. For what the Law could not do, weak as it was through the flesh, God did: sending His own Son in the likeness of sinful flesh and as an offering for sin, He condemned sin in the flesh, so that the requirement of the Law might be fulfilled in us, who do not walk according to the flesh but according to the Spirit.* (Romans 8:1-4, NASB)

Probably no passage of scripture is any more concise in describing the Gospel than these first four verses of Romans, chapter 8. Many key words associated with the Gospel stand out in these scriptures.

But first is the phrase, "Now no condemnation." To be condemned means to be guilty, accountable, responsible, and judged. The Bible declares the great truth of the Gospel that in Christ there is "NO condemnation." That means that we are no longer guilty, no longer accountable, no longer judged or condemned; but the truth is that, in Christ, we have been set free. Other scriptures tell us we are free from all things. Here, the specific freedom deals with the demands of the Law of Moses. The Spirit of Christ has set us free from the law of sin and death brought about by the demands of the Law of Moses.

How was that possible? It became reality when God sent Jesus, His own Son in the likeness of sinful flesh, as an offering for sin. Jesus paid for our sin nature on the cross. He condemned sin in the flesh, His own flesh, in order that the requirement of the Law of Moses would be fulfilled. No one ever was able to do that except Jesus.

Your walk is no longer a walk of condemnation for sins and your sin nature but a walk in the Spirit of God. God's Holy Spirit within makes it possible for the requirements of the Law of Moses to be fulfilled in you, by the Christ who is in you.

~~

Who Is This Man?

April 15, 2014

> *"Therefore having overlooked the times of ignorance, God is now declaring to men that all people everywhere should repent, because He has fixed a day in which He will judge the world in righteousness through a Man whom He has appointed, having furnished proof to all men by raising Him from the dead." Now when they heard of the resurrection of the dead, some began to sneer, but others said, "We shall hear you again concerning this." So Paul went out of their midst. But some men joined him and believed, among whom also were Dionysius the Areopagite and a woman named Damaris and others with them.* (Acts 17:30-34, NASB)

The setting was Mars Hill in Athens, Greece. The speaker was the apostle Paul - the man named Saul who was converted to Christ on the road to Damascus, Syria. The audience was a very religious group of people of all persuasions who prided themselves on their intellectual approach to all of life, especially their religious beliefs. As Paul walked around Mars Hill, he found shrines and centers of worship to gods of all varieties. In the midst, he found an inscription that addressed "The Unknown God." The apostle used that phrase to tell them about the true God. This unknown God, he declared, brings about life and being.

From the beginning of his discourse, Paul let them know that the true God declares to everyone everywhere of the need to repent. He told them that this God demands repentance because He is going to judge the world in righteousness - that righteousness based on the perfect Son of God, Jesus Christ.

This Man, Jesus, proved He could be the judge because He arose from the dead. This declaration of the resurrected Jesus was not only sneered at by the crowd but outright rejected by most. Because of their willingness to at least listen, they told Paul they would talk about this later. Some believed in the message of the resurrected Savior - others did not.

The resurrection is the proof of the deity of Jesus and His saving power. It is still true today. Do you believe in the living Christ? He arose from the dead to give you life.

~~

A Sacrifice Was Made

April 23, 2014

> *After this, Jesus, knowing that all things had already been accomplished, to fulfill the Scripture, said, "I am thirsty." A jar full of sour wine was standing there; so they put a sponge full of the sour wine upon a branch of hyssop and brought it up to His mouth.*

Therefore when Jesus had received the sour wine, He said, "It is finished!" And He bowed His head and gave up His spirit. (John 19:28-30, NASB)

These two verses possibly contain the most important word in the entire New Testament. In the English language it is three words, but in the Greek language it is only one. The Greek word "Tetelestai" means "it is finished."

Jesus had been hanging on the cross for almost six hours. His body was already beaten, bleeding, and racked with pain; and death was near. Dehydration was causing Him to be extremely thirsty. He spoke from the cross the words, "I am thirsty." Sour wine was placed on a sponge and placed on a long pole. The pole gave the men at the bottom of the cross the ability to reach the mouth of Jesus. He tasted the sour wine and then refused it.

His next word was "Tetelestai." "It is finished." The word was, to the people watching, a word of defeat; but actually, it was a great word of victory. What Jesus said was not, "I am finished." It was not "I am dead." The word from Jesus meant it was finished. It was the third person singular perfect tense. It referred to the completed work that Jesus had come to earth to accomplish. He knew that all things had already been accomplished to fulfill the Scripture. He gave up His spirit. He died, but it was finished - the death of Jesus procured salvation for all mankind.

Jesus' death was for the sins of all people. The sacrifice and substitutionary death of Jesus meant that anyone who believes would be forgiven and given eternal life. "IT IS FINISHED" meant that a sacrifice had been, once and for all, completed. No longer was another sacrifice needed. God sent His Son as the substitute for every sinner.

> *He made Him who knew no sin to be sin on our behalf, so that we might become the righteousness of God in Him.* (2 Corinthians 5:21)

He died for you. No other sacrifice is needed. "IT IS FINISHED."

~~

He Is Trustworthy
April 30, 2014

Trust in the Lord and do good;
Dwell in the land and cultivate faithfulness.
Delight yourself in the Lord;
And He will give you the desires of your heart.
Commit your way to the Lord,
Trust also in Him, and He will do it.

He will bring forth your righteousness as the light
And your judgment as the noonday.
Rest in the Lord and wait patiently for Him;
Do not fret because of him who prospers in his way,
The steps of a man are established by the Lord,
And He delights in his way.
When he falls, he will not be hurled headlong,
Because the Lord is the One who holds his hand.
(Psalm 37:3-7, 23-24; NASB)

What are you worried about today? It is likely whatever you are thinking about right now. Worries have a way of controlling our thoughts. They fill our minds with the negative possibilities of every situation in life, without a single thought of God's amazing ability to meet our needs and hold onto our hand no matter what is transpiring in our life.

King David knew what it was like to worry, or as he called it "FRET." In his own life, he found himself worried about his enemies. As he often did, he reminded himself, as well as the reader, that trust is the answer to worry, fretting, and anxiety. Jesus even told us not to be anxious about anything.

Well, what is the antidote for fretting? Can we find an answer to our worrying? The psalmist said the answer is "trust." "Trust in the Lord." Delight yourself in Him instead of dwelling on the cause of your worry. Commit your way, or your steps of life, to God. Then you must rest in that trust and commitment. Why does that work? It works because God is trustworthy. He establishes your steps and delights in His way for you. So when you have a difficulty, you will not fall headlong - because He holds onto you. Don't fret or worry or be anxious. Trust God.

~~

Finding Life

May 7, 2014

Now there were certain Greeks among those who came up to worship at the feast. Then they came to Philip, who was from Bethsaida of Galilee, and asked him, saying, "Sir, we wish to see Jesus." Philip came and told Andrew, and in turn Andrew and Philip told Jesus. But Jesus answered them, saying, "The hour has come that the Son of Man should be glorified. Most assuredly, I say to you, unless a grain of wheat falls into the ground and dies, it remains alone; but if it dies, it produces much grain. He who loves his life will lose it, and he who hates his life in this world will keep it for eternal life. If anyone serves Me, let him follow Me; and where I am, there My servant will be also. If anyone serves Me, him My Father will honor." (John 12:20-26, NKJV)

Have you ever had someone tell you they only believe the "red letter" parts of the Bible? Many Bibles highlight the words of Jesus in red letters. It identifies what Jesus actually said. Some people who desire to reject the Bible as the Word of God, will often resort to saying they only believe the words of Jesus. In this section, Jesus did speak. He shared words of truth that, for many, are hard. In this case, there were a group of Greeks who came to worship at a Jewish feast. They had only one request: "Sir, we wish to see Jesus."

Jesus communicated through several of the disciples who heard the request. Undoubtedly, they were not prepared for His statement. In prediction of His death on the cross, He said these words, "The hour has come that the Son of Man should be glorified. Most assuredly, I say to you, unless a grain of wheat falls into the ground and dies, it remains alone; but if it dies, it produces much grain."

Jesus compared Himself to a plant - in order to produce fruit, it has to germinate. The grain that is planted dies. He was preparing to die, in order to give life. He then said that if anyone wants to find life, they must die. The great words from Jesus were simply, "You must die in order to live."

~~

Simply Believe

May 21, 2014

> *Jesus answered them and said, "Truly, truly, I say to you, you seek Me, not because you saw signs, but because you ate of the loaves and were filled. Do not work for the food which perishes, but for the food which endures to eternal life, which the Son of Man will give to you, for on Him the Father, God, has set His seal." Therefore they said to Him, "What shall we do, so that we may work the works of God?" Jesus answered and said to them, "This is the work of God, that you believe in Him whom He has sent." So they said to Him, "What then do You do for a sign, so that we may see, and believe You? What work do You perform? Our fathers ate the manna in the wilderness; as it is written, 'He gave them bread out of heaven to eat.'" Jesus then said to them, "Truly, truly, I say to you, it is not Moses who has given you the bread out of heaven, but it is My Father who gives you the true bread out of heaven. For the bread of God is that which comes down out of heaven, and gives life to the world." Then they said to Him, "Lord, always give us this bread." Jesus said to them, "I am the bread of life; he who comes to Me will not hunger, and he who believes in Me will never thirst." (John 6:26-35, NASB)*

Jesus often did miracles that were considered by the people to be "signs." The proof of someone's leadership and authenticity was their ability to perform. Jesus had just fed 5,000 people with five barley loaves and two small fish. The people were astounded at the sign but were more impressed that their hunger was satisfied.

Jesus told the crowds that their interest in Him was not about signs but the fact they were fed. He mentioned the work of God, and the people responded with the question, "What shall we do, so that we may work the works of God?" Jesus' answer was FAITH - simply to believe is the work of God. They were not satisfied and wanted some proof in order that they might believe. Remember, they had just seen Him feed thousands. They then told Him that Moses gave a sign by providing manna out of heaven. They asked, "What then do You do for a sign, so that we may see, and believe You? What work do You perform?"

Jesus told them Moses did not provide the manna but that God the Father did. Jesus then announced that just as God provided manna from heaven, He was now providing Jesus - the Bread of Life - and that whoever believes in Him would have eternal life. Do you have Jesus today? Why not believe in Him as the only Son of God? Jesus revealed the Father to all humanity. His greatest sign was His death and resurrection. The work God wants from you is to believe in Him.

~~

Lord, Teach Me to Pray   May 28, 2014

It happened that while Jesus was praying in a certain place, after He had finished, one of His disciples said to Him, "Lord, teach us to pray just as John also taught his disciples." (Luke 11:1, NASB)

"So I say to you, ask, and it will be given to you; seek, and you will find; knock, and it will be opened to you. For everyone who asks, receives; and he who seeks, finds; and to him who knocks, it will be opened." (Luke 11:9-10)

Jesus' disciples had undoubtedly heard John the Baptist's followers pray. They discovered that John had taught his followers to pray, so they asked Jesus to teach them to pray in a similar way. Jesus taught them three things. He taught them a model prayer that we often call "The Lord's Prayer." This model prayer has been used for all of Christendom.

He then taught them to be persistent in prayer. The story He told was of a man who had guests show up at midnight, and then went next door and awakened his neighbor to ask to borrow three loaves of bread. The neighbor refused, but the man who needed the bread kept on asking. Finally, the neighbor gave him what he wanted. "I tell you, even though he will not get up and give him anything because he is his friend, yet because of his persistence he will get up and give him as much as he needs" (Luke 11:8).

In order to continue His emphasis on persistence, Jesus said that if you will keep on asking, keep on seeking, and keep on knocking, the answer will come. "For everyone who asks, receives; and he who seeks, finds; and to him who knocks, it will be opened" (Luke 11:10).

Jesus further explained to the disciples that God is not like the neighbor who was unwilling. God is your Father who desires to meet your needs with what you ask. "If you then, being evil, know how to give good gifts to your children, how much more will your heavenly Father give the Holy Spirit to those who ask Him?" (Luke 11:13)

Are you persistent in prayer? Are you asking and believing that your Heavenly Father will answer your prayers? Don't ever give up!

~~

Do You Hear the Whisper?   June 4, 2014

> *Now when evening came, His disciples went down to the sea, and after getting into a boat, they started to cross the sea to Capernaum. It had already become dark, and Jesus had not yet come to them. The sea began to be stirred up because a strong wind was blowing. Then, when they had rowed about three or four miles, they saw Jesus walking on the sea and drawing near to the boat; and they were frightened. But He said to them, "It is I; do not be afraid." So they were willing to receive Him into the boat, and immediately the boat was at the land to which they were going.*
> (John 6:16-21, NASB)

Jesus and His disciples had just observed one of the most remarkable miracles recorded in the Bible - the feeding of the five thousand with five loaves of barley and two small fish. Jesus, in a somewhat usual pattern, went into the wilderness to be alone. Likely exhausted from ministry during the day, He retreated for some time to be alone.

The disciples moved toward the sea, their place of retreat. Jesus was not with them as they climbed into their boats to travel to Capernaum. It was already dark. The sea became restless as the strong winds began to blow. Three or four miles out into the sea, they saw Jesus. He was not in another boat but was walking on the water - another incredible miracle.

Seeing Jesus walking on the water and coming near the boat, caused them to respond with fear. Jesus, in His concerned way, simply told them, "I am here. Do not be afraid." He climbed into the boat with them and soon they were in Capernaum.

How often are you afraid? Fear is a driving factor in most people's lives. The fear includes family, jobs, health, spiritual needs, and a plethora of life's dilemmas. What do you hear when you are afraid? You, more than likely, have thoughts in your mind that make it even worse. The need is to listen to the voice of Jesus. He is whispering in your ear, "I am here. Do not be afraid." Jesus has promised to never leave you or forsake you. He is here with you right now.

~~

No "Shrinking Violets" Here

June 11, 2014

But the eleven disciples proceeded to Galilee, to the mountain which Jesus had designated. When they saw Him, they worshiped Him; but some were doubtful. And Jesus came up and spoke to them, saying, "All authority has been given to Me in heaven and on earth. Go therefore and make disciples of all the nations, baptizing them in the name of the Father and the Son and the Holy Spirit, teaching them to observe all that I commanded you; and lo, I am with you always, even to the end of the age."
(Matthew 28:16-20, NASB)

The number of disciples had shrunk from twelve to eleven. Jesus had asked them to meet Him on the mountain. The thoughts going through their minds had to be greatly mixed. They may have considered that it was now the time for the overthrow of the Roman government. It could be they knew that something of major consequences was about to transpire. No matter what they were thinking, it was obvious they were meeting with the One who had risen from the dead and was promising to leave them. Their reaction was worship and yet doubt. Is Jesus really God? Was He expecting something from them? Whatever would greet them when Jesus arrived, was going to be overwhelming.

It was just that. Jesus announced that He had all authority in heaven and on earth, and then spoke to the disciples with the authority that let them know He was giving them the same authority. The words from Jesus could more likely mean, "As you are going about life, MAKE DISCIPLES!" They were disciples but Jesus wanted the message passed on to others. How was that to happen? It would be accomplished as the existing disciples followed Jesus' instructions: "As you go, make disciples of all peoples on the earth. As the nations believe, baptize them. But more than that, teach them everything I have taught you." Three years of following Jesus was not just to learn but to learn in order to pass it on.

The promise of Jesus to them was simply, "I will be with you to the end of the age." For all of their lives, the person of the Holy Spirit would empower them with the authority of Jesus to make disciples, much like they had become disciples. That command from Jesus has not changed. You are still called to make disciples.

~~

~ Personal Message from Dennis ~ June 30, 2014

Greetings from home in beautiful Tempe, AZ

Sorry I have been unable to send out The Encourager for the past couple of weeks. Due to being in the hospital and recovery at home, it was just not possible. This is going to be abbreviated.

The hospital stay was for 11 days during which time I had 5 surgical procedures. As of today I am still jaundiced, on antibiotics, quite weak, still struggling with pain, and awaiting an outpatient procedure tomorrow. Another major procedure is tentatively scheduled in another 2-3 weeks. I so desire your prayers for that important procedure.

I am doing basically nothing - just not able. Please forgive me if I am unable to answer your emails. They are so important. Blessings to all of you. Love you much.

~ Dennis

~~

Only Trust Him July 15, 2014

> *Now faith is the assurance of things hoped for, the conviction of things not seen.* (Hebrews 11:1, NASB)

Dictionary.com defines "trust" with these words:
1. reliance on the integrity, strength, ability, surety, etc., of a person or thing; confidence.
2. confident expectation of something; hope.
3. confidence in the certainty of future payment for property or goods received; credit: *to sell merchandise on trust.*
4. a person on whom or thing on which one relies: *God is my trust.*
5. the condition of one to whom something has been entrusted.

Where, or in whom, do we put our trust? Obviously, God Himself is the only One worthy of our trust, our hope, and our confidence. But what is our choice?

The choice is to trust God alone. The book of Hebrews proclaims that is done by faith. Faith itself is the assurance of the future hope. Faith is the conviction of that which we don't even see. Otherwise, it would not be faith.

What is going on in your life for which God is the answer? Likely everything. What a great time to trust and have faith in God! When all you have left is Jesus, you will find He is the only One you ever really needed. Blessings to you, as you trust God.

~~

Why Exult in the Lord? August 6, 2014

> *Though the fig tree should not blossom and there be no fruit on the vines,*
> *Though the yield of the olive should fail and the fields produce no food,*
> *Though the flock should be cut off from the fold*
> *And there be no cattle in the stalls,*
> *Yet I will exult in the Lord, I will rejoice in the God of my salvation.*
> (Habakkuk 3:17-18, NASB)

Over forty years ago, a friend wrote those two verses on a small piece of paper. I have carried it in my wallet. Every so often I read it and remind myself that the reason for exulting is the Lord Himself and my joy is in the God of my salvation.

The past seven weeks have been a time for me to exult and rejoice in the Lord. My physical situation is still not good. I still struggle with pain, have had seven surgical procedures, and have weight loss and weakness. Your prayers, cards, phone calls, visits, and emails have been an encouragement to me. Thanks so much. I love all of you and appreciate your love.

~ Dennis

~~

Our Confidence August 13, 2014

> *Such confidence we have through Christ toward God. Not that we are adequate in*
> *ourselves to consider anything as coming from ourselves, but our adequacy is from*
> *God, who also made us adequate as servants of a new covenant, not of the letter but*
> *of the Spirit; for the letter kills, but the Spirit gives life.*
> (2 Corinthians 3:4-6, NASB)

FINALLY AN ANSWER:

Surgery is scheduled for next Monday, the 18th. I am to be at the hospital at noon for surgery at 2 p.m. The surgery should take extra time (4-6 hours). Please be in prayer.

Any time you are struggling, humor always seems to help. I was with grandsons Bennett, Burke, and Collin and decided we needed a Gang. Now we call ourselves the "Cane Gang."

~ Dennis

~~

~ Note from Sandy ~

Dennis' surgery went even longer than predicted... but he was released from the hospital after eight days, and the following week he was able to resume his writing of the Encourager messages and enjoy the coffee shop visits to reach out to so many people. Dennis and I took our three older grandsons to the mountains just after the lengthy hospital stay. The family was not in favor of the trip but the boys promised to be very helpful - they wanted to go to the mountains and so we did. We laughed a lot, watched crazy movies, and ate out every meal. The short trip was just the medicine that Dennis needed. As we returned to the valley, Dennis' mind and heart refocused on his mission: sharing the love of Christ with anyone who would listen.

~ Sandy

~~

Have You Met the Enemy?   August 25, 2014

> *Be serious! Be alert! Your adversary the Devil is prowling around like a roaring lion, looking for anyone he can devour. Resist him and be firm in the faith, knowing that the same sufferings are being experienced by your fellow believers throughout the world. Now the God of all grace, who called you to His eternal glory in Christ Jesus, will personally restore, establish, strengthen, and support you after you have suffered a little. The dominion belongs to Him forever. Amen.* (1 Peter 5:8-11, HCSB)

Do you have a roaring lion growling at you from the bushes, behind the rocks, and is he loud and scary? He is there only to make loud noises. He was defeated at the cross and in the resurrection of Jesus Christ. He is your adversary but a defeated one. Then what is really happening? Satan, the devil, wants to distract us from our faith. He tries to get us away from our faith in Jesus Christ and trust the world around us. He wants us focused on our problems, our sufferings, and trials. Of course, none of those things can happen apart from God allowing them to enter our lives.

God also has a purpose. The God of all grace will meet the enemy head on, and will do something to and in us. He called us to bring glory to Jesus Christ. Through all we suffer or struggle with, it is God who will Himself personally restore us, establish us, strengthen us, and support us. "AFTER YOU HAVE SUFFERED A LITTLE WHILE." This too came to pass.

How do you know? Because the Bible says that all the dominion, or the control, belongs to God forever. It then finishes with "AMEN"!!! LET IT BE!!! Praise the Lord.

~~

Where's Your Hope?   September 1, 2014

> *Now in this hope we were saved, yet hope that is seen is not hope, because who hopes for what he sees? But if we hope for what we do not see, we eagerly wait for it with patience.* (Romans 8:24-25, HCSB)

In the Spiderman 2 movie, Spiderman's girlfriend, as a valedictorian, makes a speech to her college class. Her theme is "hope." Her words are very much in tune with the biblical concept of hope. It is not a feeling but a determined belief that things will be good, be okay, and have positive results. When you say the word "hope," what are you really thinking? Is it like saying "I sure hope it rains today"? Or "I hope I win that contest." "I hope I get the raise." Is there an uncertainty to your hope? Biblical hope is never uncertain. It is based on truth and trust.

In the Hebrew Bible, there are 10 words translated "hope." The most common is "to wait with great expectation for something that will happen." There are only two words in the New Testament translated "hope." They mean "the act of expecting or trusting." The hope we have for future life and eternal life is because we hope in what we don't even see. It is "eagerly waiting" for what is coming but with patience. Are you hoping for something right now? You may not see how, when, or where the answer is coming but you are trusting that God is faithful.

Hope is a vital part of life. You will find that scripture says three things remain: "faith, hope, and love" (1 Corinthians 13:13).

Let us hold on to the confession of our hope without wavering, for He who promised is faithful. (Hebrews 10:23)

Never give up your hope.

~~

The Morning Is Coming
September 8, 2014

> *Weeping may spend the night, but there is joy in the morning.*
> (Psalm 30:5b, HCSB)

Ever go to bed with pain in your heart, your mind filled with "stinking thinking," and an overall attitude of catastrophizing? Did you discover the tears trickling off your cheek onto your pillow, and you just knew there was no hope? Don't feel badly. You are not alone. It is a common dilemma to see things darkly at night. It is not because it is dark outside or because the sun has gone down. It is because night is a time to dwell on the negative things of life.

But just wait! The morning is coming, and the light will shine in the darkness and overwhelm it. JOY comes in the morning even after a dark night. Someone has likely said to you, "Why don't you just go to bed and get a good night's rest? Everything will be better in the morning." Guess what? It will be.

The more important question you may struggle with is: "Why do I have to wait until morning?" There is a story in the New Testament of a "night of doom" that overcame the disciples. They were in a boat out on the Sea of Galilee when a terrible storm came up. They were catastrophizing. They were sure they would all die a horrible death.

> *Immediately He made the disciples get into the boat and go ahead of Him to the other side, while He dismissed the crowds. After dismissing the crowds, He went up on the mountain by Himself to pray. When evening came, He was there alone. But the boat was already over a mile from land, battered by the waves, because the wind was against them. Around three in the morning, He came toward them walking on the sea. When the disciples saw Him walking on the sea, they were terrified. "It's a ghost!" they said, and cried out in fear.*
> *Immediately Jesus spoke to them. "Have courage! It is I. Don't be afraid."*
> (Matthew 14:22-27)

You don't have to wait for morning. Remember, Jesus knows what is happening. He is prepared to come to you at any time. He is THE LORD OF THE NIGHT

WATCH. Even though you may be full of fear in the night, He will come to you anytime. He tells you to take courage, "It is I. Don't be afraid."

~~

God's Approval

September 15, 2014

> *By faith Enoch was taken up so that he would not see death; and he was not found because God took him up; for he obtained the witness that before his being taken up he was pleasing to God. And without faith it is impossible to please Him, for he who comes to God must believe that He is and that He is a rewarder of those who seek Him.* (Hebrews 11:5-6, NASB)

At the heart of mankind is the need for acceptance, approval, and to be pleasing. The very taproot of our need is to have other people approve of us. The more important issue is this: does God approve of you? You may be one of those people who just give up because you say that you can never receive God's approval. You may be one of those who try and try just to do the right things, or not do wrong things, to receive approval from God. Biblical characters, as well as most believers, really desire God's approval.

How do we know if we are pleasing to God? It is not in trying, or giving up. It is faith. Enoch is used as one of the examples in Hebrews chapter 11, as a man who was approved of by God. The Bible is quite clear that it was because of his faith. He never died but was taken up by God to heaven. How did that happen? It was because he believed that God is, and that He is a rewarder of those who seek Him.

The Bible is clear that we are saved from our sin and given eternal life by faith. "For by grace you have been saved through faith; and that not of yourselves, it is the gift of God" (Ephesians 2:8). Without faith it is impossible to please God or to even know Him.

The Bible also says, "The just shall live by faith" (Habakkuk 2:4, KJV). We are not only saved by faith, but we are kept in a relationship with God by faith. It would appear that our number one need is to trust God all the time.

The enemy would do anything and everything to destroy our faith. Be alert. Watch out for those times when your faith is tested and the enemy lies to you about your relationship with God. Faith is the answer!!

~~

Dealing With Others September 22, 2014

But we request of you, brethren, that you appreciate those who diligently labor among you, and have charge over you in the Lord and give you instruction, and that you esteem them very highly in love because of their work. Live in peace with one another. We urge you, brethren, admonish the unruly, encourage the fainthearted, help the weak, be patient with everyone. See that no one repays another with evil for evil, but always seek after that which is good for one another and for all people. Rejoice always; pray without ceasing; in everything give thanks; for this is God's will for you in Christ Jesus. Do not quench the Spirit; do not despise prophetic utterances. But examine everything carefully; hold fast to that which is good; abstain from every form of evil.
(1 Thessalonians 5:12-22, NASB)

The Bible often gives us words of encouragement, admonishment, counsel, and requests. In the apostle Paul's letter to the Thessalonians, he gave a long series of words of advice and counsel. He was writing directly to believers in Jesus Christ. First of all, he told them to appreciate their spiritual leaders. His encouragement was to esteem them very highly in love because of their labor towards the believers.

Then Paul gave advice as to how to deal with different types of fellow believers. He urged the believers to admonish the unruly, encourage the fainthearted, help the weak, and be patient with everyone. There are some within the flock who need to be reprimanded, some who are discouraged and need to be uplifted, and some who are so weak they cannot do anything for themselves. Paul said that we need to deal with each one as needed. He added a way to show love to everyone - simply being patient with everyone.

He quickly reminded them to not "get even" but to seek what is good for everyone. And then in five short but to-the-point verses, he said: rejoice always, pray without ceasing, give thanks in everything, do not quench the Spirit, do not despise prophetic utterances, examine everything carefully, hold on to the good, and abstain from evil. Good advice for you, as you find purpose for your life today.

~~

At the Right Time September 29, 2014

But when the fullness of the time came, God sent forth His Son, born of a woman, born under the Law, so that He might redeem those who were under the Law, that we might receive the adoption as sons. Because you are sons, God has sent forth the Spirit of His Son into our hearts, crying, "Abba! Father!" Therefore you are no longer a slave, but a son; and if a son, then an heir through God. (Galatians 4:4-7, NASB)

Everything just came together perfectly. That could be said of a football game. The penalty that cost the other team that precious fifteen yards was just perfect. The catch in the end zone in the last fifteen seconds of the first half was likewise just perfect. What timing!! But the fumble, recovery, and eighty-yard run clinched the game. Your team won because everything came at just the right time. Ever think, of the things in your life, that timing was everything? If it had not been just the right time, you would have missed meeting your wife or husband. Timing saved your life as the car sped across just seconds before you, instead of directly into your path.

The greatest timing that ever existed is found in this short passage in the book of Galatians: "When the fullness of the time came…" Not a coincidence but at just the perfect time, God sent His Son, Jesus, into the world. God became flesh and dwelt among us.

He was born to a human being, a woman under the Law, in order that He might save us, who were condemned by the Law. That perfect timing allowed us to receive our adoption into God's family. The birth, life, death, and resurrection of Jesus made a way possible for us to become children of God.

We no longer just call Him "God" - we call Him "Abba, Father." Although we were slaves to sin and the Law, we are now free to a new relationship with God. He is our Father, our Abba. The amazing part is that it happened at the perfect time. The time was God's choosing. It was the fullness of time. We became heirs of all God has for us. We received an inheritance from God, through God.

Rejoice in God's timing, God's plan, God's provision of His Son, and God's relationship with you as His child. Live in the freedom you have from the condemnation of the Law, and the newly found inheritance you have in Jesus.

~~

From the Inside Out

October 6, 2014

Ephesians 3:16 -
I pray that out of His glorious riches He may strengthen you with power through His Spirit in your inner being, (NIV)

I pray that from His glorious, unlimited resources He will empower you with inner strength through His Spirit. (NLT)

... That He would grant you, according to the riches of His glory, to be strengthened with power through His Spirit in the inner man, (NASB)

"How did you make it through? How did you survive? Where did you find the strength to endure?" You likely have heard someone asked such questions. Usually it means that person has experienced a difficult trial or struggle in life that most people would not have survived. Instead, the person not only survived but, in turn, actually thrived.

The answer for Christians is that there is an inner strength, an inner power, something beyond them but still in them. Likely you have experienced something in your life where an inner strength or power overcame you, and you found strength to rally and make it through.

The apostle Paul, writing to the Colossian church, reminded them of his prayers for them in order that they would discover the glorious unlimited resource of God: HIS HOLY SPIRIT WITHIN EVERY BELIEVER. God the Holy Spirit is in you to give you the power you will need for whatever comes your way.

The Holy Spirit is not just an ethereal power but a real person - God Himself living in you. Next time you face something overwhelming in your life, just remember that you are not alone. God is in you to strengthen you from the inside out. I am praying that you would be empowered by His unlimited resources for your life today. To Him be the glory.

~~

Bold Curiosity   October 13, 2014

The New Birth
Now there was a man of the Pharisees, named Nicodemus, a ruler of the Jews; this man came to Jesus by night and said to Him, "Rabbi, we know that You have come from God as a teacher; for no one can do these signs that You do unless God is with him." Jesus answered and said to him, "Truly, truly, I say to you, unless one is born again he cannot see the kingdom of God."
Nicodemus said to Him, "How can a man be born when he is old? He cannot enter a second time into his mother's womb and be born, can he?" Jesus answered, "Truly, truly, I say to you, unless one is born of water and the Spirit he cannot enter into the kingdom of God. That which is born of the flesh is flesh, and that which is born of the Spirit is spirit. Do not be amazed that I said to you, 'You must be born again.'"
(John 3:1-7, NASB)

Someone has said, "Curiosity killed the cat." I assume that means the cat was curious and stuck its head into someplace where it could not get loose. Curiosity doesn't always kill - in fact, often it is the beginning of life. Nicodemus was curious. He had an inquiring mind. He wanted to know more about this man, Jesus. The stories were circulating about His healing, His teaching, and His holy ways. It was because of this, Nicodemus asked for a night meeting. His desire to know more about Jesus led him to make a bold statement: "Rabbi, we know that You have come from God as a teacher; for no one can do these signs that You do unless God is with him."

The statement from Nicodemus indicated he recognized Jesus as more than an ordinary man, but still he did not go beyond the description of Jesus as a great teacher sent from God. Jesus immediately threw a statement back to Nicodemus: "Truly, truly, I say to you, unless one is born again he cannot see the kingdom of God." The response from Nicodemus was typical. To paraphrase, "How can I be born when I already am?" Jesus then answered that to enter the kingdom of God, you have to be born physically and spiritually.

Jesus' emphatic statement, "You must be born again" indicates that every human being needs to experience a new birth to gain eternal life. Believing that Jesus was a great teacher, prophet, humanitarian, or full of good works is not sufficient.

Jesus claims Himself to be the Son of God. Faith in Jesus as God Himself is necessary for new birth and eternal life. If you have not placed your faith in Him, why not right now?

~~

God's Character
October 29, 2014

> ...(As it is written, "A father of many nations have I made you") in the presence of Him whom he believed, even God, who gives life to the dead and calls into being that which does not exist. (Romans 4:17, NASB)

Do you struggle with faith? Do you feel that your faith is weak or non-existent, and yet you have a relationship with God? Maybe the real issue is not your faith but your understanding of the character and nature of God. It just might be that your struggle with trusting God is based on a misconception of who God is. The apostle Paul, in writing to the church at Rome, recognized their struggle with faith. He used Abraham as an example of someone who trusted and had faith in God. Because of Abraham's faith, God blessed him and made of him the great nation He had earlier promised. The answer to that promise came not as a result of Abraham's deeds but his faith.

Outward evidence would have indicated to Abraham that the promise would never be fulfilled, but because Abraham knew God, he still believed. It is impossible to trust something or someone we don't know. We need to understand the character of God and His attributes in order to have faith in Him.

> The Lord also will be a stronghold for the oppressed,
> A stronghold in times of trouble;
> And those who know Your name will put their trust in You,
> For You, O Lord, have not forsaken those who seek You. (Psalm 9:9-10)

The word "name" means far more than we would mean when we say we know someone's name. It means we know Him and His character, and acknowledge His attributes. He is a stronghold. Thus He can be trusted.

Once we get to know His character, we learn to trust Him and express our faith in Him. Like the story of the little boy who was on the roof of the house, and the ladder broke. A man on the ground said, "Jump, I will catch you." The little boy's response: "Go get my Daddy - I know him."

Do you know the character and nature of God? The more you know Him, the stronger your faith will become.

~~

Intended for His Glory November 10, 2014

> For everything comes from Him and exists by His power and is intended for His glory. All glory to Him forever! Amen. (Romans 11:36, NLT)

> For God wanted them to know that the riches and glory of Christ are for you Gentiles, too. And this is the secret: Christ lives in you. This gives you assurance of sharing His glory. (Colossians 1:27)

The book of James teaches that "every good and perfect gift" comes from God. In Romans, the apostle Paul gives us the truth that everything is from Him and exists because God holds it together. Why would He be involved in your life? Why would He exert His power in your life? The reason for our existence is to bring glory to Him. Thus it is logical that in His power, He directs everything to bring that glory to Himself.

We might like to place some things into the category called "God did it," and other things into another where someone or something else did it. As life comes from Him, so does His power. Not that God causes bad things to happen to people - it is that all things are for God's glory and comes with His allowing it.

His power directs all things. His power allows things to exist but always with His hand on them.

We may wonder why "all to bring glory to Him?" God can take our most difficult moments and He "causes everything to work together for good" (Romans 8:28). It is so hard for our finite minds to grasp. What is the outcome of all things that come into your life, and that are controlled by the power of God? God gets the glory. Your life brings glory to God.

Christ is in you. This is what gives you the assurance (one definition of faith) that God is at work through every trial in life. You will not only observe His glory but will share in it. Sharing in the glory of God will be for all of eternity.

God wants all people on earth to know that the glory and riches of Christ are for them. Although we are undeserving, unworthy, sinful, selfish, and rebellious, the glory and riches of Christ are for each of us. To Him be the Glory.

Praise God that everything comes from Him, exists by His power, and is intended for His glory. And that means you.

~~

Enslaved to Him   November 23, 2014

The Truth Will Make You Free
So Jesus was saying to those Jews who had believed Him, "If you continue in My word, then you are truly disciples of Mine; and you will know the truth, and the truth will make you free." They answered Him, "We are Abraham's descendants and have never yet been enslaved to anyone; how is it that You say, 'You will become free'?" Jesus answered them, "Truly, truly, I say to you, everyone who commits sin is the slave of sin. The slave does not remain in the house forever; the son does remain forever. So if the Son makes you free, you will be free indeed." (John 8:31-36, NASB)

You likely have never been to prison, or maybe you have. If you think about what feelings that would produce, the greatest fear would likely be losing your freedom. You cannot do what you want, go where you want, see those you want to see, or experience life aside from a barred room. Jesus taught the disciples to remain in the Word because it would make true disciples of their lives. The result of being His disciple is freedom. If we are controlled by sin, then we are not free.

The Hebrews bragged about never having been enslaved - although the statement was not correct. Jesus knew that the true loss of freedom did not come from being a slave of another person. He knew that true freedom was a relationship with God, broken from sin.

The Son of God, Jesus Himself, would set us free from the Law, from self, fear, insecurity, insignificance, failure, and a host of other things that may be binding us to a life of bondage. It is Jesus that sets us free through His life, death, and resurrection.

So if the Son sets you free, you shall be free indeed. Why not give that which enslaves you, to Him?

~~

~ Personal Message from Dennis ~
December 13, 2014

Greetings from Home,

I am really weak and in lots of pain. My cancer is growing at a rate 7 times faster than normal. I met with my doctor and received more information than I could comprehend. My doctor wants me to go to Houston, Texas, for the next actual treatment for my cancer.

Our home church will open an account for donations to defray the expenses of the actual treatment, including travel, meals, hotel, and follow-up. It is possible that the Medicare and health insurance I currently have may pay for part of it. The cost will be 40-70 thousand dollars with all the tests and other procedures that will be necessary. Any changes and I will let you know immediately. I will also follow-up with another update later this week or early next week. I am waiting for more information about dates and actual costs. We plan to be in Houston December 28 to January 10, unless times change.

I pray God will bless you with His amazing Grace. Love all of you so much.

~ Dennis

~~

Where's Your Focus?
December 21, 2014

That is why we never give up. Though our bodies are dying, our spirits are being renewed every day. For our present troubles are small and won't last very long. Yet they produce for us a glory that vastly outweighs them and will last forever! So we don't look at the troubles we can see now; rather, we fix our gaze on things that cannot be seen. For the things we see now will soon be gone, but the things we cannot see will last forever. (2 Corinthians 4:16-18, NLT)

Don't give up!! Don't lose heart!! Never become discouraged!! Faint not!! These are just a few of the admonitions of the Bible related to present troubles. At some point in time, everyone will face "troubles." How can we have any victory over our problems? The writer says it is because we have something that is more powerful than our troubles. That "something" is God at work in our lives. We, too, often look at the present and forget there is a future where God receives all the glory.

Our current troubles are small and won't last long compared to the glory that is to be ours for all of eternity. That glory will last forever.

So why keep our focus on the present when the future is so bright? What we see and experience now is just temporary. In order to look past trouble, we must look at that which, in reality, we cannot even see.

For that reason, we live by faith and not by sight. We focus not on troubles that are so real in the present, and look to the unseen. Fix your gaze on the things you cannot see. Live by faith, "for without faith it is impossible to please God" (Hebrews 11:6, NIV).

Faith in the unseen is what gets us through trouble. Trust what you cannot see.

~~

~ Personal Message from Roger Wood ~ January 16, 2015

Encourager Family,

It is with a mix of both great joy and great sadness that I write to let you know that Dennis went on to be with Jesus last night, January 15, 2015. He fought long, hard and oh so well in his battle against cancer, and he never grew tired of encouraging all of you. Not a day or a week went by that he didn't tell us about a question you had emailed to him or with a word of your love and support.

He would want me to tell you all how much he loved and cared about each of you. Many of you first met him years and years ago, and others only met him recently. However, all of us can say that at one point in time, "Dennis encouraged me."

I know Dad was devoted to only a few simple things: his Savior; my mom, Sandy; his family; his church family; and God's Word. He would not want me to leave any of you without this hope and this encouragement for us all today. Galatians was perhaps his favorite book in the Bible and this message is particularly comforting and challenging to me today. I can almost hear Dad reading it to me and I hope you can too:

> *... but the one who sows to the Spirit will from the Spirit reap eternal life. And let us not grow weary of doing good, for in due season we will reap, if we do not give up. So then, as we have opportunity, let us do good to everyone, and especially to those who are of the household of faith.* (Galatians 6:8b-10, ESV)

Much love and thanks to you all,

~ Roger

~~

~ Personal Message from Sandy ~ January 29, 2015

It is with a heavy heart I write this note to all of Dennis' faithful readers. He was an amazing man and I will truly miss him, but I must express my gratefulness to all of you for your encouragement to Dennis. He, himself, was so encouraged when you would drop him an email and share how God's Word came alive to you. He rejoiced with you and diligently prayed for you because he truly cared.

I wish I could individually thank each one of you for the emails, texts, cards, phone calls, visits, gifts, food, coffee, Facebook "likes" and posts, but I was overwhelmed with the countless number of messages.

Again, thank you to many who shared in Dennis' Homecoming Celebration last week. As I said, he would have loved every minute of it!

Many of you have asked, "Will someone continue the weekly devotion?" Others have said how much you will miss the family updates and photos of our grandchildren that Dennis often attached. I know that however God chooses to encourage you, it will be exactly what you need because He is ALWAYS faithful.

Thanks to each of you. May God bless you with grace and peace.

~ Sandy

~~

Have You Lost Something? March 23, 2015

> *Though the fig tree should not blossom*
> *And there be no fruit on the vines,*
> *Though the yield of the olive should fail*
> *And the fields produce no food,*
> *Though the flock should be cut off from the fold*
> *And there be no cattle in the stalls,*
> *Yet I will exult in the Lord,*
> *I will rejoice in the God of my salvation.*
> *The Lord God is my strength…* (Habakkuk 3:17-19, NASB)

Loss is uncomfortable, unsettling, and a challenge to work through in our lives. No matter what kind of loss we encounter, we each must work through it on our own. In this passage, Habakkuk speculates about the possibility of coming war for the nation of Israel with the Chaldeans. The prophet talks of no food, no fruit of the vine, no oil, no grain for bread, no meat because the cattle perish, and no flock for meat and coverings.

What in your life has been taken from you? What loss have you incurred? Not many of us are in want of food and drink, but we do have things we have lost or people we love and care about that have been taken away. Habakkuk says that even though all the creature comforts and every necessity of life are removed, he will exult in the Lord and rejoice in the God of his salvation.

In Habakkuk's life, his worship of God was not affected by his circumstances. Even though a loss may be deep and painful, we should be moved to our source of strength, God Himself. That happens through worship. But worship is a choice that we have to make. Twice in the verses Habakkuk says, "I will." Habakkuk moves to the positive rather than the negative. Worship is personal, and Habakkuk took ownership to change his focus. Worship is not just a feel-good experience we enjoy together. It is a choice we make to glory and triumph in the Mighty God of the Universe. Worship of God is the answer to loss. It takes the focus off our troubles and puts our emphasis on the One who knows and who cares about our situation. Really, God should always be our strength - in good times and in hard times, and definitely in times of loss.

Will we, as God's people, stand with Christ when we go through loss? When jobs fail, the economy goes south, sickness strikes, shortages occur, when storms threaten, or a loved one dies? Will we continue to worship God? Worship is a choice. Rejoice! The answer is in worshiping our amazing God who never fails to supply our needs and heal our hurts.

~ Sandra M. Wood

~~

DENNIS G. WOOD

~ Note from the Editor ~

It has been a truly amazing privilege for me to work so closely with the devotional thoughts that Dennis authored. Though looking primarily to evaluate punctuation and grammar, I could not help but be overwhelmed by Dennis' unchanging and persistent messages of God's love, truth, and grace – all given to us freely through Christ Jesus our Lord.

While in the midst of this project I came upon a quote by Oswald Chambers taken from *My Utmost for His Highest* that struck me very powerfully:

> "*In the year that King Uzziah died, I saw also the Lord*" (Isaiah 6:1). Our soul's history with God is frequently the history of the "passing of the hero." Over and over again God has to remove our friends in order to bring Himself in their place, and that is where we faint and fail and get discouraged.

In personal application of this truth, Chambers said, "In the year that the one who stood to me for all that God was, died – I gave up everything? I became ill? I got disheartened? Or – I saw the Lord?"

It is our prayer that through reading the journey of this "hero," you would see the Lord and be drawn closer to Him through deeper understanding of His love, His truth, and His grace. Indeed, to God be the glory.

~ Nancy

~ Your Relationship with God ~

Some people think a personal relationship with God is something only theologians can comprehend. Actually, God's plan of salvation is simple enough for everyone to understand. Here are the ABCs of salvation:

Admit to God that you are a sinner.
"For all have sinned and fall short of the glory of God" (Romans 3:23, NIV).

Believe in Jesus Christ as God's Son and receive Jesus' gift of forgiveness.
"For God so loved the world that He gave His one and only Son, that whoever believes in Him shall not perish but have eternal life" (John 3:16).

Confess your faith in Jesus Christ as Savior and Lord to others.
"If you confess with your mouth, 'Jesus is Lord,' and believe in your heart that God raised Him from the dead, you will be saved. For it is with your heart that you believe and are justified, and it is with your mouth that you confess and are saved" (Romans 10:9-10).

Printed in the United States
By Bookmasters